PARTISANS AND MEDIATORS

Partisans and Mediators

The Resolution of Divorce Disputes

Gwynn Davis

CLARENDON PRESS · OXFORD
1988

Oxford University Press, Walton Street, Oxford OX2 6DP

Oxford   New York   Toronto
Delhi   Bombay   Calcutta   Madras   Karachi
Petaling Jaya   Singapore   Hong Kong   Tokyo
Nairobi   Dar es Salaam   Cape Town
Melbourne   Auckland
and associated companies in
Berlin   Ibadan

Oxford is a trade mark of Oxford University Press

Published in the United States
by Oxford University Press, New York

British Library Cataloguing in Publication Data
Davis, Gwynn
Partisans and mediators: the resolution
of divorce disputes.
1. England. Divorce. Mediation
I. Title
344.2061'66
ISBN 0–19–825612–4

Library of Congress Cataloguing in Publication Data
Davis, Gwynn.
Partisans and mediators: the resolution of divorce disputes
Gwynn Davis
Bibliography: Includes index.
1. Divorce mediation--Great Britain.   2. Divorce--Law and
legislation--Great Britain.   I. Title.
KD764.D38 1988   346.4101'66--dc19   [344.106166]   88-5381
ISBN 0–19–825612–4

Set by Pentacor Ltd.
Printed in Great Britain
at the University Printing House, Oxford
by David Stanford
Printer to the University

To My Parents

Preface

This book represents the fruits of five research studies undertaken over a period of eight years. The first of these, the 'Special Procedure' project, was funded by the Joseph Rowntree Memorial Trust. The other four were funded by the Nuffield Foundation and I should like to express my heartfelt thanks to the Nuffield Trustees and Secretariat for their support throughout this period. I am especially grateful to Pat Thomas, for all her encouragement.

It will be evident, to those who read beyond the first two chapters, that I draw heavily on the experience of divorcing couples interviewed in the course of our various researches. I should like to thank them all for their frankness and for giving me their time.

At each court where we carried out the various studies we were given generous access and treated with the utmost courtesy by court staff. I have been a thorn in the side of Registrars Parmiter, Bird, Price, and Dunford for several years, but they have continued to give me every possible assistance. I was also granted generous access by Fred Gibbons and his colleagues at the South-East London Conciliation Bureau, and by Rosemarie Fraser and her fellow mediators at the Bristol Courts Family Conciliation Service.

Throughout the 'Conciliation in Divorce' study I was guided by a Research Advisory Committee, chaired by Lord Justice Dunn MC, and I am grateful to all the members of that Committee for their advice. Sir John Arnold, President of the Family Division, also lent active encouragement to my various research enterprises. In addition, I have benefited from the advice of several experienced solicitors and divorce court welfare officers. I cannot mention them all by name, but I am especially grateful to John Westcott and Tony Wells, who commented (sometimes in strongly critical vein) on draft chapters of this book.

In the course of these researches I have been assisted by several highly skilled research interviewers, notably Margaret Borkowski, Jenny Bagley, Alison Jackson, Carole Moore, and Petula Smith. I have also been helped at various times by two friendly and efficient research secretaries in Pat Lees and Liz Young.

Researching the same field over a number of years can be an uncomfortable experience, as new insights (whether one's own or other people's) undermine old positions. Marian and Simon Roberts have been particularly influential in this respect and I should like to thank them both for sharing their ideas with me. Marian was a colleague on the study of the Bromley Conciliation Bureau, undertaking most of the interviews in connection with that project, and I learnt a great deal from her. Two eminent colleagues, Stephen Cretney and Roy Parker, have also offered wise counsel at various times.

My greatest debt is to two former colleagues in the Department of Social Administration in the University of Bristol who have been collaborators on several of the research projects relied upon in this book. Mervyn Murch gave me my start in research and helped me understand what it was all about. We enjoyed a productive working relationship over some ten years. Kay Bader is a valued colleague and friend who has likewise worked with me on several research projects. I have learnt to place great reliance upon her. She also, as an additional chore, typed and re-typed this book.

GWYNN DAVIS

Faculty of Law
University of Bristol

Contents

1

Introduction

THE term 'divorce' may be understood in a number of different ways—most obviously, as an event which entails massive disruption and reorganization for individuals and families. But 'divorce' may also be conceived as an area of substantive law destroying the status of marriage, or as a legal process (involving visits to solicitors, court appearances, and so on). As far as these latter aspects are concerned, there is a growing tendency to view divorce in administrative terms (Freeman 1976), with courts seeking to respond as quickly and efficiently as possible to the parties' private decision to end their marriage. But whilst obtaining a decreee may be, for most couples, a relatively straightforward and uncontentious matter, there are relatively few divorces which do not involve, in at least some aspects, conflicts of interest or perception. Fulfilment of the parties' hopes for the future may also, to some extent, depend on the co-operation of their former spouse. So divorce, far from being purely 'administrative', is also a time of conflict and of negotiation.

Evidence for the persistently conflictual nature of divorce is found in the growing numbers of contested applications to the courts over so-called 'ancillary matters,'—that is to say, money, property, and children.[1] (This is in apparent contradiction of the trend towards administrative decree proceedings.) Furthermore, it would appear that the number of contested applications understates the extent of the conflict over these issues (Davis, Macleod, and Murch 1982*a*). The majority of divorcing couples, even though they may not contest these matters through the courts, find themselves in dispute over one, if not all three. Some do indeed resolve their differences without outside assistance, although such settlements may reflect fatigue or domination as much as genuine agreement. But the great majority of divorcing couples will seek help in negotiating or, as it might appear, in battling with one another. This book is about that help, and about the partisans and mediators who provide it.

[1] The number of contested applications relating to children rose from 35,992 in 1977 to 108,305 in 1983, a period in which the divorce rate remained constant. *Judicial Statistics*, Annual Reports 1977, Table C. 13(m) and 1983, Table 4. 8, HMSO.

The former group are legal practitioners, either solicitors or barristers. They enjoy high status and have their own special language. Their responsibilities lie exclusively with one party to the conflict, although it has to be understood that their tasks include negotiation as well as advocacy, the former responsibility being one which they share with another group of 'helpers' who are of more recent origin and, generally speaking, have lower status.

This second group—the new mediators—offer themselves to both sides to the dispute, saying to them in effect, 'we see you cannot agree—why not let us help you sort out the problem?' Their claim to specialist expertise lies in the area of negotiating skill, although some will also be 'expert' in other areas, for example in counselling, or in knowledge of child developmental psychology. The partisan may likewise be a skilled negotiator, although the negotiations in which he engages will be of a rather different kind. But the professional partisan will also be expert (and have qualifications) in law and legal processes. The mediator's knowledge of these matters is likely to have been built up informally.

The recent rapid growth in the number of informal mediation schemes[2] has been accompanied by expressions of dissatisfaction with the formal legal process (Glendon 1981, 120). But whether this weakening of belief, or 'legitimation crisis' as it is sometimes termed, is actually felt by the parties to divorce proceedings is not easily established. (It could be, for example, that many of these criticisms emanate from rival practitioners, notably the new mediators.) Whether that is true or not, one difficulty faced by those who posit a general dissatisfaction with family law and practice is the need to explain the increased resort to litigation to which reference has already been made.

One possible counter-argument is that the mere fact of people using a service (the courts) does not mean that they are happy with it. They may feel that they have no alternative. That would be true in one sense, but false in another. In so far as litigation is viewed as a last resort, with the emphasis placed on the need for an *adjudication* of the dispute, there is indeed no alternative. But reference to lawyers 'bargaining in the shadow of the law' (Mnookin and Kornhauser 1979) points to the inaccuracy of this view of the legal process. Only a small proportion of initially contested applications are finally adjudicated. For the most

---

[2] See the *Report of the Inter-departmental Committee on Conciliation*, Lord Chancellor's Department, 1982, para.3.8ff.

part, the law and the court provide a framework for negotiation. If we place the emphasis on negotiation, rather than adjudication, it can be seen that divorcing couples have a great deal of choice, although they may not be aware of all their options. Even within the framework provided by solicitors and the court, there tend to exist what might be regarded as two separate but parallel negotiating processes: first, that which takes place 'on the record' through affidavit and preliminary hearing; and second, that which is conducted orally or by means of 'without prejudice' correspondence. In both cases the negotiations tend to be carried forward by professional legal advisers, with the parties remaining very much in the background.

To view legal process in terms of negotiation, as much as adjudication, is helpful also in that it suggests that it might well be a mistake to concentrate all our reforming energies on the substantive law, although it is here that the fiercest moral battles are fought. Statute and case law offer certain general principles to guide legal advisers—a series of signposts indicating the room for manœuvre. But the law cannot do more than this. Indeed, as far as disputes over money and children are concerned, it offers surprisingly little help.

That is why significant reforms are as likely to come about through *procedural* innovation, one might almost say through stealth, as they are through changes in the law. The gradual introduction of the 'Special Procedure' through the 1970s was one example. This enabled the divorce decree to be granted on the basis of affidavit evidence alone and had a profound impact on the experience of most divorcing couples. Nevertheless, it provoked only a fraction of the controversy surrounding the 1969 Divorce Reform Act.

One general trend encompasses both law and procedure. This is towards making separation and divorce less acrimonious than was formerly the case. For example, it is pointed out that certain aspects of our family law no longer conform to an 'adversarial' model of justice.[3] Recent procedural developments designed to encourage and institutionalize negotiations on court premises also reflect this trend.[4] These changes may be observed, not only in this country, but in many others with a common law tradition.

[3] This is true, in particular, of s. 41 of the Matrimonial Causes Act 1973, under which courts have a duty not to grant a decree absolute without first checking on the proposed arrangements for the children's future.
[4]   See in particular the *Report of the Matrimonial Causes Procedure Committee* (Booth Committee), Lord Chancellor's Department, July 1985, in which it is proposed that there be an 'initial hearing' in most categories of divorce case.

It is consistent with these developments that we should have recently witnessed a mushrooming of services geared to resolving family disputes through informal negotiation. Our legal system is trying to reform itself from within, whilst at the same time its monopoly of dispute resolution services is being challenged by these new mediators, a breed of expert which did not exist ten years ago.

One way to locate and understand this latter development is to place it in the context of a general movement towards 'informalism' in the resolution of disputes (Abel 1982*b* and Auerbach 1983, 3 ff.). The application of 'mediation' to family conflict is a relatively recent phenomenon, but in relation to other kinds of quarrel, mediation is well established and probably universal. The essential characteristic— a non-aligned third party who attempts to bring about settlement through negotiation and persuasion—is to be found amongst several cultures (Roberts 1979, 164 ff.).

The movement towards informalism has been criticized on the grounds that, in the absence of a coherent community with shared values, there is no possibility of justice outside the legal system (Auerbach 1983, 16). It is suggested that without a shared commitment to common values, informal dispute resolution will reflect 'the historical forms, but not the historical substance of non-legal dispute settlement' (Auerbach 1983, 67).

On this view, there are grave problems whichever way one turns. In heterogeneous societies, where there may well be no 'community' of shared values, law is all we have left—but that law is bound to be unsatisfactory since it is not sustained by shared norms; accordingly, to some groups and individuals, it will appear arbitrary and unjust. But in these circumstances, to look for justice *outside* law is to follow a chimera. The success of informal mechanisms depends entirely upon shared values; they cannot even fall back on the *trappings* of legitimacy, as may the law itself.

These criticisms of informalism were developed in the context of the 'de-legalization' movement in the USA, a country which is heterogeneous, individualistic and aggressively materialistic, perhaps more so even than our own. But can the critique be said to apply to the informal resolution of *family* disputes? Members of a family might well be expected to have a system of shared values and, therefore, to meet the definition of 'community' advanced as a prerequisite for informal dispute resolution. On the other hand, there is the strongly articulated view that men and women do indeed have different aspirations within marriage and different perceptions of any problems that emerge (Bernard 1982, 5 ff.). This poses a problem for the mediation 'movement', although the challenge to the aura of consensus surrounding mediation is based not so much on these supposed differences in ways of seeing the world, as on the alleged structural inequality between men and women. It is this analysis in terms of gender which has led to the image of mediation as empowering *both* parties to the conflict coming under strong attack (Bottomley 1984). The argument is that 'mediation' provides a forum in which the dominant spouse (usually the man) will continue to hold sway, unchecked by judicial authority. This enables a false image of equality to be assumed, so that the real inequality between the parties is both masked and perpetuated. It is also feared that hard-won gains achieved by women through the courts (in domestic violence, property on divorce, and property acquired during cohabitation) will be undercut as men resort to these informal modes of dispute resolution.

Whilst feminist critics of mediation tend to assume that the woman is more vulnerable than the man in these negotiations, the essential criticism relates to the alleged imbalance of power, no matter in which direction it operates. The same criticism may be applied to informal resolution of other types of conflict, such as disputes between consumers and large suppliers of goods or services; disputes between individual employees and a corporate employer; or disputes between an injured person and an insurance company.

But is the relationship between former marriage partners likely to be marked by this degree of power imbalance? There are indeed several potential sources of inequality, the most obvious being: control over financial resources; *de facto* custody of children; intellectual or emotional dominance; and violence, or the threat of violence. The latter can serve to provide one illustration of the potential difficulties. It has been suggested that anyone who attempts to 'mediate' following violence by a husband against his wife, is doing no more that maintain the status quo. Thus, if a policeman who is called to a domestic 'incident' merely cautions the husband (and a 'mediator', generally speaking, has no power to do more than this) he is, in effect, acting in the interests of the stronger party. This is because the home circumstances will be essentially unchanged after he has left. This view has been taken by representatives of the Women's Aid Federation:

Where there was intervention, the whole emphasis was on conciliation—with the aid of valium, a psychiatrist, some casework—rather than on the challenge to violence that . . . the woman actually sought[5]

Equally, it should be acknowledged that the power balance between men and women may change upon separation and divorce. That is why many women leave. Also, the sources of male and female power are likely to be different with, for example, the man having the economic power derived from his position as principal wage earner, whereas the woman may be better placed to draw on her children's allegiance in any conflict that arises. Each may feel powerful in different circumstances. Power in one area may compensate for powerlessness in another. It is also important to recognize that most people have a tendency to feel powerless, rather than powerful. Either party may fail to recognize the power which they hold and so not understand why this is resented by their former spouse.

It is also slightly incongruous to find our notoriously male-dominated legal institutions being presented as upholders of women's rights, in opposition to mediation services with their predominantly female staff. However 'bourgeois' the latter may be to some eyes, they probably have a better appreciation of, say, the problems of single parenthood than do most judges.

None of this is to deny that, in many important respects, men occupy a privileged position in family life. They may also, following separation, be hoping to recover some of the power which they have lost. Thus it is not altogether fanciful to regard men as 'fighting back'. But on the other hand, the *need* to resort to mediation is to some extent a refutation of the view that the man tends to retain this more powerful position; after all, it is usually the weaker party to a dispute who seeks outside help (Schattschneider 1964, 4). The fact that over 50 per cent of self-referrals to the busiest mediation services in this country come from *men* (Davis and Roberts 1988) offers therefore a two-edged message, suggesting the man's vulnerability, but also a strategy for recovering power and influence against which women may need to be on their guard.

Meanwhile, there are a number of other key ideas which have encouraged the development of mediation services, some of them providing further ammunition for feminist and other critics. Perhaps the first of these is the desire to promote *compromise*, almost as a worthy

---

[5] The *Guardian*, 7 October 1981. Report of DHSS Seminar on Domestic Violence by A. Shearer.

objective in itself. This ties in with the present reluctance to assign blame for marriage breakdown. The resulting emphasis on incompatibility, rather than fault, has encouraged all forms of negotiation, but this aura of compromise appears to cling, above all, to mediated settlements. This pursuit of compromise has a pragmatic element since it is often claimed that compromise agreements, in being more 'amicable' (itself a questionable assumption) are more likely to be adhered to (Murch 1980, 222).

Secondly, there is the view that disputes between divorcing couples cannot be taken at face value: the legal issues serve as a channel through which the couple express their anger at past hurts and mourn for what may seem wasted years. This view of divorce-related disputes may appear somewhat patronizing, but it is certainly the case that many custody and access disputes reflect long-term family problems which courts cannot finally resolve. The legal framework may appear clumsy and inappropriate as a means of settling issues which have such a high emotional content and which stretch back over many years.

Thirdly, it is argued by some that mediation may assist the parties in adjusting to the shock of the marital breakdown, enabling them to share feelings of distress and uncertainty which would have little relevance in arriving at a settlement defined purely in legal terms. Taking this argument one stage further, mediation is even seen (by what might be termed the 'therapeutic' wing of the movement) as a means of transforming 'the crisis of divorce' into an opportunity for personal growth and fulfilment. Influential research conducted in the context of a divorce counselling service (Wallerstein and Kelly 1980, 157) has encouraged some mediators to think of their work in these terms.

Descending rather abruptly from these rarified aspirations, a key plank in the case made *to government* on behalf of mediation schemes is the claim that they offer a *cheaper* means of settling disputes. As far as officials in the Treasury and Lord Chancellor's Department are concerned, personal growth is something that they shave off each morning. For them it is sufficient that mediation offers the prospect of a higher rate of settlement of contested applications, reduced congestion of court lists, and finally, most important, a saving to the Legal Aid Fund. This preoccupation with 'savings' has arisen largely because the sheer numbers involved in divorce have led to escalating legal costs. Divorce is now the resort of the humble many, rather than the privileged few. In the past, the actual number of litigants was small.

This kept total costs within bounds, whereas now the Legal Aid Fund makes a respectable contribution to our national debt.[6]

Nor is it simply that the numbers are greater; the *kind* of case, it may be said, does not merit the full panoply of the law. Most divorcing couples have a limited income and (at most) one mortgaged home. In their financial, as in their child-care arrangements, they have little room for manœuvre. In these circumstances, procedures designed to unravel complicated family fortunes can seem wasteful and irrelevant. The provision of legal and welfare services to oversee what, in legal terms, are humdrum divorces, has become unduly expensive for the state.

However, it is by no means clear that solicitors are tending to divert their poorer clients towards mediation services. Some indeed would say that the verbal skills which they believe to be required lead them to do the very opposite. But the fact remains that government interest in mediation, such as it is, rests on the premiss that legal aid savings may be achieved by these means. To that extent, mediation in family disputes is vulnerable to the same criticism as has been levelled against the whole 'informal justice' movement, namely, that those being channelled away from the courts are relatively low status, disadvantaged people, feeding little of their own resources into the legal coffers.

This does not mean that savings will in fact accrue. Indeed, there is good reason to believe that mediation services, even if successful in securing agreements, are unlikely to achieve a major impact on legal aid expenditure. After all, for a large section of the legal profession, the Legal Aid Fund is, quite literally, their bread and butter. Many solicitors are feeling disgruntled because the scope of the scheme has been cut back in recent years.[7] They already consider that they receive meagre payment for the preliminary work which they do on their clients' behalf. Understandably, they will be resistant to further loss of income. Given that there is an element of 'robbing Peter to pay Paul' in the compilation of most legal bills, it should not be too difficult for solicitors to ensure that any loss of income from a few successfully mediated cases will not be reflected in their *overall* level of remuneration.

It is also necessary to bear in mind the burden which conciliation

---

[6] Legal Aid expenditure in matrimonial disputes totalled over £71.1 million in 1984/5, as compared with £32.1 million in 1980/1. *35th Legal Aid Annual Reports (1984–85)*, The Law Society's Report, Appendix 4H(ii), HMSO.

[7] Legal Aid (as distinct from the more limited 'Legal Advice and Assistance') was withdrawn from undefended decree proceedings from 1 April 1977.

schemes may impose on the Exchequer—since it is clearly their *intention* to impose such a burden. In Britain, at present, these services are provided free. This is possible thanks to a combination of volunteer effort, *ad hoc* local funding, and subsidization by the divorce court welfare service. Unlike the USA, there is no significant fee-for-service sector (Dingwall 1986). This means that government is under continual pressure to find *additional* resources to finance conciliation schemes. There are signs that the Lord Chancellor's Department now recognizes that not much can be expected from extra-legal mediation schemes in the way of 'savings'. Hence its dilatory response to the various campaigns aimed at securing government funding.[8].

One other anxiety, or preoccupation, has contributed to the current interest in mediated divorce settlements. There is hardly an article written on the subject which does not express concern about the well-being of children whose parents divorce. This anxiety is on two levels: there are fears for the happiness and psychological health of these children; and secondly, there is concern about the impact on future generations who may experience even more instability. Mediation has become identified with a greater concentration on the needs of children, bringing home to parents the hurt and perhaps even the long-term damage which may result from their continued quarrelling, or the abandonment of all links between the child and the non-custodial parent.

In the recent past this concern has led to various forms of investigation, or treatment, or supervision of the family by qualified experts. Indeed, since 1958, following the Royal Commission's recommendations, a child welfare check has formed an integral part of divorce proceedings, the court having a duty to satisfy itself about the proposed arrangements for children before granting a decree absolute.[9] This investigation has been shown to be perfunctory at best. It also meets with a decidedly ambivalent response from parents (Davis, Macleod, and Murch 1983). It is not too fanciful to suggest that we are entering a climate of scepticism with regard to both surveillance and treatment approaches. Assistance with negotiation may be more

---

[8]   This coolness was apparent throughout the *Report of the Inter-departmental Committee on Conciliation* (see n.2), not least in the Committee's recommendation that a further three-year research project be set up (paras. 5. 19 and 5. 20), thereby ensuring that no decision need be taken on funding new services until the end of the decade.
[9]   This provision was originally s. 2 of the Matrimonial Proceedings (Children) Act 1958. It was later re-enacted in s. 33 of the Matrimonial Causes Act 1965 and has since been consolidated in s. 41 of the Matrimonial Causes Act 1973 (see n.3).

acceptable and also, more realistic. But it is one of the contentions of this book that surveillance and treatment have not simply disappeared, or even become less popular with those trained to practise them. They find expression within the current enthusiasm for mediation. Many of the new mediators have a social work or counselling background. It is by no means clear that they will be keen to abandon their authority as experts in child welfare or family dynamics. In some cases it was the prospect of applying these skills in a new context which led them to take on a mediating role in the first place.

But it is not immediately clear why *mediation*, more than any other form of dispute resolution, should have something special to offer in the way of safeguarding children's interests. Mediation is said to provide the parties with encouragement and opportunity to retain control over their own case. It is true that this concept, usually termed 'client self-determination', also forms part of the rhetoric of social work. But it is by no means certain that it imbues the practice. Indeed, there is good reason why it should not do so, as social workers have to balance their clients' wishes against the constraints imposed on them by limited resources and agency responsibilities (such as, in certain circumstances, removing children from the care of their parents). They are used to *exercising* authority, rather than ensuring that this is retained by parents.

The same may be said of divorce court welfare officers, most of whom have had a generic training in social work. Like many other professionals in this field—including some solicitors—they are attracted by the aura of consensus which surrounds 'conciliation'. But welfare officers are used to excercising considerable influence with the court. It is only to be expected that they should seek to extend their traditional child-protective responsibilities so that they are applied to this supposedly new discipline. Certainly it is asking rather a lot of them that they be child-welfare experts for one half of their time and mediators, lacking any kind of formal authority, for the other half. Some welfare officers claim that they can perform both roles, even that they can perform them both at the same time (Shepherd, Howard, and Tonkinson 1984). But it has been demonstrated convincingly that these tasks and their associated objectives are theoretically quite distinct and may, in practice, conflict (Roberts 1983).

This usefully prompts the question: who is behind the recent chorus of support for mediation? The answer is that most of the press articles and television and radio reports flow from the strenuous efforts of a few articulate people who have taken it upon themselves to proselytize on behalf of the mediation cause. Interestingly enough, this group includes a number of lawyers, although it should not surprise us, given the many different aspirations which underlie the mediation concept, that it should attract the backing of at least some partisans. Also, eminent lawyers such as the President of the Family Division (one notable supporter) are already established in the public eye, whereas if one regards the ideal mediator as an *unobtrusive* figure, the 'professional' expert on the subject is something of a contradiction in terms, although one does now find several high-profile exponents of the art.

Meanwhile, it is clear that if the existing network of independent schemes were to achieve a secure financial base, there would be no shortage of would-be mediators. Abel has pointed ironically to the fact that 'there are even professionals at informalism' (Abel 1982*a*). Whilst his analysis is of informalism *in general*, it also fits the emergence of family mediation, although we are not nearly as 'advanced' in this respect as is the USA. The same phenomenon has been observed by Brigitte and Peter Berger, although they are not concerned, as are Abel and Auerbach, to point up the ironic juxtaposition of informalism and the development of professional ideology. But they do identify the aggrandizing tendency exhibited by members of what they term 'the professional camp' (Berger and Berger 1983, 9).

Robert Levy has reminded us that supporters of mediation tend to espouse a number of other causes, most of which offer opportunities for intervention by appropriately trained and qualified personnel (Levy 1984). One possible parallel is with the 'child-saving' movement in nineteenth-century USA, this being concerned primarily with juvenile delinquency. This also had career implications for its adherents; it tended to be the domain of women; and it was primarily a middle class (or 'leisure class') movement, launched on behalf of those less fortunately placed in the social order (Platt 1969, 76 ff.).

A degree of scepticism is probably appropriate in relation to most professional growth industries, but this does not in itself undermine the case for informal mediation as a means of resolving some family disputes. What has to be avoided is the imposition of 'problem' status on all separated families. This is the effect achieved by those journal and newspaper articles which begin with a litany of divorce statistics showing how the divorce 'rate' has risen to its present level and citing the number of children affected. This is presumed, generally without supporting argument, to point up a major social problem which would be ameliorated through the offer (or, as it may transpire, the imposition) of social work or counselling skills.

The actual extent of this problem and the nature of the 'help' sought by the families themselves forms the background to this study. Meanwhile it is important to recognize that the distinction between 'formal' and 'informal' justice in relation to family disputes is becoming blurred. This applies especially to the preliminary stages of the legal process. The assumption underlying traditional legal forms has been that an application to the court is the point at which the parties' authority is superseded, either by judicial authority, or at the very least by the authority of professional advisers. In practice that is still the case, but there has of late been growing support for the idea that the values and strategies underlying mediation may be applied to the pre-trial negotiating process.

Roberts has argued that this linking of law and mediation will 'sap the vitality of both' (Roberts 1983). But whilst it may be correct to claim that registrars and court welfare officers cannot act as 'mediators' in any strict sense, it is difficult to justify such a strong commitment to the creation of informal services, whilst leaving the vast edifice of the courts, the legal profession, and the financing of the system virtually untouched.

In practice, attempts are now being made to institutionalize a framework for negotiation on court premises (Parmiter 1981). This takes the form of a 'mediation appointment'(or similar title) under the eye of the registrar. The parties' representatives are normally present at these discussions and this is one reason why the negotiations are of a different order to those conducted through an 'out of court' mediation service. These appointments call for settlement-orientated negotiation, the timetable for which is controlled by the court rather than by solicitors acting in their own good time, as some would prefer. The object is to reduce costs. This is also reflected in the Report of the Matrimonial Causes Procedure Committee, with its suggestion for an 'initial hearing' in every disputed case.[10].

These developments bear out Auerbach's glum thesis that 'alternatives' to law tend, in their turn, to be legalized (1983, 15). It does not take a great deal of imagination to see that a greater emphasis on the achievement of 'settlement' could lead to an erosion of the parties' right to seek judicial determination. Registrars, in their enthusiasm to

---

[10] *Report of the Matrimonial Causes Procedure Committee* (see n.4). The 'initial hearing' proposal forms the cornerstone of this document.

secure legal settlements, may bring pressure on the parties, leading in some cases to a reluctant (and probably short-lived) compromise agreement. The claim that preliminary hearings on court premises will promote 'participation' (Murch 1980, 259) will be turned on its head if the object is simply to achieve quick and cheap settlement of what are often complex issues. It is an inevitable limitation of our legal process, not by any means confined to these 'in-court' mediation appointments, that considerable pressures exist which direct the parties to 'settle' in circumstances which may leave them to cope on their own with major areas of disagreement.

The same may be said of extra-legal dispute resolution. Early attempts to achieve justice without law were supported by Christian values, notably by a desire for harmony within the community as a whole. But that does not mean that these early experiments in informalism were marked by friendly cajoling and a spirit of cheerful self-denial. These informal mechanisms, just as much as the law itself, could be discretionary, arbitrary, and domineering. This was possible because the community good was placed above the wishes of the individual. However, in so far as this vision of community was shared by all, 'the meaning of justice was clear to its members' (Auerbach 1983, 16).

Japan in the early part of this century offers another compelling illustration of a society in which people were expected to conduct themselves harmoniously (Kawashima 1969). The rigid social stratification amongst the Japanese discouraged litigation and judicial decision-making, whilst the traditional Japanese view of family life was that the law was intended to maintain family solidarity, rather than define the rights of individual members. Isono's account of the 'Conciliation Committee' in the Japanese High Court clearly illustrates the limitations of a mediation-dominated approach to family disputes (Isono 1975). He notes that the Committee was expected to persuade the parties to reach agreement, rather than to make legal judgements. When the mediator suggested conditions for settlement, his prestige and authority were such that the proposed solution was usually accepted.

Preservation of the family unit and subjugation of the interests of the individual to the good of the whole cannot be said to be dominant values in our society, or at least, not to the same extent. However, the state does have a financial interest in promoting legal settlement. One finds, as a result, that certain forms of mediation are effectively imposed on the parties. These negotiations are underpinned by a kind of sociology of effectiveness in which efficient processing looms as the dominant, not to say the only value. The practical consequence of this is that argument in open court gives way to the definitions of professionals, advanced in private. The parties may feel bound to accept this strange hybrid—a form of joint arbitration by registrars, welfare officers, and their own partisans.

One may infer from this growing interest in procedural reform that it is in fact legal partisans around whom the 'savings' argument principally revolves. Conciliation has become a hurrah word, but solicitors continue to provide the gateway to divorce for the overwhelming majority of couples. There is also a growing tendency to embark on divorce proceedings within a few months of separation, if not sooner (Davis, Macleod, and Murch 1982*b*). Solicitors are therefore even more likely to be involved from a very early stage.

It can be argued that the legal profession has done its best to bring about this dependence on their services. Having been around so long, they tend to be taken for granted. Visits to lawyers have long been seen as the 'right' way to respond to marital conflict (Roberts 1983); not to consult a solicitor is seen as risky, even, one sometimes gathers, indicative of an obsessive or overwrought reaction to the marital breakdown. But even if one regards the present dependence on solicitors as a successful piece of marketing, or job creation, there is little doubt that in the view of most divorcing couples, such dependence exists. They feel they need technical advice and they also—many of them—want someone who can speak on their behalf. As far as they are concerned, the solicitor plays a crucial role.

From the point of view of the new mediators, this is rather galling. They are having to accept judgement in terms of their cost-effectiveness, whilst the costs which they are supposed to affect (and which no one thinks to challenge directly) are the salaries of members of the legal profession. To some extent this is due to the fact that solicitors and barristers got in first. As a result, there is not much research done on them—and certainly none that challenges their very existence.

But there is a much more fundamental question underlying the legal profession's grip on the divorce process. Partisan support may be necessary for one of two reasons. The first is that despite the simplification of decree proceedings, there is a highly technical side to divorce (especially when it comes to settling financial questions) and the people who possess this technical competence happen, by virtue of the traditionally adversarial character of the proceedings, to be partisans. On this interpretation, solicitors are central to the whole process, not because of their partisanship, which is incidental, but because they are technically skilled.

The other view would be that given the conflicts of interest that arise on divorce, not to mention the stresses involved and the possibility that one party may be able to dominate the other, partisan support is a vital safeguard against injustice (mediation, in contrast, may appear almost a luxury, reflecting a belief in 'reasonableness' held by middle-class liberals).

Whether one puts the emphasis on solicitors' partisanship, or on the parties' need for technical legal advice (which is what 'the new breed of matrimonial lawyer' would seem to prefer), there is every likelihood that negotiations will continue to be conducted either alongside, or through, solicitors and barristers. They dominate the scene. That is why this book is concerned as much with them, the partisans, as it is with the new mediators.

2

Research

IN writing this book I have drawn on evidence from five separate research studies. The first of these was the Special Procedure in Divorce project, funded by the Joseph Rowntree Memorial Trust, which ran from 1978 to 1982. This research was undertaken in seven courts in the south-west of England and South Wales. It was directed by Mervyn Murch and in the course of it we examined 3,000 court files, observed 1,500 Children's Appointments[1], and carried out 398 interviews with parties to divorce proceedings. This was a large-scale study of 'routine' (in the sense of uncontested) divorce, focusing primarily on judges' examination of the proposed arrangements for children. It provides a useful backdrop to the later projects, all of which involved dispute.

Also in this period I undertook two studies of the Bristol Courts Family Conciliation Service (BCFCS),[2]. In the first of these, I examined BCFCS records over the first six months of the service's operation (84 cases in all) and interviewed forty local solicitors. The second study was intended to discover BCFCS's impact, if any, on applications to the court and legal costs. This involved an examination of records maintained by BCFCS and the local Law Society, as well as contacting solicitors who had acted in each of the 184 cases included in the sample.

From 1981 to 1985 I was engaged in a study of the negotiation and settlement of legal issues. The original stimulus for the research was the opportunity to explore 'mediation' on court premises, but in

---

[1] By S. 41 of the Matrimonial Causes Act 1973, courts have a duty not to grant a decree absolute without first declaring that the proposals for the children's future are 'satisfactory or are the best that can be devised in the circumstances'. The substance of this provision has remained largely unaltered since it was introduced in 1958. From April 1977, the provisions of S. 41 have been met through a system whereby judges examine divorcing parents in private about their plans for their children.

[2] This was the first 'out of court' mediation service in this country. It opened in February 1978 and from May 1979 received a grant from the Nuffield Foundation which enabled it to operate on a fully funded basis.

practice this involved studying the work of partisans (principally solicitors) just as much as that of mediators (in this context, welfare officers and registrars). The research was undertaken at Bristol, Newport, Gloucester, Yeovil, and Wandsworth County Courts, and at the Principal Divorce Registry in London. It included a detailed study of case files at each centre, whilst at Bristol we also sat in on mediation appointments and so observed part of the process at first hand. We spoke informally to a range of solicitors, welfare officers, and registrars, as well as conducting a postal survey of solicitors in the Bristol area. The final stage of the fieldwork, carried out in 1983 and early 1984, was a programme of interviews with recently divorced couples, all of whom had been in dispute concerning their children or the divorce decree. We conducted 299 interviews in all, 277 in the Bristol area and the remainder in South Wales. It is from these interviews that I derive nearly all the directly quoted material employed in succeeding chapters.

Finally, in parallel with this study of contested applications, I have been monitoring the work of the South East London Conciliation Bureau, based at Bromley. Like BCFCS, the Bromley Bureau runs an 'out of court' mediation service, but it is organized (and in part staffed) by divorce court welfare officers, thus offering an immediate point of comparison. The Bromley study included: examination of the service's case records; observation of mediation appointments; and follow-up interviews with fifty-one parents who had attended the Bureau.[3]

The research evidence on which I choose to rely most heavily is that drawn from face to face interviews with divorcing couples. With my colleagues, I deliberately set out to discover the parties' reaction to every aspect of the legal process. My interest was in disputes, but a representative cross-section of the divorcing population was desirable if only because, in trying to understand conflict, it is helpful to observe 'non-conflict' or 'conflict resolved'.

The three separate 'consumer' studies on which I am able to draw were arrived at in different ways and, broadly speaking, they represent different points along a continuum from 'amicable' divorce to legal contest (although, in practice, there was considerable overlap between the three groups).

The 'Special Procedure' survey comprised *undefended* divorces, i.e.

---

[3] The bulk of these interviews were undertaken by Marian Roberts. We have jointly written a book which gives a detailed account of the work of the Bromley Bureau (Davis and Roberts 1988).

the decree itself was unopposed. Furthermore, the bulk of the sample had been drawn from the court lists of Children's Appointments which meant that most cases in which there had been a contested application in respect of custody or access were excluded from the sample. It is safe to say that the most difficult, conflict-ridden cases were significantly underrepresented in this survey.

In contrast, the interviews undertaken as part of the study of contested applications comprised precisely those cases which had been excluded from the earlier project. All had involved at least the preliminary stages of legal contest in respect of the divorce decree, custody, or access.

Thirdly, the fifty-one former clients of the Bromley Bureau, whilst they had been unable to agree some aspect of the arrangements for their children (usually, the terms of 'access' for the non-custodial parent), had opted for mediation as a means of trying to resolve the dispute. It is reasonable to suppose that, on the whole, this group were more inclined to negotiate than were those (a minority of the divorcing population as a whole) who took their quarrel to court.

The fact that I regard these three sets of interviews with 'consumers' as the most illuminating element in the research should not be taken to imply, as has been suggested elsewhere (Smart 1984, 150), that divorcing couples (with all their problems) are themselves the object of study; on the contrary, my subject is the way in which law and legal procedure both define and respond to family conflict. My concern is with those who practise either within or on the edge of the legal system. To ask the parties about courts and legal practitioners is, in a sense, to make a political statement. First, it implies that 'problems' in the delivery of legal service have to be located within law, court procedure, and legal practice, rather than amongst 'consumers' of these services; secondly, it suggests that the parties are legitimate arbiters of legal performance; and thirdly, it acknowledges that there may be a conflict of interest between 'consumer' and professional 'producer' (Shaw 1976).

There are of course ways in which consumer evidence can be played down, but in considering the parties' response to the court and to legal services generally, it is all too easy to assume that these are 'unreasonable' people, or 'self-centred', or any of the other criticisms which are sometimes levelled against those who cannot manage their divorce arrangements neatly and tidily. The argument is sometimes put that the parties' anger and distress leads them to 'project' these feelings onto the legal process, taking in various convenient scapegoats such as judges, registrars, and welfare officers. There may be an element of truth in this, but the charge is all too easy to make and may serve to defend insensitive and self-serving professional practices.

In our interviews we did indeed encounter the occasional person who displayed a kind of baffled resentment towards all aspects of the legal process. No matter how their case had been handled, they would probably have blamed someone for their unhappiness since they could not understand any system of justice which did not come down on their side. But in many cases it was not the fact that they had 'lost' that people were complaining about; they considered that they had been dealt with in an arbitrary, insensitive fashion.

There were, on the other hand, a great many positive accounts; it is not true that people are more articulate about professional practices which give rise to anger and dissatisfaction than they are about those which they find helpful (Rees and Wallace 1982, 73). We found that people could distinguish between good and bad practice; between a conscientious solicitor and one who was abrupt or slapdash; between a dictatorial welfare officer and another who was 'family-minded'. So it simply will not do to lump everyone together and say of those who complain, the fault lies with them.

There is also the question of divorcing couples' differing interpretations of their own case. Marvin Michelson (world famous 'palimony' lawyer) has remarked that 'everyone lies in divorce'.[4] But one might equally well say: 'everyone tells the truth in divorce'; it is just that this 'truth' is told from a particular perspective. It may well be a somewhat selective truth; nevertheless, it is the version which runs through that person's mind, day after day, often for years.

Our sample of cases drawn from the Bristol court included seventy-one in which we interviewed both parties. We found, not surprisingly, that accounts differed marginally in some areas—or, more commonly, that a different emphasis was given to certain events (it was interesting to see, for example, what each person chose to tell and what to leave out). But in our experience it was unheard of for anyone to be found telling downright lies. There was almost always a good 'fit' between the stories, although, hearing them separately, they might excite our sympathy and interest for very different reasons.

The contradictions which we *did* uncover reflect the problems inherent in truth-finding within the judicial process. As researchers,

---

[4] In the course of a television interview with Alan Whicker.

we set out to discover 'what really happened' (and, in particular, what really happened on court premises). In doing so, we occasionally had to grapple with the same contradictory versions of 'truth' as, at some earlier stage, had the court itself.

One cannot of course regard the parties' account as the *only* valid perspective on professional performance. But this is no argument against consumer research. Without it, there is no effective means of monitoring the development of legal policy; we are reliant on the good instincts of a few officials in the Lord Chancellor's Department and on the opinions of practitioners and their professional bodies. On that system, the parties are represented only by pressure groups (who are almost bound to be *un*representative) and by the Lord Chancellor's postbag (equally so).

It should however be recognized that 'consumer' surveys can take a number of different forms (including postal questionnaires, or a highly structured interview format in which the interviewer seeks immediately codifiable answers to specific questions). Our interviews took place in the parties' homes, lasted on average between one and a half and two hours, and were tape-recorded. Many of the questions were open-ended and we were happy for our informants to take us wherever they wanted in terms of what was important to them (rather than confining them to points which *we* believed ought to have been significant).

In presenting this material, I rely heavily on individual accounts—on what is generally termed qualitative or 'soft' evidence, rather than on counts of answers. This is at odds with a common view of social science research findings which holds that quantifiable results provide a yardstick against which to judge the other 'softer' data, thus ensuring that the researcher does not simply include material favourable to his particular argument. Such a view ignores the extent to which the researcher's perceptions are embedded in the design of a question-naire, so that the answers which he gets are used primarily to support (or, more occasionally, to refute) his prior assumptions. Even a question like 'what did you think of the registrar?', whilst it may appear innocent enough, is requiring the person interviewed to furnish an opinion of an official who may have been so marginal to his experience of the legal process that he has to be reminded of who he was. Nevertheless, that reply will be given the same weight as that of other informants who were simply burning to recount their experience of a hearing before the registrar.[5]

[5]   I am grateful to Simon Roberts for a very useful discussion concerning different forms of 'consumer' research.

In presenting the transcribed 'quote' material, I have striven to achieve a balanced presentation of the weight of opinion and experience across the range of interviews. Apart from this, my only selection criterion has been—in line with the point made above—to choose material which flows directly from the parties' experience and which is not simply a response to a direct question.

Finally, it should be noted that we only asked our informants about their own experience, not about legal or welfare *policy*, or about professional practice in any general sense. This was because it could not be assumed that they would have any knowledge of the possible alternatives upon which such questions might be based. For example, we did not ask them whether they favoured the introduction of a 'Family Court'. Their views on that question would be of no greater interest or relevance than those of any other group.

The Parties

3

Private Troubles

BEFORE considering the role of partisans and mediators in family disputes, it is important to gain some understanding of the history of these conflicts. How have the parties behaved towards one another 'in private'? What was their experience of trying to negotiate together? To what extent did either feel under threat?

A quarter of the couples interviewed in the course of the 1980 'Special Procedure' survey reported that there had been little or no tension between them in the period following their separation. It was not uncommon for us to hear remarks such as the following:

Not bitter at all . . . say he called in here . . . I can sort of say anything to him, class him as a friend.

In the last eighteen months everything has been on a friendly basis. He will be the strongest friend I have until the day I die.

These couples did not wish to remain as husband and wife, but they had salvaged something from their marriage; the relationship that endured was a source of satisfaction to them both.

At the other extreme, more than a hundred of the parents in the 'Special Procedure' sample (31 per cent) told us either that their divorce had been 'not at all amicable' or that there had simply been no communication between them throughout the divorce period.

There was also a large middle group, comprising 40—50 per cent of those interviewed, who had experienced a variety of tensions and disagreements but who had nevertheless struggled to behave in a 'civilized' or 'adult' fashion, partly for their own sakes, but also for the sake of their children. Whatever the basis for these couples' reluctance to allow their divorce to degenerate into a legal battle, they were not helped by the common assumption, reflected in court procedure and in the approach of some legal advisers, that on divorce the parties *separate* interests should necessarily be regarded as paramount. We found, on the contrary, that for many divorcing couples, separate and mutual interests coexist. This element of mutuality centred on their children, whom they both wished to see and bring up. But in addition it was apparent that some couples still cared for one another, whilst others felt it important to behave in what they regarded as a reasonable fashion. We formed the view that there was insufficient attempt to differentiate and cater for those who did not seek an adversarial solution to their problems (Davis, Macleod, and Murch 1982*a*).

The Fighters

It is upon the above thesis, expounded of course by many other commentators, that the mediation 'movement' has largely been built. But in the course of the later 'Conciliation in Divorce' research project, when we interviewed 299 parties to contested legal proceedings, I was forced to recognize that many couples had no sense of there being a 'middle ground' which might be tapped by a skilled mediator; they saw their divorce in terms of an unashamed conflict of interest. It was in the realm of finance and property disputes that this tended to find undiluted expression. The following accounts sum up the spirit in which many of these negotiations were conducted:

There was no suggestion that I could put forward, or anybody else could put forward, that my wife would agree to. She was out to take me for every cent that she could possibly screw me for. As my solicitor put it, 'She wanted my left testicle'—half of everything.

All the way through our divorce, it's always been seconds out of the ring, and I'm in the red corner and she's in the blue.

There was no actual conflict between us, there was only, speaking for myself, resentment and acrimony.

The 'rethink' that occurred as a result of this later project illustrates the importance of the point made earlier, that everything depends on whom you ask. I had moved from a sample of 'routine' divorces to one of legally contested applications; the difference was striking. For the remainder of this chapter, I shall concentrate on these disputed cases, all of which are drawn from the 'Conciliation in Divorce' research study.

It is probably a mistake to regard these highly charged public quarrels as reflecting simply a conflict of interest. The threat posed in many of them was more serious than that. Although not put in these terms, it often appeared that one party had come to pose a fundamental threat to the other's psychological health and well-being:

My solicitor advised me if I tried to stay in the house, then maybe he would go and I would be able to stay on. But the situation was that bad that in the end it made me quite ill, you know—just used to get very nervous; so that whenever I used to see him, I used to practically shake from head to foot—and if he just said anything at all, you know, that would be it, so we just didn't talk. The less we had to do with each other, the better—as far as I was concerned anyway.

The same pattern emerged in many other cases. The element of 'threat' which we perceived was seldom mentioned directly, but it could often be inferred from the parties' violently hostile reactions towards one another whenever they came face to face. Anger, shouting, 'letting rip' can be useful defence mechanisms and this was how many of these couples had learnt to deal with one another:

Never sees her. Never sees her at all. She don't bother even to come up here and see the kids. Every time I sees her she jumps down my throat. The less I see of her the better. If I do it all through solicitors, there's no rows and no arguments and she can't blame me for nothing, so that's why I does it. I always does it through the solicitor.

[different case]

Well, it was a waste of time, because every time we started to talk about it, I'd have to see things from his point of view; I could never have a point of view of my own. So, you know, it just erupted into a row. It was just a waste of time— sheer waste of time.

In many of these cases the parties were so locked into competing, antagonistic positions that the battle proceeded in the same way, no matter what ground was being fought over:

He will tell you his story, so I'll tell you mine. If I say no, he says yes. It's that sort of relationship. His attitude was that if I wasn't going to stay with him, he wasn't going to let me stay with anybody else. If I wanted the children, no, I wasn't going to have them. If I didn't want the children, I could have them. It was just the opposite, you know. We've now been separated three years and I still can't talk to him over the phone. We don't talk, we row. It's abuse. And I've now got to the stage where I put the phone down. Now, if I want to have the children for an extra day or an extra weekend, I do it through my solicitor.

Several of the women whom we interviewed felt that they had been dominated and undermined throughout the marriage; that was their reason for seeking a divorce—they wanted to get away:

There's *always* been ill-feeling. He thinks he owns me—that whatever he says is right. He can do no wrong. We're not the sort of couple who can discuss things. We've always had a love/hate relationship. We don't talk—we quarrel.

As far as I'm concerned, we should be able to speak to each other on a friendly basis. But that's not possible for my husband. He despises me.

It is possible to view conflicts of this kind in terms of a failure of communication, with costs to both sides. In some cases this does seem a reasonable interpretation. But some of the women whom we interviewed in Bristol described years of psychological domination by their husbands, often reinforced by physical violence. One woman simply refused to answer the question 'What would be your husband's version of these problems?'—she couldn't bear to think of it. Another's skin turned red and blotchy in the course of the interview under the strain of recounting her former husband's behaviour towards her.

This kind of background may explain why in many of these cases it was the *wife* who refused to entertain the possibility of any direct negotiation. The psychological dominance of the man was such that negotiation as equals was simply not possible. In fact, for many of these couples, both men and women, the biggest problem as they saw it was to get judges and registrars, or whoever else was involved in the case, to recognize who was telling the truth (that is to say, that *they* were). They wanted someone (a lawyer) to protect their rights and they wanted the court to decide the case in their favour. The idea of *negotiating* with their spouse (even with solicitors present) seemed almost incomprehensible.

Needless to say, if one party wishes to talk over the problems and the other refuses, this can be very frustrating for the 'negotiator'. But it is important to understand the reason for such reluctance and not simply to regard it as evidence of intransigence. The following accounts, taken from a case in which we interviewed both husband and wife, may give some insight into this:

Mr A: Principally, although she wants as much as she can get, she doesn't want the acute discomfort of actually doing the negotiating—she hands everything over to her [second] husband, including every letter that I write to her—so that whatever happens, there's a solicitor's letter, even though I would rarely want to call in the solicitors, partly because it's expensive. But if there's any kind of hitch, then there's a solicitor's letter. I've written to say, 'Look, for God's sake, call off your legal bloodhounds', and I remember saying in a couple of letters, 'Of course I'll pay the maintenance, it's the law of the country—and in any case, I see the moral obligation, so don't go on like this.' But actually, she never reads the letters—she passes them straight to [second husband] who passes them straight to the solicitor, who writes to my solicitor . . . and that does rile me something terrible.

Mrs A: I don't think 'bitterness' is the word that characterizes my feelings. I mean, my feelings are of enormous relief that I no longer live with this scandalous human being—I'm very angry because I think it's tragic that there has been so much ill-feeling because, after all, it's the children who suffer as a result. And that I will always regret. I mean, he's done immeasurable damage—he really has.

One way of attempting to reconcile these accounts is to see them in terms of a power imbalance which the 'weaker' spouse has opted to rectify (quite successfully, it would appear) through the involvement of third parties. The woman's refusal to negotiate directly was only possible because she had at last achieved a physical separation from her husband. She also felt, given the man's past behaviour, that she had a moral right to distance herself from him. This question of moral right is, of course, a tricky one; we all have a tendency to feel that we're right most of the time. Stripped of that element, the woman's behaviour in this and other similar cases would begin to look much more like the exercise of power—a power which derives from having control over a key 'resource' in the conflict. Mrs A had a court order for maintenance and knew that, quite apart from the legal sanctions, a reputation as a defaulter would have been damaging for her husband.

It is impossible for an outsider to make a judgement of 'fairness' in such a case. But what does seem clear is that where one party exercizes control over a key area of the conflict, there is often a reluctance to compromise this position through negotiation. In the following case the husband was totally cast down by his ex-wife's refusal to meet with him or compromise in any way. His tone throughout the interview was lugubrious and depressed:

My wife is very . . . she seems frightened to negotiate on her own with me. She seems to appear to think that I'm going to be able to pull a fast one over on her. When she goes to her solicitor, she always goes with her father, so perhaps she feels the same about the solicitor. I think she lacks confidence to work out things and negotiate on her own behalf. She's obviously given guidance, I think, from her parents because of that. I think if we could have gone along to an office, even if she brought her solicitor along for her own confidence—and me bring my solicitor along—I think a lot of things could have been thrashed out and settled, because no matter what happened at the end of the day, you've got to get a steady situation where you can enjoy life. I'm sure she's not getting anything out of life at the moment. And I'm certainly not.

Whilst the wife in this case was thought to fear negotiation—in one sense, a sign of 'weakness'—her response can also be understood in terms of her having a fragile grasp on a certain kind of power. Following separation, the woman, perhaps for the first time since the marriage, may find that she is both relatively independent of her husband and even, as far as the children are concerned, in quite a strong position. This was another father's account:

It was just one-sided. It was me against a brick wall. She just was determined to do what she was going to do and literally, physically, you could see a steel shutter drop. It wasn't just me. It was anybody who wanted to discuss the situation she was going into. She didn't want to discuss it with anybody, to discuss the children being moved. As far as she was concerned, it was going to be all right for the children to be moved, it was going to be all right for her to move, and she just literally would not discuss anything.

This newly acquired power is peculiar to divorce. We were often told that the man had occupied the dominant position in the marriage—the term 'a brick wall' was used by some wives to describe their husbands' attitude towards them when they were still living together. But on separation the woman may, perhaps for the first time, have the upper hand in relation to the children; it is then she who becomes 'the brick wall'.

For those not used to exercising power, the only feasible strategy may be one of avoidance. There is no reason why these women should have had confidence in their own or anyone else's ability to control the outcome of a negotiation; everything had to be fought for, with all the limited strength at their disposal. This may serve to explain the view advanced by some men that women make poor negotiators. Our evidence lends support to Mary Ingham's argument that ' . . . if women haven't learnt the art of negotiation, it's because they've not had much experience of having negotiating power. Women are accustomed to having to act the injured party, rather than the put-out partner, prepared to give way a little' (Ingham 1981, 184). Also, it should not be assumed that in pursuing 'negotiation', these husbands were genuinely wanting to understand their wives' point of view. They were not disinterested; some, indeed, were extremely hostile. They may have been seeking an opportunity to cast blame, or exert pressure. Certainly this was suspected by some wives.

There are, however, other reasons for not talking. In some cases the decision to separate had been taken completely unilaterally. This had often come as a devastating blow to the abandoned spouse, compounded by their partner's subsequent refusal to discuss the marriage, or even the separation arrangements. The 'flight' that was exhibited in such cases (usually, it appeared, by men) was occasionally justified in terms of their spouse's refusal to accept the inevitable. But an alternative explanation might be that these men, knowing the effect that their action would have, could not bear to face the terrible distress of their wives. One example concerned a middle-aged woman who had obviously fought tooth and nail following her husband's sudden departure to live with another woman. She was thoroughly 'frustrated' (her word, which she used often) at his refusal to discuss either the marriage or any arrangements for his seeing the children. He only resumed contact after his wife (by then divorced) had met and started living with someone else; prior to that, one might suppose, he had been afraid of being swallowed up by her desperate need of him.

This frustration on the part of the spouse who is 'left' and then faced with a complete refusal to talk over the problem was evident in several other cases:

For me, the most unsatisfactory element in the whole business is that it is so impersonal. My husband left home without warning, after twenty-one years of marriage, and has never given any explanation. He writes directly to our son to arrange meetings; I am not allowed to speak to him; and his solicitor wrote to say that (husband) would not open any letters that I wrote—everything was to be done through his solicitor. At the very least, I have found this most impractical, and also enormously frustrating and hurtful. I would have given anything to have a meeting with him.

It was unusual to find men being left quite as suddenly as this. But in any event, it seemed that men who were abandoned by their wives were less likely to respond by making these frantic attempts to reopen communication; some, indeed, were consumed with anger and indignation. In the following case, both parties agreed that the man's reaction had been one of rage:

Mr B: She doesn't exist as far as I'm concerned. To begin with we were able to talk to each other, but nine times out of ten we had a mediator; I was likely to lose my rag and go for her, which I did a couple of times.

Mrs B: We couldn't speak. He would shout and rave. It was as though my voice and my being there just sparked something off in him, just unpredictable and terrible rage. In the end the only way I could get him to sit round the table and talk was if I had someone else in the other room. It was as though he couldn't face it—and that was his reaction, looking back now. He's lost so much in being bitter and not trying to understand. His pride ... as far as he's concerned I could never survive on my own, but I've proved I could.

Possibly as a defence against the pain of rejection, some of the men we interviewed regarded their divorce in exclusively (even ruthlessly) adversarial terms. One had been battling for twelve years over the terms of access to his son, following a marriage which had lasted a few months. He had no conception of what his wife's view of the matter might be, but took pride in his determination to go on fighting. He arrived for our interview with a briefcase full of legal documents. Another, equally combative character explained his position as follows: 'It was a business thing. I was wronged: from then on I was going to be righted'.

What was striking in many of these cases was not just the man's determination to win, but the cool and calculating way in which he went about this—reflected, for example, in the 'game' metaphor which some men employed when discussing their divorce. A few were encouraged to think in this way by their solicitors; for others, the legal process itself seemed stylized and rule-bound:

It seems to me that there's a routine to the game, that is, the wife tries to claim everything; the husband's solicitor then turns round and says we're not accepting that; then you go through another phase of coming to a mutual agreement. That's the game, or so it appears to be.

But there's no doubt that some men find it *easy* to respond to the impersonality of the law; they settle down to play the game for all it is worth. The most remarkable demonstration of this 'game' orientation was provided by a husband whose job entailed regular negotiation. His professional life had provided him with the skills necessary to conduct a successful, 'winning' divorce:

We spent quite a long time negotiating over the property, how much she should have, how much she shouldn't have. I mean, my job—I'm negotiating all the time. I'm negotiating over £5 or £100,000 for various companies. I'm well versed in the ways of negotiating: how much brinkmanship to use, how far to push the opposition, what to hold out for, because like I said before, when you get to that stage it's a battle, it's a game, a gigantic game. Somebody's going to win, somebody's going to lose; you might draw in the end, you know, but when you're looking out for your own interest, self-preservation takes precedent over everything else. It's a game, you've got to be game-orientated. I'm a good draughts player. It's a very good game. I really like to play that game with somebody who can also really play that game. And that game is based on moves and it's based on thinking,—if you move this way, the partner is going to move that way. And now if they move that way, you've got a chance to go *that* way, make them fall into the trap. Now to me, the whole divorce was based on a game of draughts and I played it. My finest hour was playing all the way through for three years until we got to the settlement stage.

This man had been very upset when his wife left him for someone else; his pride, if nothing else, was badly hurt. But in the marvellously efficient way which some men appear to have, he set about reconstructing his support system. Almost immediately, he found himself a new partner; that accomplished, his regret for the loss of his wife appears to have vanished like spring snow; she became another business opponent. If his response suggests a certain emotional shallowness, one might equally well say that an element of calculation and some degree of armour-plating are necessary in order to withstand the rigours of matrimonial litigation.

But although several people acknowledged their own ruthless or manipulative approach to property and financial matters, there was usually, implicit in these accounts, some explanation or justification for their behaviour. This was often in terms of the emotional damage inflicted on them by their spouse, accompanied, in the case of some men, by notions of betrayal, or the breaking of a contract:

Emotionally I was shattered. I mean shattered. It was my 17th birthday [when they met], she was 15, we were true to each other until she started messing around. I was hurt. Material-wise, didn't worry me at all. I won't say I played the dirty on her, but I played a crafty move, material-wise. She had this bungalow in _____ , but she never had nothing in it and she came down with a list stating, 'I want a sideboard, a dressing table, a wardrobe, a this and a that', and I thought, 'After all the years I've been putting into this place . . . ' So I went to a local market, furniture market, and I bought a sideboard, a table, a dressing table. She never said which one she wanted specifically. And then I put them out in the driveway and I put a lorry tarpaulin over, canvas tarpaulin you know. And when she came down, I said, 'There it is. There's a dressing table', ticked off, 'a sideboard', I had it all ticked off, it was there. It cost me about £15, I think.

If a researcher were to regard one party's account as providing the whole truth about any of these cases, he would have a very jaundiced view of a large section of the divorcing population. But the image of the vengeful, manipulative spouse which was sometimes presented to us seldom survived our actually meeting that person. For example, where fathers were applying for care and control of their children, we found that one reason for going on fighting—seldom appreciated by their wives—was that they simply could not bring themselves to 'give up' their children:

I've got a very strong relationship with my children and I felt that I could bring them up, to say the least, as well as she can. And I don't think they wanted to be parted from me—I certainly didn't want to be parted from them. I couldn't bring myself to leave them and I thought, if we've got to be parted, it's going to be the law of the land that does it, because I couldn't, I couldn't bring myself to leave—so that's what I fought for.

Other husbands and wives displayed remarkable forbearance in circumstances where there must have been a strong temptation to take revenge for past hurts. This was typified by those custodial parents who, despite being engaged in a legal contest over other aspects of the divorce, were determined that this should not damage their children's relationship with the non-custodial parent. This ability to 'compart-mentalize' the various issues was most impressive.

Just as remarkable, it seemed to us, were those couples who fought with great determination over the custody of their children, but whose approach to financial and property matters was entirely non-litigious. There were several cases in which one or other spouse accepted less than their legal entitlement. This may have been through a sense of guilt, that person believing that he or she had broken up the marriage, but whatever the motive, such behaviour tends to soften the starkly black and white picture which emerged from many individual accounts. It serves to remind us that there is no reason to suppose that these people were in any way out of the ordinary: given different circumstances, they would have been no more grasping, ruthless, or manipulative than the rest of us.

4

Informal Mediation: Family, Friends, and Others

THE resolution of family disputes is, these days, seen as a matter for professional experts. Many separating couples have learnt to think in terms of court proceedings as the only remedy for their difficulties. Mediation has likewise become a matter for professional organisation and trained (or at least accredited) personnel.

But it should be recognized that, even without specialist assistance, divorcing couples are unlikely to be struggling with their problems in total isolation. The probability is that they will have a number of potential 'partisans' and 'mediators' already to hand. Foremost among these will be other family members (especially parents), but they may also be able to call upon friends, colleagues at work, and, in some instances, new partners. These networks are truly *informal* in that they bring in people who usually have no claim to expert status; they are 'on a level' with the divorcing couple. The part played by these unsung 'partisans and mediators' is the subject of this chapter. The data relied upon will again be that derived from our 'Conciliation in Divorce' study of contested legal applications.

Family

50 per cent of those interviewed in the course of our study of these disputed cases said that they had discussed problems arising from the divorce with members of their family (usually parents). Of these, approximately two-thirds thought that their parents had been 'helpful', although the extent of that helpfulness varied considerably.

It may seem surprising that only half of those interviewed had spoken to their parents about these problems, but this reflects the fact that in many of these cases the parties were estranged from their parents in any event. Others felt that their parents were embarrassed by the depth of unhappiness which they wanted to express:

I found that most of my family treated me—this may sound really over the top—like some sort of leper. They couldn't cope with the whole situation and they couldn't cope with my grief, if you like, because it was grief, it was tremendous grief. I was really distraught. Had I been the happy-go-lucky type who said 'Right. I've lost a husband. I'll go out there and sock it to them', they could have coped with that, but they couldn't cope with the fact I was hankering and yearning after someone who'd gone. I didn't find them supportive.

It is probably true of many families that parents and children do not talk easily about personal matters. On the other hand, some parents offered their adult sons and daughters unconditional acceptance and support:

She [mother] said to me she thought it was coming because she'd stayed with us weekends when he'd been very brutal towards me. She must have known— she was in another bedroom but mothers being what they are . . . She never said anything to me before we split up, but she said, 'For years,' she said, 'I've known that you haven't been very happy.' I said, 'Well you never said anything.' She said, 'Well, when I changed from the house to the flat, that's why I wanted a two-bedroomed flat, because I knew that sooner or later you'd be coming'.

The issue of partisanship does not enter into this kind of unquestioning offer of help; the mother's view of her son-in-law is more or less irrelevant. Other parents had carefully resisted the temptation to take up a partisan position; although well aware of their children's marital difficulties, they had succeeded in remaining above the battle:

She [mother] said, 'Look, it's between you two', and she wouldn't interfere. She said, 'It's entirely up to you, you know your own minds, the both of you— you get on with it', kind of thing, you know—which, to me, I was grateful for that. She's never been the one to interfere with our marriage at all.

(different case)

They [parents] stayed out of it, you know, except for somebody that I wanted to talk to, they were sort of there. If [husband] was to walk through the door now, my mum would say, 'Oh, hallo. Put the kettle on'—she's that sort of person.

It might appear from such comments that these parents, in their non-partisanship, were 'uninvolved' rather than supportive. In fact, in the context of the interview as a whole, it was clear that this was not so. They had been a source of great strength, whilst yet resisting the temptation to become involved directly. This suggests a commitment to the independence or 'separateness' of their children, even when they were going through a very difficult time. It was clear that this belief in 'separateness' did not imply—and was not taken to imply—any lack of love. But there were other parents whose response had been fiercely partisan. As a result, they had effectively disqualified themselves from playing a useful mediating role. Their loyalty had been fierce and their response unambiguous, but the son or daughter directly concerned often displayed (at least to the interviewer) a more ambivalent reaction, perhaps retaining some loyalty or affection for their spouse, or being disinclined to view the marital breakdown in terms of guilt and blame. As one young woman explained:

I didn't want them [family and friends] involved—I knew what would happen if they were. I'm sure they'd be trying to help but they'd immediately want to take sides, and it wasn't like that. People don't understand—there were no 'sides' to be had.

Another of our informants, asked whether her parents had been helpful, replied as follows:

They thought they were. My mother was very, very protective—over-protective—like mothers are. I'd done no wrong, it was all his fault. He was always in the wrong. I just couldn't discuss anything with her. He was in the wrong, he was the one who went off, this, that, and the other. It was always . . . she was anti-him. Whatever the conversation, she was always coming down on him. She would never listen and try to think things through logically—which I think I needed at that time. I think in circumstances like that you just need to talk to somebody—not necessarily to be offered advice at the end of it, just to talk, without somebody putting their point of view to you. I've met other women who've been through divorce and they've said the same—they haven't wanted advice, just someone to talk to.

Whilst the kind of immediate leap to partisanship displayed by these parents was found to be unhelpful, there were other cases in which this was precisely the reaction sought. Partisanship is not some quirk of the older generation. We discovered that where this support was *not* forthcoming—if, say, a parent or brother or sister remained friendly with 'the other side', that person might be placed firmly in the 'enemy' camp. But on the whole there was a strong tendency for parents to side unambiguously with their own son or daughter. This is understandable if we accept that 'unreasonable' partisanship is an important benefit of parenthood, this being contrasted with the *impartiality* which is the normal aspiration of community or institutional care (Newson 1978). This may help to explain parents' response to the marital difficulties of their children—and also why our evidence concerning the kind of 'support' which the parties were seeking from other family members is fascinatingly contradictory. For example, many of those interviewed implied that their parents had been *too* partisan—and yet others were at pains to point out that the balance of parental approval (that is, including the reaction of 'in-laws') had been on their side.

They were several graphic accounts of the part played by parents and parents-in-law at the height of the conflict. In the following case it is interesting to note the very different roles played by the two parents-in-law. It seems that to be the beneficiary of unsolicited partisanship can at times be irritating, but to be the victim of it may give rise to thoughts of murder:

Several years before, my wife said, 'I want a divorce.' I thought, oh crikey, oh hell—I didn't know what it was all about. Well, quite honestly, I thought I was heading for a nervous breakdown because I just didn't know what to make of what had gone wrong—she wouldn't tell me, or couldn't tell me—I didn't know the words to say it and I got really way, way down—I was doing really potty things. I went to see her father and I said, 'I don't know what to bloody make of it all, she just wants a divorce.' And I said, 'For Christ's sake, don't say anything, I'm just putting confidence in you—I don't want you even telling your wife, because it may just blow over.' But of course, he did tell his wife— and well, my ex-mother-in-law was a bit of a boozer anyway and . . . we were in bed one night—it was a Saturday night I believe—and her mother was on the phone, 'Oh, Bob's been over talking to your dad about a divorce and I just wanted you to know kid, that I'm all for you, you know, you can depend on me.' I thought, 'You evil cow—she really was evil anyway . . .

We came across several other cases in which there seemed to be an affinity between the person interviewed and the parent-in-law of the same sex. This bond of common experience and understanding cut across the concern which that person felt for his or her own son or daughter, leaving no clear pattern of family alliance. The following account was given to us by a woman who had left her husband to live with another man:

They [parents-in-law] were very, very upset. It put his father in hospital. They just couldn't believe that it could happen to their son. . . . I had a talk to his mother before I'd filed for the divorce and I said to her that I'd walked out the house and I was terribly upset. I said, 'I just can't live with him any longer, he's just tormenting me to such an extent, I just can't take any more.' And she said,

'You know, he was just his father's son.' And that was exactly how his father had treated her and she could quite understand. She knew his faults and she'd been through an awful lot herself, but she didn't have the courage to do anything about it.

Friends

In assessing the part played by friends of the divorcing couple, some of the same patterns emerge as with parents and other family members— that is to say, the friendship and 'support' that are offered can take many different forms, although it is likely that most people choose to confide only in those friends who will respond in a way which they would consider appropriate. For example, we discovered that a kind of 'pull your socks up' approach went down well in certain circumstances:

Yes, I was very lucky (a) with my family and (b) with a very good friend who'd been through it all himself and he was able to put me on the right path by not giving me too much sympathy. He put me onto a counsellor who I had a little chat with but basically this friend put me back on my feet. He said, 'It's no use crying over spilt milk, life has got to go on and you've got to make something of it', and he really put a bomb up my backside and made me decide that I had to do it for myself. And I suppose I sorted myself out in about three months.

An interesting question in relation to friends' support (as with that of parents) is the extent to which this is unqualified. One or two people said that they had confided in friends, *rather* than parents, precisely because friends took a one-dimensional view. Parents, it was suggested, were also concerned for their grandchildren and anxious about their own position as grandparents. But friends' support may also be conditional, perhaps reflecting a judgement as to which spouse was responsible for the marriage breakdown. This throws a new and interesting light on the significance of 'guilt' or 'innocence' in these matters:

People said to me, 'Ray, it wasn't you that broke your marriage up, it wasn't you that ran off with somebody else, and your children will know that when they get older', and that helped me. Now if it was me that broke the marriage up I probably would have felt an awful lot of guilt as my kids were growing up, but seeing as how it is my wife that done it, it really helped me. Irrespective of what they say in the courts, neighbours and friends, they know, and that's a terrific help. I talked to everybody and anybody. I didn't keep anything in. I think a lot of people felt sorry. They were helpful, tremendous. They backed me up mentally, physically, everything. Friends took me out and came round to see if I was all right. I think it's because it wasn't me that went off with someone. It may have been round the other way if I'd left my ex-wife; maybe all my friends would have gone round there. A lot of *her* friends came to see me as well. It was her best friend who told me that she was carrying on with the bloke. People were ever so good to me. If I'd run off and left my wife and the three children, perhaps they wouldn't have been so nice.

But not everyone whom we interviewed had been seeking unqualified support; indeed, as we found in relation to parents, some of our informants had been embarrassed to receive it:

I gave up talking to other people about it because I found that people are very eager to take sides. Anyone I wanted to talk to, I found they couldn't be objective about it. Very few people seem to know how to be both supportive and objective at the same time.

The above extract sums up the problem admirably: few people know how to be both supportive and objective at the same time. Friendship or 'support' are defined in terms of a partisan commitment. But again it has to be acknowledged that friends may be responding to what appeared to be the parties' *demand* for partisanship. The man quoted below was one of the few who acknowledged that in discussing his marital difficulties with friends, he was not presenting them with the plain unvarnished truth:

Obviously, advice which people give you is fairly dubious because, I mean it's only human nature, we always argue cases from our own point of view and make it sound so reasonable that nobody could possibly disagree with us. I mean, that's human nature to do that. So when I'm telling my friends, I'm not presenting the best viewpoint from somebody else's point of view, I'm presenting the best viewpoint from *my* point of view. So I don't tend to trust advice which people give me, because I know that we automatically present biased information—you can't accept advice from somebody on a biased set of information.

One possible inference to be drawn from this is that if friendship is based on the perpetuation and mutual endorsement of flattering accounts and images, it is essential, when it comes to divorce, to seek more disinterested advice. Unfortunately, the same problem is faced by professional partisans; they too may have to deal in laundered accounts of motive and behaviour.

For others whom we interviewed it was not the *quality* of the advice or support received that was the problem; as far as they were concerned, there was literally no one to whom they could turn. There were frequent suggestions to the effect that, everybody's circumstances being different, you cannot look to your mates to grapple with problems which are peculiar to you. We found that men were more likely to express this view, perhaps reflecting their greater sense of social isolation. In some instances it appeared that this withdrawal was a reflection of their whole personality; their divorce had made each of them that much more of an outsider, less trusting and more lonely:

I tended to make it all inwards. I still do, actually—yeah, rather take it all on myself. Hard to explain really, but I don't really talk about it to other people.

I don't think I've ever told anyone the complete picture because if you spread the agony, people soon get pissed off with you.

I don't think anyone else can give you an answer. You've got to experience it. To be honest, I don't think you can expect anyone else to care very much.

We encountered few women who felt themselves to be as isolated as this, although one or two had been so distressed by their friends' reaction that they cut themselves off from all contact—a kind of forced isolation which, in retrospect, they felt had delayed their recovery from the trauma of the divorce:

I shut myself away all on my own . . . Well, they were all against him, so all I ever heard was about him . . . what he'd done and what they'd do to him, and I didn't want to know. So I just kept away and did it all on my own, which probably now was wrong. If I'd had a bit of guidance from somebody else, I could have come out of it a lot better off.

There were other cases in which the woman's natural reticence about sharing details of her marital relationship with outsiders had meant that no-one else really knew what was going on: such, it appears, is the awful privacy of married life:

Friends say, 'I wouldn't do this' and 'I wouldn't do that'. It's interesting to sit back later on and watch them go through very similar circumstances and see how they cope. I think that's the basic problem. I think you're so emotional and you're so influenced by other people that you're scared of making the wrong decision, although deep down you know what you're doing is right. People pressure you—friends, family, they pressure you for the wrong reasons because they don't really know what you feel. I think it's a very difficult time. Everything's traumatic and everyone's emotional and you're tipping up a whole life, everything . . . People can see you together and say, 'Well, you always seemed all right', but you don't go out and start having a stand-up row—that's not always what's wrong with a marriage. People think, like they did with my ex-husband—he went abroad and came back very wealthy, and people said, 'You've got that lovely home'—but they didn't have to go to bed with him.

New Partners

Amongst our sample of legally contested cases, the men were much more likely to have formed a new relationship than were the women (74 per cent as against 49 per cent). The same pattern was found amongst former clients of the Bromley Conciliation Bureau. Over half the men in that sample were cohabiting, as against 5 of the 22 women. Both groups reflect what would appear to be the standard pattern following separation (Leete and Anthony 1979), with men being quicker to embark on a fresh cohabitation or remarriage.

Not surprisingly, we found that new partners were a very important source of 'support'. But because some of our interviews took place several years after the time of greatest upheaval associated with the marriage breakdown, we cannot assume that this same level of support was available at the point of separation. Nevertheless, where a new partner *had* been on the scene, he or she had often played a vital role during the period when issues were being contested through the courts. As one young woman explained:

I'm quite a strong-minded person, but emotionally, it broke me when I realized I'd lost custody of the children. I really couldn't have cared less what happened. I think if I'd left and been on my own, I wouldn't have got through it, but having (new partner) behind me, he has helped 100 per cent—pulled me through it.

On the debit side, it was evident in several cases that these new relationships had led to further conflict between the former marital partners. Of the 230 people interviewed in Bristol who told us that either they or their former spouse had formed a new relationship, 98 (43 per cent) considered that this had led to increased tension, whilst only 8 (3 per cent) told us that new partners had contributed to *improved* relations. It was apparent that even after years of separation, one spouse's acquisition of a new partner could disrupt previously harmonious access arrangements:

I could have them whenever I wanted. He never stopped me until I met [new partner] and then everything seemed to go wrong. It was as if, while I was working and had my little flat, he had the control of my life. He had his woman, he had his children, and he had what I wanted more than anything— which was my kids. So he had the control of everything. It wasn't till I married that things started to go wrong.

It was also common for us to be told, from the other side, that the new partner was unreasonably possessive, so that he or she disrupted communication between the former husband and wife. It is little wonder that these situations provide the inspiration for so much television drama—usually distilled into comedy. In real life they provide a considerable test of anyone's resources. There were a number of accounts which suggested that this tolerance and understanding may have to be *learnt*:

I said to [husband] when he came to pick Angela up, he could maybe come in and have a cup of coffee. And knowing [new partner] was going to be there, to be fair I said, 'If you want to bring your girlfriend with you . . . ' And secretly I wanted to meet her anyway because I wanted to know what the woman was like who was looking after my daughter every weekend. It was a very tense and awkward moment but I thought quite beneficial really that we had that meeting. I had a little chat with her and I said, 'I know what Angela can be like.' She looked at me and I said, 'Don't worry, she can be a little cow when she wants to be.' I said, 'I'm not like her father who thinks she can do no wrong. You have my total permission to do whatever you think's necessary to her if she's naughty.' And I think that made her more relaxed towards me. Mind you, I'm the 'other woman' as far as my boyfriend and his children are concerned—he's got custody but they've got a mum. I suppose I was a little bit more understanding towards her because I knew what it felt like.

Mediation

If one accepts that the best mediators are those on a par with the disputants themselves (Roberts 1983), one might expect to discover that family members, friends, neighbours and new partners were all active in helping to secure a resolution of disputes arising from marital breakdown. In fact, we found very little evidence of such activity. Perhaps, these being cases which had involved a contested application to the court, they were a particularly entrenched group for whom 'mediation' did not appear a viable option. This in turn may be a reflection of the marked power imbalance which was apparent in several cases.

On a more general level, one might also point to the characteristic *privacy* of family life. We are now used to the idea that in certain dramatic circumstances (ill-health, divorce) these barriers may need to be breached by professional outsiders; we are less attuned to their being breached by relative intimates who are not sanitized by professional training and ethos.

There is also the apparently *idiosyncratic* nature of each couple's domestic arrangements. This is in part a function of privacy, but it is also important in its own right because it may be felt that non-professional mediators will import their own experience and value judgements, neither of which may be relevant to the particular circumstances faced by the parties. This was how one man explained the problem:

> You tend to try and keep it to yourself, basically, because it's down between [wife] and myself as regards *we* got married, *we* had the children—although you tend to accept a certain amount of advice. Your individual family unit— which are different from next door and next door—they do things in different ways. It takes a certain someone to be completely fair or whatever. So no, I don't think we speak to other people who've gone through it, but no one else's case is exactly the same as yours—no one I knew had this type of house or had a business—wanted to keep the children, this sort of thing. So I was sort of in a minority of one, if you like, as regards my situation.

Finally, there is the problem that most of these potential 'mediators' will be identified with the position of one or other party to the divorce. It was this which bedevilled the few attempts at 'parental mediation' which we heard about, none of which had proved notably successful:

> My parents did try to get us back together at one point. They tried to discuss it with us but it ended up with them having a fight in the kitchen. My dad got taken to court and he was told to stay out of it.

This is not to deny that parents may adopt a conciliatory stance (although for most 'family' it would appear that the attractions of a committed partisanship overrode any impulse to be conciliatory). But we found that parents seldom made any *direct* contribution to negotiations between husband and wife. Their influence was more likely to be exerted through advice given to their own son or daughter. A typical example might be where, as grandparents, they wished to continue seeing their grandchildren and so urged their son to maintain contact with his family at a time when he was tempted to abandon access visits.

Nor, amongst these litigated cases, did we hear of many *friends* who had played an effective mediating role. The following was one exception:

Yes, a friend. He acted as a sort of mediator when we were splitting up. Everything in the house: she said what she wanted, I said what I wanted. He was a good friend of both of us and still is. He's just one of them blokes.

Friends who can maintain good relations with both parties are no doubt extremely useful. But we did not hear of many such 'natural mediators' in the course of our survey. (Nor, for that matter, should it be assumed that there are many natural mediators amongst the staff of conciliation services, but that is another story, to be explored in subsequent chapters).

There were rather more occasions when a new partner had served as a useful conduit of information between disaffected spouses. These were also the most successful examples of 'informal' mediation that we encountered. In the following example, the man's embarking on a new relationship had initially served to exacerbate what was already a thoroughly acrimonious divorce. But as it turned out, this second wife (as she became) was able to distance herself sufficiently from her new husband's continuing resentment to prove acceptable to the former spouse as a mediating figure. Since she managed to retain her new husband's confidence at the same time, this suggests that she knew a thing or two about mediation, This is the *former* wife's account of the way in which the negotiations were conducted:

Our solicitors were taking so long in sorting out the maintenance and Jean phoned up one day and we settled the maintenance in forty minutes on the phone and it had taken the solicitors about two years. It was amazing: I was saying something to her and she'd say it to him and then the answer would come back. Between us we sorted things out and we said, 'You write it down. I'll write it down. You get yours to your solicitor and I'll get mine to mine.' And that was it. And we said, 'That's what we want.' The solicitors didn't really settle anything. It seemed to be up to us to settle it. The same happened with the selling of the house. It was Jean who sorted the majority of the problems out with that. Bill [ex-husband] never writes to me. Any notes about access— she writes them.

Other Sources of Informal Help and Advice

It will be clear from the preceding sections that many of the people we spoke to had found their divorce a thoroughly isolating experience. Whilst some had regarded this as inevitable, others had been desperate to find someone in whom they could confide. Men and women may experience this isolation in different ways, but both sexes experience it. Whilst women's freedom to act as they wish in some social situations is more constrained, they may also have a greater capacity to ask for help. We found that men tended to rely heavily on acquiring a new partner. For those who had not done so—and some men seemed to have lost all 'drive' or confidence in their ability to manage this—they might literally have no one else. In these circumstances, the financial and emotional burden which they were under had brought some men to the point of breakdown. As one man recalled:

I got extremely depressed back in May. My previous job—they were losing money every month and they were putting me under extra pressure. Even though the divorce was going on, I was bringing a lot of work home. And then I was trying to keep up correspondence on this business with the solicitor. Financially, I was rapidly going broke. I was still trying to keep up payments on the house. My wife wasn't very interested in the size of the bills any more—you know, I'd go home at 5 o'clock and the first thing I'd have to do was to go upstairs and switch all the lights off upstairs. There'd be every light in the house on. And I'd get gas bills, electric bills, telephone bills. Financially, I was up against it, but first of all what I wanted in the whole world was somebody to talk to, somebody to sort out the situation.

In these circumstances, voluntary organizations such as Gingerbread provided the kind of support which some people were seeking. In the words of another of our male informants:

That's where I found Gingerbread brilliant—just to be able to sit down and talk to someone else and they look up and say, 'Oh, I went through that. That'll pass', because at that precise moment in time you don't believe it'll pass.

Voluntary organizations may also have a part to play in dispute management. Indeed, some see their role primarily in these terms. However, the stance adopted by group members was often strongly partisan. This occasionally provoked bitter criticism of these bodies from the other spouse:

There's an organization—Families Need bloody Fathers—honestly, it's dreadful. They're not doing anybody any good, least alone the child. I asked what on earth they thought they were doing. They're just bitter men, really up there to cause as much trouble, get as many rights for the man as possible. Even the welfare officer's better than them; I mean, at least she's unbiased.

Of course, this particular organization would not claim to be non-partisan. It may nevertheless fulfil a useful function in offering unqualified support to its members. But the fact is that not everyone wants unqualified support. Families Need Fathers may suit the embattled temperament and circumstances of some men, but it does not suit others. Other organizations are perhaps more likely to contain members who have that rare capacity to offer support with objectivity. These people did not act as mediators as such, but they nevertheless provided low-key, non-inflammatory advice which was found to be helpful:

I talked it over with some members of Gingerbread—this was after I'd decided to go to court, because it seemed the only answer to the problem, and they said, if you go along quietly and state your case, then you'll be all right. And that's why I instructed [solicitor] to be very low-key in his approach to the court. You don't get that kind of advice from everybody down there, mind. Some of them will only see it from their point of view. It was a question of picking the right one.

Having noted the extent of truly informal (in the sense of unorganized) mediation, I now turn to what is arguably the most dramatic development in the field of family law for several decades, namely the rise of the 'conciliation' movement and the emergence of the new mediators.

The Mediator

5

Mediation: Background Ideas

A MEDIATOR is someone who tries to help parties to a dispute settle their quarrel, without having the power to impose a settlement upon them. By convention, we would not expect him to be identified with, or overly sympathetic towards the case advanced by either side. The use of this term therefore implies something more specific than merely being 'conciliatory'. The latter description could be applied to almost anyone: the parties may be conciliatory in the attitudes which they adopt towards one another; the approach of solicitors or barristers may also be conciliatory, as may that of a welfare officer conducting an investigation for the court; even a judge may encourage the two sides to reach agreement in the course of a hearing, or try to reconcile them to his adjudication. But solicitors, barristers, welfare officers and judges cannot, in the course of their normal duties, act as mediators— either because they are partisan, or because they possess adjudicatory power, or, in the case of welfare officers, because they have a degree of influence which is close to being 'adjudicatory' in many instances.

Having emphasized the non-coercive character of mediation, it is important to acknowledge that there are cases on the margins, where the degree of 'party control' is in doubt. Epstein has described processes which are both 'a mode of adjudication' and 'a settlement by consensus' (Epstein 1971), whilst Gulliver refers to cases in which the parties were unable to settle their dispute but nevertheless agreed to abide by the adjudicator's suggestion when persuaded that to do so would be to conform to norms of behaviour which they themselves upheld (1979, 27). Even in our present-day County Court, the boundary between exploration and persuasion on the one hand and coercion on the other can easily become blurred. This is particularly true in the field of family law, where judges now recognize the importance of achieving consensus.

Anthropologists have demonstrated that 'mediation' has a long history and is to be found in a variety of forms amongst many different cultures. It is tempting, as a result, to draw on these accounts in order to create the impression of a cross-cultural mediation tradition. But in many respects the comparisons are not apposite, and even where there are some parallels, the inferences that may be drawn are not always positive ones. For example, Merry's (1982) account of dispute resolution in non-industrial societies suggests that, in general, mediation takes place promptly, soon after the incident which provoked the quarrel; is time-consuming; is held in public; is conducted by powerful and respected community members, known to both parties; and is usually followed by payment of damages. In our culture, mediation in family disputes takes place in private, the mediator tending to rely on professional wisdom rather than community consensus. If there is coercion, it is likely to be based on the mediator's claim to specialist expertise, rather than on peer group pressure.

Given that there is no long history of divorce mediation, why has the conciliation movement, in the 1970s and 1980s, attracted such remarkable levels of professional interest and support, both in this country and in North America? It is obviously difficult to explain the precise timing, but one can certainly point to a remarkable conjunction of projected benefits. (The problem, as already noted, lies in reconciling all the competing claims.) The first thing to be said is that the word 'conciliation' summons up comforting images of consensus ('adversarial', of course, does the opposite), the implication being that, by these means, conflict may be satisfactorily resolved. It is significant that the term 'mediation' is comparatively little used in the UK, 'conciliation' being preferred, although the latter is sadly unspecific when it comes to crucial questions of third party alignment and authority. 'Mediation', on the other hand, clearly implies disputant control, and one can identify this (where it exists) as the one distinctive feature of 'conciliation' which gives these independent services much of their appeal. One central aspiration, therefore, is that couples who would otherwise have to submit to outside decision-making will be able to retain a greater measure of autonomy, and perhaps dignity, than is normally possible within the legal arena. But it is clear that the development of divorce conciliation in this country reflects a much broader and more confusing range of objectives than is conveyed by this bald statement of principle. Aside from any desire to promote party control (and sometimes quite clearly at odds with it) one may discern several other arguments or ideas which have given life to the conciliation 'movement'. For example, there are those who emphasize the need for counselling and advisory services at the time of separation and regard 'conciliation' principally as a means of meeting this need. Such a view is often advanced by members of the legal profession, perhaps because, consciously or otherwise, they continue to regard dispute resolution as their own preserve. As one solicitor put it, referring to BCFCS:

> It has time to talk, to counsel, advise and warn. It is generally much too expensive to treat your solicitor as a father confessor.

Some would argue that counselling is in any event best offered under the guise of dispute resolution, this being because the conflict orientation of these services means that they are free from stigmatic associations of weakness or dependency (Murch 1980, 35). This is reflected in the caseload of the Bristol service: a significant proportion of their clientele (25 per cent or more in the early days) appeared to be seeking individual advice rather than mediation in dispute, and indeed it was in this vein that the service responded to them.

But leaving aside some mediators' interest in individual counselling, the case for family mediation has largely been built upon the twin pillars of *cost reduction* and *child welfare*. It is held that mediation may achieve a higher settlement rate of contested applications to the court (or reduce the number of such applications), thereby saving court time and perhaps bringing about a corresponding reduction in legal costs. Secondly, mediation is identified with a greater concentration on the needs of children. There is a view that divorce gives rise to a 'diminished capacity to parent' (Wallerstein and Kelly 1980, 36) and the new mediators are motivated, at least in part, by their perception that conflict between separated parents is bad for children; indeed, this is a quite explicit part of the case advanced on behalf of most mediation services.[1] This reflects the fact that the conciliation 'movement' in Britain is very much a social workers' movement—and one which, moreover, appeals to the less 'radical' wing of the profession (Dingwall 1986).

In fact, there is no simple relationship between the practice of

[1] In the introduction to their 'Guidelines for Parents', the South-East London Conciliation Bureau state that: 'The way you cope with your divorce will in large part determine how your children cope with it. Try to use the experience of divorce as an opportunity for personal growth not defeat. In this way you can continue to be effective as a parent and to not only effectively meet your children's needs, but just as important, your own needs as a person. Continuing conflict between you and your marriage partner during and after divorce can interfere with your effectiveness as a parent.'

mediation and the pursuit of either of the above objectives. If we believe that children of divorcing parents are 'at risk' and also that the State is in a position to do something about this, then it might be supposed that we should tackle the problem directly, by instituting a more rigorous welfare check. The problem with this, of course, is that we already have a welfare checking mechanism in the s. 41 Children's Appointments. This form of surveillance has proved largely ineffective, whilst also being very unpopular with those on the receiving end (Davis, Macleod, and Murch 1983). An emphasis on negotiation and counselling may appear more realistic than surveillance, whilst possibly achieving some of the same ends.

Mediation offers the prospect of an *agreed* outcome in cases where parents may otherwise be faced with an unattractive choice between litigation and frustrated withdrawal. It is reasonable to suppose that a negotiated settlement, provided this is entered into voluntarily, will contribute to an improved atmosphere between the parties and, as a corollary, a greater likelihood of continued satisfactory contact between children and the non-custodial parent. It has to be said, of course, that this favourable outcome is not guaranteed and there is an inevitable tension between vigorous pursuit of child welfare objectives and the achievement of 'party control'. The more zealously the mediators pursue their *own* goals, the more likely they are to alienate parents (who are themselves concerned for their children's welfare) and the greater the risk that their intervention will lose its mediatory character.

The second claim, that mediation will secure legal aid savings, is even more questionable. In recent years the number of matrimonial legal aid applications, and the cost of these, has risen sharply. Since many people cannot get access to the legal services which they feel they need (Davis, Macleod, and Murch 1982*a*) and since solicitors and barristers will wish to continue to make a living, it is not easy to imagine this trend being reversed. In any event, it is taking the economic principle of 'trickle down' to considerable lengths if we are to imagine that a significant reduction in court business will be achieved by means of these extra-legal services, eking out their precarious existence at the edges of the legal system. If this is indeed a symbiotic relationship, the image presented is not a flattering one, the mediation schemes being cast in the role of those intrepid little birds which supply a tooth-cleaning service for alligators.

At the same time, it is hardly surprising that preoccupation with survival has led the new mediators to invite assessment largely in terms of their usefulness to the court: that is, in reducing the demands placed upon judge and registrar time, and secondly, in achieving 'savings' to the Legal Aid Fund. This in turn has encouraged a form of false accounting under which mediation *appears* to be cheap because it is performed by volunteers, or by divorce court welfare officers whose costs are absorbed within the Probation Service's overall budget. If the present crop of volunteer mediators were to be paid, as many aspire to be, then these schemes might well prove quite expensive.

There are, fortunately, rather better arguments than this in support of family mediation. In summary, the case can be said to rest on the three main planks of: (a) the alleged highly personal, idiosyncratic nature of family conflict; (b) the fact that contact between family members may need to be sustained after divorce, thus requiring the parties to look forward, as well as back; and (c) the fact that family members are presumed to share a number of key *values*, although their individual *interests* may in certain respects conflict.

In divorce, as in other areas of our civil law, justice has long been regarded as based on precedent and commonly accepted norms of behaviour, so that a reasonable and disinterested person may decide what is just in a given case. Justice in these terms is seen as absolute—difficult to establish, no doubt, but capable of objective assessment. However, the present interest in negotiated settlements suggests that it is often impossible to resolve disputes between divorcing couples on the basis of legal precedent. One reason for this is that a marital relationship will have its own history, a culture in which some behaviour is accepted as reasonable and some is not. What is defined as reasonable may appear bizarre to an outsider. Any third party who becomes involved in the conflict will therefore need to come to terms with the assumptions upon which the relationship is based.

If such a view is accepted, it follows that the parties themselves should exert a large measure of control over the negotiation process, the object being to achieve flexible solutions tailored to the particular case. This implies an informal procedure, rather than fixed rules or any kind of ceremony which would appear to elevate third-party decision-makers above family members.

The second key argument in support of family mediation is that the mediator is not required to arrive at a judgement based on past events, ensuring comparability with other decisions arrived at in roughly similar cases; she can afford to look forward to future arrangements and so may focus on the long-term consequences of any proposal. Adjudication may be very much a last resort where conflict arises between parties who have many mutual interests and dependencies which are likely to survive over a long period.[2] Former marriage partners often have to maintain some kind of relationship and this puts negotiation at a premium, particularly when it comes to agreeing maintenance, or the terms of access to children. It may be impossible for an adjudicator in these circumstances to devise precise and detailed instructions which will cater for all eventualities. Unless the parties are to go back to court time and time again—'perennials' as they were referred to by one judicial officer—they are almost bound to have to sort these matters out for themselves in the end. It may therefore be better for them to be involved from the outset, thus, it is hoped, developing some capacity to negotiate together.

The third argument in support of family mediation is that negotiation (of which mediation is but one form) is *most* likely to be successful where there is a clash of interests—a situation of scarcity where the parties are seeking the same resources without there being enough to satisfy both (Gulliver 1979, 8). If this supposition is correct, one might conclude that financial adjustment (and, to a lesser extent, access arrangements) are best dealt with through a process of narrowing, compromise-seeking negotiation, whereas the issue of care and control, or disputes over which parent should retain the matrimonial home, are much less negotiable.

Taking this one stage further, it may be that in order to secure more general acceptance of mediation in divorce, *more people may need to be persuaded to think in terms of interests* (children's interests, as well as their own), so abandoning their perception of the dispute as resting on a clear value judgement. As will be seen in Chapter 7, some mediators do indeed try to bring about this shift in perception. Whether that is desirable or not depends on how we conceive these issues. It is at least arguable that family disputes are more appropriately addressed within a framework of rights and responsibilities; a discussion framed in terms of 'interests' may seriously distort the true nature of the conflict (Merry and Silbey 1984).

---

[2] This point is made in a Memorandum submitted by the Legal Aid Advisory Committee to the Inter-departmental Committee on Conciliation, *32nd Legal Aid Annual Reports 1981–2*, Appendix D, para. D 3.

Influences Upon Negotiation

In almost any divorce dispute, but especially in relation to financial matters, an important influence on the negotiations will be the court's response, as far as this is known, to other similar cases in which there has been an adjudication. This is what is meant by the well-known phrase that the parties bargain 'in the shadow of the court' (Mnookin and Kornhauser 1979). This legal framework exerts a strong influence upon negotiations conducted by legal advisers, but 'the shadow of the court' will fall across any form of third-party intervention. Even for the mediator, an ability to predict the outcome of an adjudication may be as important as the capacity to relate to the parties on their own terms, understanding their views of what a fair outcome might be. So, in relation to finance and property disputes, the mediator would appear to require a detailed knowledge of case law in respect of tax, trusts, mortgage payments, and legal costs.

This brings us to one of the key questions in the debate as to the rival merits of mediation on the one hand and adjudication (or lawyer negotiation) on the other. The question might be put in terms of whether one believes that these matters have to be resolved by reference to a public standard, or alternatively, whether there is scope for negotiation which rests on the parties' 'private' perceptions of their quarrel. Were husband and wife to negotiate on their own, there could, arguably, be a problem of lack of informed consent. On the other hand, negotiation through legal advisers may lead to a settlement which takes virtually no account of the parties' own interpretation of the issues in their case. It might be argued that mediation offers a middle way between exclusively 'private' and 'public' forms of settlement-seeking; for example, it is difficult to imagine mediators responding to questions concerning the relevance of the parties' 'conduct' simply by reference to the leading cases in that field. But one should be careful not to exaggerate the new mediators' commitment to negotiating on the basis of these 'private meanings'. Even if one accepts that mediators, by virtue of their operating outside the legal framework, will be better placed than solicitors to take account of the parties' own interpretation of their differences, it would be naïve to imagine that professional interest in mediation is inspired solely by visions of party control; the contradiction is all too plain to see. Empowering the disputants may be *one* aspiration, but it is equally plausible to regard the practice of the new mediators as underpinned by their strongly 'pro-child' and 'pro-family' values. This is not simply a matter of seeking to identify and promote children's interests; it reflects a vision of *the whole family as needing help*. This is consistent with the view of some commentators that, following separation, the family is still a family—and should be treated as such (Murch 1980, 93). Many of the couples who present themselves for mediation are likely to endorse this. They are to a large extent self-selected and the fact that, like the mediators themselves, they tend towards the 'middle-class' may well reflect this value identification.

We should not infer from this that it is only the new mediators who endorse these 'pro-family' values. Many partisans feel the same way. But it is difficult for partisans to reflect this in their actual practice, as one Bristol solicitor explained to me:

A conciliation service can react to problems in the family as a whole. Under the adversary principle, the lawyer's job is to represent the client *on that issue*. Support and counselling is part of that role, but you need someone for whom it is their sole job.

Some solicitors evidently feel torn at the legal system's endorsement of the single-minded pursuit of separate interests. For them, 'conciliation' is doubly attractive—an undoubted good in itself, but also a much needed counterweight to the individualism of the law. One can imagine therefore that mediation has even more appeal for those non-lawyers who have long been in business as experts on the family. Thus we find, for example, that a form of 'conciliation' is undertaken by practitioners whose principal concern is with the repair of family relationships on a 'family therapy' model. Apparently, mediation is regarded as an appropriate extension of these activities, if not actually synonymous with them. This of course sits uneasily with any desire to promote 'party control'; the greater the emphasis on professional expertise, the more the parties will tend to be confirmed in their inferior 'client' role.

The current organization of mediation services reflects the uncertainty in this area, as well as the professional interests involved. As far as extra-legal services are concerned, there are two main models. In the first, the scheme operates as an offshoot of the divorce court welfare service, although possibly employing volunteer staff, many of whom will have a professional qualification of some kind. In the second, the scheme is independent of any other organization; once again the staff may have qualifications in counselling or social work, although, depending on funding arrangements, they may work for little or no pay. The Bromley Conciliation Bureau is an example of the former model, whilst BCFCS in Bristol is the best known of the 'independents'. The staff of *both* types of scheme tend to have a background in counselling or social work. This inevitably colours their approach, as well as determining those issues which they feel competent to take on. Thus we find that very few of these services feel able to mediate on property and financial issues. This is despite the fact that custody disputes are bound up with decisions concerning the matrimonial home, whilst problems over access to children are often related to non-payment of maintenance. These divisions reflect the fact that mediation has been developed in such a way as to promote the interests of one professional group, whilst not posing any fundamental threat to the boundaries of another. When interviewing solicitors in Bristol, I found that very few were prepared to consider that a service staffed principally by former social workers might be competent to mediate on financial matters. As one explained:

I don't think BCFCS can help resolve capital settlements because the conciliator does not know if the parties have disclosed all assets and because, I imagine, the conciliator does not know the legal rules and precedents to apply.

Given the background of these particular mediators, one can hardly quarrel with this view. But the fact that mediation services are staffed by social workers and marital counsellors tends to put on one side the question of whether, in principle, financial issues might appropriately be resolved through mediation. In fact, as discussed earlier, these disputes might well prove to be the *most* suitable. Nevertheless, the assumption appears to be that custody and access disputes are best resolved collaboratively, whilst financial and property issues are appropriately 'settled' by means of negotiation between legal partisans.

The Demand for Mediation

The fact that most of these schemes concentrate on custody and access disputes makes it difficult to assess the potential demand for mediation across the whole field of marital breakdown. Another problem is that most of these services have been operating for only a short time, often with inadequate local publicity. Thirdly, mediation schemes tend to rely heavily on solicitors for their supply of cases; only a minority of their clientele come in 'off the street'. Accordingly, demand is largely in the hands of the legal profession, of whom some are enthusiastic and others not.

As it is, BCFCS and the Bromley Bureau deal with several hundred cases each year, but other services may attract fewer than twenty couples over the same period.[3] In 1983, of 144 cases included in our sample of contested custody or access applications to the Bristol court, 48 (33 per cent) had at some stage been referred to BCFCS. Clearly this is a not insignificant proportion. But even BCFCS has had trouble in attracting both parties to the dispute and one gathers that at other centres lack of demand is seen as a major problem. The same difficulty arises in the USA, where one finds researchers expressing the rather plaintive hope that their study might lead to a better understanding of 'the causes and cures for the pervasive underutilization of mediation services by the general public' (Pearson and Thoennes 1984).

The Inter-departmental Committee on Conciliation tried to assess 'demand' simply by comparing the number of referrals to mediation services with the number of contested applications to the court.[4] This was misconceived. In the course of our 'Special Procedure' study of uncontested cases we found that 18 per cent of parents expressed themselves dissatisfied with the current access arrangements, but few, if any, had sought redress through the court. It would appear therefore that some people avoid court proceedings come what may. Fear of costs is one reason for this, but there is also the tension and feeling of impotence which is engendered by the legal process.

It may appear surprising, in these circumstances, that the 'demand' for formal adjudication appears to be rising.[5] But there are two reasons why we should *not* be surprised at this: first, because contested legal applications are necessary in order to secure lawyer income through the Legal Aid Fund; and secondly, because many couples have learned to think in terms of court proceedings as the only remedy for their difficulties. It is possible that if they were introduced to other services, they would come to find those equally necessary. It is worth noting, in this connection, that the Bromley referral rates built up gradually over several years as legal advisers and the general public became more aware of what was on offer.

[3] *Report of the Inter-departmental Committee on Conciliation*, Lord Chancellor's Department, 1983, para. 4. 4.

[4] *Report of the Inter-departmental Committee on Conciliation*, para. 4. 3.

[5] See ch. 1, n.1.

The only safe conclusion to these arguments is that, no matter what the forum, everything depends on the quality of justice that is available within it. It is for this reason that I believe the family mediation 'movement' has done itself a grave disservice by its concentration on 'settlement rates'. Given the need to demonstrate cost-effectiveness, schemes have felt bound to employ the same measure of effectiveness as does the court itself, but 'settlement' (in the sense of an agreement that can be enshrined in a court order) need have little to do with justice. The most attractive features of mediation—immediate response, informality, flexibility, and absence of coercion—could easily be lost through this slavish adoption of the court's criterion. 'Settling' as an end in itself does not occur to most people. It is much more important in their eyes that someone, judge or mediator, should fully understand their case.

Finally on the subject of 'demand', there is the question of whether this falls evenly across the social and employment categories. Critics of informalism, especially in the USA, have argued that organizations such as the Neighbourhood Justice Centres cater for disadvantaged groups who cannot afford access to the legal process (Abel 1982*b*, 274). Whatever the basis for this criticism, it is fair to point out that in the USA people expect to have to pay for professional help which they value. This is not the case to the same extent in Britain, where the National Health Service and the Legal Aid Scheme go some way towards enabling working-class people to have the kind of non-stigmatized access to highly regarded professional services which are denied them in countries where these people are available only as a commodity—that is, for a fee. Accordingly, the assumption that any service provided free is of a lower order and therefore stigmatizing to its recipients may not apply, or at least, it may not apply to the same extent.

As far as can be judged from our surveys of BCFCS and the Bromley Bureau, the clientele of mediation services in this country are not confined to the low paid. As already noted, there is, if anything, a tendency towards the 'middle-class', although it would appear that the *most* privileged members of our society are not represented. If it is correct to assume that 'the privileged classes will not submit to judgement by inferiors' (Abel 1982*b*, 274), one might well expect this kind of class distribution. This is because the staff of mediation services themselves have intermediate professional status. As for the under-representation of the very poor, this may be because their legal costs are paid in full, so that 'mediation' offers them no financial saving. There is also the fact that some solicitors consider that these clients are more vulnerable than their middle-class counterparts in any negotiation conducted without benefit of legal advice.

6

Authority, Neutrality, and Gender

THERE are two potential inequalities which, it has been argued, undermine the mediation case. These are the 'twin hooks' of—first, an imbalance between the parties; and secondly, an imbalance between the parties and the professional mediator (Bottomley 1984). These two issues are not easily separated, particularly now that a form of 'mediation' is being practised on court premises. Given the difficulty in securing access to judicial determination (for which see Chapter 12) the 'choice' which some people may face is either to accept the authority of the mediator, or else to submit to the will of their spouse.

In this chapter I shall explore these questions, drawing on illustrative material derived from the 'Conciliation in Divorce' research study. I shall rely principally on the interviews with 51 former customers of the Bromley Bureau; and on the large study of contested applications to Bristol County Court, many of these couples having had prior experience of the Bristol Courts Family Conciliation Service (BCFCS).

Parkinson (1986, 131 ff.) has identified several inequalities in bargaining power, including greater intellectual or verbal ability; emotional dominance and emotional blackmail; the physical power of actual or threatened violence; and the ability to invoke religious or moral authority, possibly with the support of other influential community members. An important question for any mediator therefore concerns the extent to which he will seek to rectify any imbalance between the parties—as reflected, for example, in the forcefulness with which they present their case. In practice, there may be a temptation to do the opposite—that is, to probe for areas of weakness in the hope that one spouse will be more 'reasonable' or less robust than their partner, so that concessions may come from that quarter. This is in line with Haynes' suggestion (1983) to the effect that power to resist making *any* settlement may confer significant advantage on one party. Merry (1982) has gone so far as to claim that 'with few exceptions, a mediated settlement reflects the status inequalities between the disputants'. She also argues that 'a mutually acceptable solution tends to be one in which the less powerful gives up more'.

The experience of the following client of BCFCS would appear to support these observations. She felt that the mediator had been intimidated by her husband, he having refused to compromise in any way. As a result, attention had been switched to her, as the more vulnerable partner:

> The only way anything could have been solved at that place was for one of us to give in and he wasn't willing to, so I did. How I felt was that they wanted a solution—they wanted to achieve something—and one of you has got to be reasonable—hopefully both of you, but if not, at least one of you. I felt that they tended to pick on the one who was the least uncooperative ... If a woman's got custody, then it's a case of, well he has a right to see his children and don't you think you ought to try and think about it and be a bit reasonable; and you're sat there thinking, 'Oh, aren't I awful?' You know, sometimes I used to come out of there thinking, well, maybe I am being a bit mean; maybe I'm not looking at it clearly.

But in the end she regretted her own capitulation:

> We were in there for hours and I really felt taken over. I came out with a splitting headache and I felt totally drained. I went home and I said, 'I've agreed to it but I don't know why.' Two months later I thought, 'Why the hell did I listen to that woman?' I was right all the time. I regret every minute of it. We went through hell because I gave in.

This extract offers some support for the feminist critique of mediation outlined in Chapter 1. It could be argued that one reason why these pressures will tend to bear on women rather than men is that our culture demands that they be less confronting, or less assertive of their own interests at a cost to someone else's (Gilligan 1982, passim; Wishik 1984). This is difficult to establish and of course some women appear well able to resist such cultural expectations. Nevertheless, it is possible that men are better able to indulge any tendency to be aggressive or domineering; the 'powerful' woman might be more constrained by the mediator's presence (again reflecting cultural expectations about how women 'ought' to conduct themselves).

A related problem concerns the different modes of argument employed by some husbands and wives. A few of the women interviewed at Bromley found it difficult to respond to their husband's reasoned, carefully argued approach—which they interpreted as coldly hostile. The man for his part might complain that the issues could have been resolved much more quickly; as one Bromley customer commented wearily: 'It was difficult, lengthy, tedious.'

The mediator often has to grapple with the contrasting verbal styles and methods of argument employed by the marriage partners, although we should not assume that it is always the man who is articulate and belligerent, the woman cowed and retreating. In attempting to respond to this power imbalance, or difficulty in communication, the mediator can call only on her own resources and on the authority vested in her by the parties. But we should not infer from this that the mediator is necessarily an unobtrusive figure, someone who assists the parties towards a negotiated settlement whilst they almost forget that she is present. She may need to exercise considerable *personal* authority, as reflected in a willingness to pursue the problem and not avoid painful issues; and secondly, in ensuring that each party has the space to make their statements. Mediation may provide a safe enviroment in which these exchanges can take place without fear that they will degenerate into a shouting match. As one Bromley parent explained:

It was very nice being able to say something and have a mediator there that could prevent fisticuffs or whatever. It was a very controlling influence. The aggression slowly faded during the interview.

'Professionalism', as far as the mediator is concerned, should not therefore be equated with aloofness or superiority. In so far as this term was employed by the parties, they used it to refer to this ability to provide a non-threatening framework which enabled them to explore issues in a way which they could not have managed on their own. Prior to their attendance at the Bureau, many of these couples had found that any attempt at reasoned discussion had degenerated into a row. In the following case, this was confirmed by both parties:

Wife. We're not the type of people to row in front of other people. You know, we're both very private people and the fact that there was another man and another woman in the room, we could sit and discuss things that we couldn't at home. Because every time we tried at home there was fights and rows.

Husband. At the beginning, obviously there was things I didn't want [wife] to know about. By the end, well, half way through the meeting, I think [mediator] had sort of put you in the position where you had to tell the truth. I think because actually he was sitting there, you could say the truth, and I didn't mind. I found it a lot easier to get off my chest and . . . I mean now I'm still frightened to tell [wife] things because obviously when you're on your own, she sort of tends to fly off the handle. He enabled us to talk.

Perhaps the best answer to the charge that mediation perpetuates a power imbalance between men and women lies in this control over the process. If the mediator simply provides a forum for the parties to get on with the negotiations, then it might well be argued that the more dominant personality will continue to hold sway. But some of our Bromley informants indicated that the mediators did more than this: they were active; they did challenge; they controlled the ebb and flow of the negotiation; in some cases, the 'weaker' party did indeed feel empowered. In particular, it emerged very clearly in some instances that the mediator had been at pains to protect women against the greater emotional force, or even physical threat, which was presented by the husband:

It was very calm. I could've said anything I wanted to there which, that was very important . . . I suppose it reassured me that in that office I couldn't be bullied, which was very nice. It was comforting to sit down and have somebody civilized, you know what I mean, rather than to be shouted at all the time because of course he couldn't shout in front of somebody else. And that's very nice to be able to go and sit somewhere comfortably because that's what I haven't been able to do with [husband] anywhere. Wherever we went it was always screaming and shouting. And [mediator] is so big, you see. It was very nice also to have a man from my point of view because that's what I needed because I was being bullied . . . for me it was important that it was a man there.

Of those interviewed at Bromley, 30 per cent reported that the exchanges had been tense or acrimonious. (Women were more likely than men to say this.) This is an important message for those who regard mediation as attractive largely because it is seen as having the potential to 'get rid of' anger and hatred. There is considerable social anxiety about such negative feelings, particularly when they are expressed within the family. The attraction of mediation to the social work and counselling professions appears sometimes to be based on a notion that all conflict is resolvable and that, given the right kind of professional help, a reasoned consensus will emerge. This is a very tempting view—and from the standpoint of those who fear conflict, a very comforting one.

Some of the interviews which we conducted amongst former clients of BCFCS suggested that whereas the mediators had found it relatively easy to be 'tough' in the context of an individual counselling session, they were much less at ease when faced with the task of controlling negotiations with both parties present. (I should emphasize that this group of cases, being drawn from contested applications to Bristol County Court, would have included a disproportionate number of BCFCS 'failures'.) Some of the women who had experienced the Bristol service felt that the discussion had been dominated by their husbands, the men being more articulate, or more forceful that they were. They suggested a lack of authority on the part of the mediator:

I felt as though she was intimidated by my husband—which a lot of women are—and she would back down from him and then, sort of, put more emphasis onto me because he just would not budge. She wouldn't pump him so much because she just wasn't getting anything from him. If that had been a woman reacting like that, I think she would have acted differently. Because a 6′ 2″ giant who's sitting there bellowing out that he's not doing this, that or the other—I do feel she was slightly intimidated by him. I think a man may have had a different effect on how he reacted. He was answering her just like he used to answer me—because he is *right*, you see—he's totally right. And all women have a place and they all should be put in it. And on a couple of occasions I saw how he was talking to her—I would have been livid if that was me he was talking to—and he was just laughing at her . . . I did feel that I would have preferred a man in our circumstances.

This was another woman's account:

He dominated the conversation all the time. She couldn't ask questions because he kept coming out with statements like—one statement that kept coming over was this: 'She's an evil woman, Mrs _____ , you just don't know what she's like, she looks like butter wouldn't melt in her mouth'—you know—finger-pointing—it was like something out of a film, so dramatic—she had no control over it at all, she couldn't tell him, 'Okay, right, let's go onto something else.' She couldn't have that sort of effect. She just couldn't get through to him. And I just got so fed up, I completely cut off and just ignored it—I just sat there and waited for him to get it out and say what he wanted to say. As far as I was concerned, it just gave him a chance to let go all that bitterness.

It is interesting that BCFCS, an all-female service, seems rather more vulnerable than the Bromley Bureau to this accusation of failing to protect the woman from being harangued and bullied by her husband. Nevertheless, it is doubtful whether the ability to control these exchanges and protect the less outspoken parent is a peculiarly male characteristic. I have seen male mediators at Bromley fail to do this, whilst some female mediators were anything but inhibited in their challenge to the husband's aggressive behaviour. This was confirmed by the following former client of BCFCS:

I reckon they're great. Because you really could put your point across to him without him shouting you down, because he was a bit of a bully. I could never speak to him, talk things out. He'd never have that, but I could do it with another person sat there, you know, and he could put his point across. I think they're very good.

The mediator's authority may be necessary both to shield the woman from her husband's verbal bullying and, in some cases, to provide physical protection, without which she would feel intimidated. But mediation is also about reconciling competing versions of 'truth' and the mediator must be prepared to take on the uncomfortable task of exploring the significance of these discrepancies as they emerge. This calls for the kind of strength of purpose which is another aspect of 'authority'. At both Bristol and Bromley this was an area where several people (men almost as much as women) felt they had been let down by the mediator. For example, some women who had attended BCFCS regarded their husband as inherently untrustworthy; the mediator, although 'very nice' (in the first of the accounts given below) or 'very fair' (the second), had failed to recognize this:

Well, they were very nice but it was totally unsuccessful because the lady who was dealing with us was always totally taken in by my former husband's story, as it were. So whatever he said, yes he'd do that or do the other, or yes, he agreed that was right, or that was right, she believed it. I don't think she was tough enough. I don't make those remarks in any way to her detriment—he is a most plausible personality and that's been the hassle at every point. I mean, he is hugely convincing, absolutely plausible, very charismatic and totally unreliable—which makes any kind of negotiation impossible. And that I found in court as well and haven't known how to handle it. So you know, any piece of information from him is quite as likely to be wrong as right.

In a different case:

I'm not very good at explaining myself, my husband was. He's got, like, the gift of the gab. He could tell you black was white and you'd believe him . . . and I felt at a distinct disadvantage because he'd say things I knew were blatant lies and I'd just erupt and the lady would say to me, 'Now calm down, calm down', and I felt like saying, 'He's telling lies, why don't you believe *me*?' I felt as if I was banging my head against a brick wall. I felt like taking my friends along, not for support, but just to tell the real truth. I couldn't really talk like that. I ended up losing my temper . . . it was just sheer frustration. Because I knew he was telling lies and he knew I knew he was telling lies and I just couldn't handle it at all. I don't really know how much she realized what he was really like. It was all pathos with him while he was in there, you know. You felt like getting the violin out, but as soon as you were outside, he had the biggest grin you've ever seen in your life. He thought he really done himself proud—that was why I was so frustrated in the meeting. I'm not really very good at putting my case, so I felt at a disadvantage there, but on the other hand, she [mediator] was very fair. It was good that you had somebody from the outside looking in, but anybody like my ex-husband who was good at putting a case would do well in that sort of setting.

The final comment to the effect that 'anybody . . . who was good at putting a case would do well in that sort of setting' has disturbing implications for mediation generally. These accounts also contradict what might be the commonsense view that a mediator will be more sympathetic to the case presented by the parent of his or her own sex. We found at Bromley, where there was almost invariably a male mediator present (sometimes in tandem with a female colleague, occasionally on his own) that it was mainly *men* who complained of their partner's successful manipulation, whereas at BCFS, an all-female service, it was usually *women* who alleged that their spouse had not been sufficiently challenged by the mediator. One inference might be that mediators are less adept at seeing through the play-acting and story-weaving of parents of the opposite sex to themselves. This in turn would suggest that for the parent of the *same* sex as the mediator, it is possible to be understood all too well; the inscrutability afforded by sexual difference may be necessary in order to construct a plausible case.

On this evidence, one might conclude that those parents who seek a mediator of the same sex as themselves are deluded. This was the reason given by some of the men interviewed in Bristol as to why they had not sought help from BCFS. In the following case, the husband had encountered female solicitors, barristers and judges. He was growing desperate. Adrift in a world of women, he approached BCFS—only to find that the place was infested with the creatures:

My solicitor mentioned something like that to me and I rang them to find out about it, but it was like everywhere else, it was all women, women everywhere. Everywhere I went, I'll tell you this, I was up against the opposite sex. Now I don't know how that's a fair system. I wanted to talk to a man, I didn't need to talk to more women. I needed to talk to a man about getting her back, like. So I asked them, 'Are you all women there?' 'Yes.' 'Well, bloody hell.' And I didn't want to know. If there'd been a bloke there, I'd have been there like a shot.

Do we conclude that this persecuted soul had got it wrong? Possibly, but I suspect that the kind of embattled desperation which is displayed by some men means that they are not really interested in mediation. We came across several, the interviewer in the end coming to feel rather like the wedding guest, fixed by the glittering eye of the Ancient Mariner. They had their tales of horror to impart, but these held such a grip on their imagination that there was no room left for negotiation.

An understanding of the importance of gender in these negotiations suggests that the question of the mediator's 'neutrality' is more complex than we might at first suppose. There is still a tendency on all sides to regard it as unproblematic. For example, the following were typical of the favourable comments made by solicitors in relation to BCFCS:

They're not retained; they're no one's advocate; absolutely independent of the courts and parties . . .

Both parties, neutral ground, a disinterested approach . . .

Even for those solicitors who did not mention the mediator's neutrality directly, it was usually implicit in other points which they made, whilst the accounts which they gave of their own clients' experiences suggested that most had accepted this without question. Similarly, most parents interviewed at Bromley accepted that the mediators in their case had been 'impartial' (although some did distinguish between the two mediators in this respect, even to the point of suggesting that husband and wife had each had their 'own' mediator).

But it is necessary to define what is meant by 'impartiality' in this context. Neutrality, in the sense of declining at all times and in all circumstances to take sides, is a concept of little practical use. Within a framework of general even-handedness, the mediator must be free to point out the effect which either party's behaviour is having on their spouse. The skilled mediator may be able to give support to *both* sides, albeit at different stages of the negotiation. This is likely to pose considerable difficulty for some would-be mediators, given their habitual approach to conflict. It may be a particular problem for welfare officers, many of whom are natural partisans. From reading their court reports, it is clear that they see nothing wrong with this; their whole approach involves first the achievement and subsequently the defence of partisan positions.

Nor can we take it that practitioners within independent mediation schemes are necessarily content to regard themselves as honest brokers. They will have their *own* goals—in Schelling's terms, 'a pay-off structure of their own' (1960, 44). This is not simply a matter of wanting to secure as many agreements as possible, although obviously the mediator's job satisfaction (and likelihood of continuing practice) will be related to this to some extent. But more significant is the fact that family mediators will see it as their responsibility to safeguard a key *third-party* interest—that of the children. This may be where problems arise, if only because parents are also concerned about the welfare of their children and, as we shall see in Chapter 7, their perceptions and views do not always coincide with those of the mediator.

It would be a mistake therefore to assume that independent mediation services are invariably staffed by gifted, self-effacing 'facilitators'. Mediators are constantly at risk of being drawn into alliances (involving, for example, frequent telephone conversations with one parent, but none with their spouse) so that it is tempting to regard the natural non-partisan as a delightful aberration, rather like an English victory at cricket. Indeed, this may be why everyone is so fascinated by the idea, and why so many people want to practise it, despite the abundant evidence of partisanship in their make-up.

7

Getting Agreements

In this chapter I pose the question: what is it that mediators actually do which enables them to secure a greater measure of agreement than the parties were able to manage on their own? Perhaps the simplest view of the mediator's art would be to say that he or she provides clarification and restatement of the parties' respective positions, and that this enables them to identify areas of possible compromise between the standpoints that develop. But whilst it may be true that some couples are very out of touch, or else so angry or distressed that they need to be encouraged to actually listen to one another, it is doubtful whether restatement *in exactly the same terms as employed by the parties themselves* would advance the negotiations very far. In fact, mediators' own accounts of these processes suggest that they do not simply assist in articulating the positions of the two sides: there is also an element of 'positive reframing' (Parkinson 1983). So, if the parties' approach to the quarrel is such as to demand 'answers' couched in terms of winner and loser, the mediator will 'reframe' the issue in such a way that both may gain something from the negotiation—or at least, both may *appear* to gain something. (Questions which Parkinson suggests are ripe for reframing include: 'Which of us is the better parent?' or 'Is access bad for the children?')

One of the clearest and most revealing accounts of divorce mediation along these lines has been furnished by Haynes (1983) who employs the concept of the 'add-on position' in order to suggest that the parties generally ask for more than they expect to get:

Usually, the parties have already indicated their add-on positions to each other when they arrive at mediation. Not only is their own add-on intact, but their concept of the other's add-on position is often inflated . . .

According to Haynes, the mediator moves the parties away from their add-on positions in two ways. The first step is to demonstrate to them that their opening gambits are at odds with their own sense of fairness. In order to do this, he asks them:'When you come to a settlement, how will you know it is fair?' and secondly, 'What objective criteria of fairness will you use?' The object, as Haynes describes it, is to help the parties 'modify their add-on positions in order to reduce the dissonance caused by the clash with their standards of fairness.' ('We might note at this point that Haynes fails to mention certain difficulties that may arise—such as that it may only be *one* party who has actively sought mediation, the spouse having attended more or less reluctantly. Secondly, and this applies particularly to access disputes, the concessions being sought may be largely *one-way*, in which case the Haynes' description of both parties retreating from their respective 'add-on' positions cannot apply.)

The second step identified by Haynes is that of attempting to redefine the issue in terms of a shared problem which has to be resolved. This calls for the kind of 'positive reframing' already referred to. According to Haynes, questions such as 'How much can I get from him?' or 'How little do I give her?' can be reformulated by the mediator in terms such as 'How can we close the gap between resources and needs?' As he describes it, '(the) important component is the mutual problem-solving that helps the disputing parties to focus on mutual self-interests, not on narrow self-interest.' Haynes argues, although it is difficult to see from his account how this is achieved, that mediation is more likely than other forms of negotiation to bring about an outcome that reflects the parties' 'mutual and overlapping self-interests . . . *in a way that does not involve compromises or concessions.*'

But, to return to the question with which I started this chapter, how does mediation help to bring about, or accelerate, these changes of perspective? Although Haynes' exposition of these processes is very well expressed (and perhaps the best available, in the divorce field) it is still not clear *why* the parties are prepared to accept their dispute being 'reframed' in this way.

At the simplest level this may occur because the mediator is able to suggest alternatives which the parties themselves had failed to consider, perhaps because they were too strongly wedded to their own viewpoint. At Bristol we found that one consequence of BCFCS's willingness to see parents separately, or even to 'conciliate' by means of interviews with just one parent, was that the mediators were forced to engage in a form of negotiation at a distance, trying to suggest new strategies which might be useful to parents when they did actually get together. The following was one case, seen from the father's point of view, where this approach seemed to bear fruit:

One of the things she did suggest actually was I write to the children and write how I feel, try to put my feelings into the letter. And that did work. What she suggested did work. She said, 'I guarantee you eventually', she said, 'it doesn't matter what other people say to your children, they will come round. You know, you're their dad. They'll eventually come round. The sourness, the bitterness, what people say, I won't go out with him, what he done, they'll overcome all that', and they did . . . I don't think I would have wrote myself.

But it is probably exceptional for the mediator to come up with a bright idea which satisfies everyone. So we have to find other explanations as to why third parties may be effective in securing agreements which could not have been managed by the disputants between themselves. One very useful attempt to do this, albeit rather perfunctory in the context of their work as a whole, has been made by Rubin and Brown (1975, 54 ff.). They suggest that the presence of third parties, even if they are inactive for the most part, creates a pressure which pushes the disputants towards accepting norms of fairness, reciprocity, and social responsibility. This happens because the parties want to be well-regarded by the mediator and therefore will do their best to subscribe to the values with which he or she is identified.

Some hint of this may be gathered from the following account of a former client of the Bromley Bureau. This woman had initially felt very bitter towards her husband; she was determined not to grant him access. But in the course of the mediation session, she began to reconsider her own motives and behaviour:

We went to the Family Reconciliation Service [sic] and they certainly solved the gap at the time. I didn't want him to have access whatsoever, not one ounce, not one iota, and I was so . . . I'd made my decision in my mind. He'd made his choice, another woman. She's got two children. Let him have her and her two kids, you know, he wasn't going to have me or my two kids and I was so on one wavelength and I couldn't see nobody else's point of view . . . and we went to this Family Reconciliation and they was very good, I must admit . . . at least I could see when somebody else was telling me it's not fair from his point of view. I then saw it, but until that point I wouldn't.

One reason for the transformation which appears to have taken place in this case was that the mediators' authority was thrown behind this new view of the problem. In these circumstances, one may suppose, it becomes status-enhancing for the parties to accede to the mediators' arguments: they are seen to be behaving as a fair person would. In support of this thesis, there have been various experimental studies which suggest that when a third party is introduced to a dispute, even if the disputants know nothing about him beyond the fact that he is meant to be neutral, the amount of co-operation between them tends to increase (Pruitt and Johnson 1970). This applies even in cases where the mediator does not intervene directly; in other words, his mere presence, coupled with some sparse information about his role, is sufficient to increase co-operation between the two sides. This was confirmed by some of the parents whom we interviewed in Bristol and Bromley. They suggested that the presence of the mediators, coupled with the fact that they (the parents) had sought this help, placed them in a position where they were expected to find a solution. As it was put by one man who had attended the Bromley Bureau:

Conciliation shouldn't really be about exercising pressure, should it? It's about talking . . . nevertheless, one feels obliged to come to an agreement because maybe there are people looking at you in a way, saying, 'Now come on, be reasonable, maybe there's a compromise, maybe there's a solution, we can't go on behaving like this.'

This is a very important point: acceptance of a mediation appointment, plus the influence of the mediators in the course of the discussion, may herald a genuine reappraisal. Some expectation of change is inherent in the process. That is not to say, of course, that this change is accomplished easily. It may take time and freedom from threat before a person who is involved in conflict such as this will be prepared to shift their view of what is fair. In the early stages, at least, a sense of their own possible destruction may prevent them doing so. But once this threat is removed, most people will *prefer* to feel that they are being fair, or even generous.

Another reason why mediation may be effective, also advanced by Rubin and Brown, is that it may permit one or other party to make a concession which, had they taken such an intitiative themselves, could have been regarded as a sign of weakness. This contention is again supported by the work of Pruitt and Johnson (1970) who suggest that mediation provides the negotiator with a face-saving device; he can retreat without feeling that he has capitulated. This face-saving is achieved through the parties being able to throw blame for their concessions onto the mediator. Rubin and Brown (1975, 56) note that any concession carries a potential for both 'position loss' and 'image loss'. In other words, the person who gives way on any point risks loss of face, in addition to the substantive concession. But if he makes the

same offer at the suggestion of a mediator, he places some of the
responsibility at the mediator's door and in so doing protects himself to
a degree against 'image loss'.

At Bristol and Bromley the mediators attach great importance to the
support and encouragement which they try to give to whoever is being
asked to make the most significant practical concessions (often,
although not invariably, this is the custodial parent). Our interviews
give some insight into the kind of 'support' which is offered in these
circumstances. They confirm that the mediators will deliberately
bolster the self-esteem of the parent who is being asked to 'climb
down' in some way. For example, they may give time to exploring the
custodial parent's feeling of resentment in areas not directly related to
the 'access' dispute. In the following Bromley case, the wife was
preoccupied with the injustice of her financial position. The anger
which she felt at her husband's attitude towards maintaining her and
the children undermined any spirit of co-operation which she might
otherwise have brought to the access question:

I don't naïvely expect that I'm going to have this meal-ticket for life that
everybody's talking about, but on the other hand I have all the commitments
with the children and I have the house to run and I do all the things that my
husband didn't do . . . His sort of commitment with regard to the children is
geared to their leisure and pleasure and very little . . . okay, he goes to the
school and he does this sort of thing, but there's no day to day nitty gritty as I
call it. . . . I did find alternative employment which fortunately still fits in with
what the children do, but if you want me to be blunt, I'm just damned if I'm
going to work myself into the ground in order to, you know, relieve my
husband of his responsibilities. I really don't think that you can say with any
honesty that you want to be a father and want to have a commitment to your
children and then opt out of what is basically, you know, the greatest thing of
all . . . which is financial support. He has never messed me about, but on the other
hand, it's like getting blood out of a stone. Despite his very much improved
situation, nothing is sort of forthcoming, nothing is volunteered, and that really
is the nub of my own feeling of very strong resentment.

Nevertheless, an access agreement was reached in this case, the
quid pro quo for the wife's granting more liberal access being the
mediators' recognition of the problems she faced and the sense of
grievance which she harboured. (She was delighted that her husband
had had a 'dressing down' from one of the mediators.) As far as the
mediators' 'support' is concerned therefore, the message is highly
equivocal. It is true that they displayed considerable imaginative
understanding of the mother's position, but the practical outcome of

the negotiation favoured her husband. (The mediators would probably say that it favoured *the children*, a point I address later in this chapter.) Parents did not always agree as to why the mediators had treated the wife so sympathetically. Some women explained this in terms of the mediators' acknowledgement of their central position as the custodial parent, or as being due to their emotional vulnerability when set alongside the husband's more dominating personality. In other words, they felt that their 'case' had been recognized and, to a degree, supported. Given the practical outcome of many of these negotiations, this would suggest that the mediators had been remarkably successful in preventing 'image loss'.

I now wish to return to a consideration of certain problematic features of family mediation not addressed by Rubin and Brown—not surprisingly, since theirs was a broad-ranging study of the nature and characteristics of all forms of negotiation. I have already mentioned that one spouse may be a reluctant participant, and that in some instances the concessions sought may appear to be all one way. There is also a strong possibility that the parties will have approached the mediation service with different agendas for discussion. In studying these processes at Bristol and Bromley (where the focus is primarily on issues relating to the children of the marriage) we found that the mediators sometimes faced a great many difficulties in even getting to the point where negotiations could begin. We came across several cases in which it appeared that only *one* spouse had really wanted to negotiate a custody or access agreement; the other (usually, it appeared, the husband) was still so preoccupied with the circum- stances of the marriage breakdown that, whatever his prior intentions, all his energy was devoted to recrimination. This was the account of one woman who had attended BCFCS:

The second time my husband was there with the two younger children. It was very bitter. He brought them there so that they could tell me that they never ever wanted to see me again—that was his whole reason for going. It was all right in the end, but the whole hour was a battle. The conciliation bit was to see if we could come to some arrangement about the children and when I could see them, but it was turned into a slanging match about what I did and didn't do—and all that had gone by the board, finished. All I was interested in was when I could see the children. I never answered back—I just let it all reel out. I thought, 'The poor woman has probably heard it all before anyway.' There's no point at that stage in raking up all the old things—it's all gone by the board and you can't make it not happen. All I was interested in was when I could see the children and are you [ex-husband] going to stick to it. And that I did—I got a couple of visits. I suggested the arrangement (meeting once a fortnight to go shopping and have lunch) otherwise I think I might have come out without anything. I mean you grab what you can, don't you?

Evidence from both Bristol and Bromley suggests that the power to resist making a settlement in relation to the children is sometimes employed by the custodial parent as a counter to their experience of rejection at the hands of their former spouse. But even if one's sympathies in the above case lie with the wife (and of course she is the one telling the tale), the question arises as to why one grievance or preoccupation is deemed relevant, whilst another is set aside. This is an area in which the mediators are bound to exercise considerable influence.

The mediators will also help to determine the focus in another sense, because they will influence *the terms in which an issue is discussed*. For example, it will be largely up to them to determine the balance between exploration of attitude or feeling on the one hand and the search for an itemized 'agreement' on the other. An excellent contribution to an understanding of this issue is Merry and Silbey's (1986) account of mediator settlement strategies. They refer to the mediator's typical opening strategy of 'broadening the dispute' which involves asking the parties to expand on their opening statements so as to encompass other events and circumstances. The object is to identify shared values and shared experience which can form the basis for a settlement. By this means the mediators will uncover a range of problems from which they will select the ones most capable of settlement. Merry and Silbey suggest that when the parties' accounts reveal fundamental conflicts of fact, the mediators will shift the discussion to feelings, morality, and an examination of how future relations should be ordered. Conversely, if the mediators are unable to achieve consensus in a discussion framed in terms of relationships and values, they are likely to return to a search for specific, practical agreements.

These authors also suggest that mediator strategies fall along a continuum between 'bargaining' and 'therapy'. The bargaining style is characteristic of negotiations which take place 'in the shadow of the court'. A central feature of these negotiations is that they tend to rest on the assumption that somewhere within the parties' competing aspirations and differing views of the quarrel lies the possibility of *compromise*. We have already observed that this bargaining perspective might be enthusiastically espoused by the parties themselves. It was especially characteristic of negotiations conducted on court premises, whether or not these were given a conciliation label. But whilst negotiation on issues of custody or access is seldom totally free from elements of bargaining or reluctant asquiescence, this does not alter the fact that the case for mediation (as distinct from adjudication) is based upon the mediator's capacity to bring parents to the point where they make concessions *without* arm-twisting, either out of a sense of fair play, or because they feel that it is in their children's interests for them to do so. Rather confusingly, Merry and Silbey refer to these less intrusive forms of mediation as 'therapeutic', but what they are actually describing is the mediator's ideological commitment to open communication and reasoned exchange, the parties being expected to take their lead from the mediator in treating one another with dignity and respect. Rather than engaging in a process of hard-boiled 'bottom-line' negotiation, the 'therapeutic' style of mediation 'attempts to recast disputants' individual experiences in terms of mutually valued relationships; it urges settlement based upon a recognition of shared experience and values.'

Merry and Silbey suggest that the nature of the mediators' claims to authority will be different, depending upon the style of mediation which is adopted. Mediators who adopt a 'bargaining' style will stress their association with the court and their familiarity with its criteria for decision-making; at the same time, they will emphasize the negative aspects of the adjudicative process, especially its arbitrariness and cost. 'Therapeutic' style mediators will tend to present themselves as experts in managing personal relationships.

The mediation processes which we have studied at Bristol and Bromley appear to combine elements of these two approaches, but the nature of the dispute (in the great majority of cases the focus is on issues of custody or access) contributes to a style of mediation which is above all *child-centred*. This means that, rather than the mediator seeking to 'influence the parties to come to agreement by appealing to their own interests' (Eckhoff 1969), it is in fact the interests of the children which become the main focus for discussion.

The mediators' claims to authority and expertise are also distinguishable from those which Merry and Silbey describe as characteristic of the 'bargaining' or 'therapeutic' modes. They tend to place less emphasis on their familiarity with the court, or on their communication skills, than on their knowledge of (or belief in) the impact of divorce on children. This applies especially to their knowledge of the impact on the child of an acrimonious relationship between the parents following separation, and to their appreciation of the costs involved in abandoning or disrupting the child's contact with the non-custodial parent. The impression conveyed in some of the Bromley cases was that the children's interests were, in effect, represented by the mediators. They tried to persuade the parents that they should put their own disappointments and bitternesses on one side, and so elevate the children's needs above their own, adult concerns (Davis and Roberts 1988). This suggests that the children were seen by the mediators as a genuinely independent element in the dispute— independent, that is, of the parents' own, 'adult to adult' preoccupations. Sometimes this approach was accepted and sometimes it was rejected, but whatever else may be said about it, it represents a peculiarly 'moral' form of mediation and one which can be distinguished from both the 'bargaining' and 'therapeutic' styles identified by Merry and Silbey.

Brigitte and Peter Berger have pointed out that in many different conflicts (not only intra-familial ones) differences are often overcome *via the children* (1983, 184). They go on to argue that values reflected in such phrases as 'let's think of the kids' form the cornerstone of the bourgeois family. Mediation services in this country exemplify this value of 'kids first', the following being an extract from the publicity material prepared by the Bromley Bureau:

As you know, a divorce or separation cannot and does not end your responsibility as a parent. Both parents should make every attempt to play a vital part in the lives of their children, no matter who has custody. Children need the on-going affection, interest, and concern of their parents. A child must feel that he has two who love him, even though they could not live happily with each other.

What we find therefore is not only that quarrels are expected to be resolved *through* the children (as noted by the Bergers), but that the exercise is conceived as being directly *for* the children, and thirdly, that the mediators apparently have a fairly clear idea about what needs to be accomplished in order to achieve this end. This, I would suggest, reflects the influence which the divorce court welfare service, with its traditional child welfare orientation, has had upon the conciliation movement in this country. It is at odds with the impression which Dingwall (1986) gained from his observation of family mediation in the USA, he having observed that even where the mediator intervened to invoke the children's interests, this was in the hope of inducing some shift in the adults' negotiating positions, rather than in order to introduce a distinctive viewpoint. Dingwall suggests that this may be a reflection of the 'fee for service' model of mediation in the USA, with the mediator in effect being employed by the parents. In the UK, on the other hand, many mediation schemes have close links with the divorce court welfare service and, as we shall see in Chapter 11, these organizational ties have contributed to a blurring of the ideological and practice distinctions between mediation and child welfare investigation.

Merry and Silbey report that in the mediation sessions which they observed, there was very little explicit discussion of norms and values: 'parties and mediators clearly assume that they share the same "paradigm of argument" (Comaroff and Roberts 1977) and therefore leave norms unstated and implicit' (Merry and Silbey 1986). Not so at Bromley, where the mediators' 'kids first' values may be expounded at some length. Perhaps not surprisingly, it emerged from our interviews with parents who had attended the Bromley Bureau that most of them strongly endorsed this preoccupation. Nor, for the most part, did they wish to challenge the mediators' assumption that parents might neglect their children's interests in order to pursue their own battles; the explicit shift away from adult grievances was greeted with approval:

There was the realization that we had got ourselves into a one to one conflict and both of us . . . had got to the point where we had stopped considering the children and were really just out to score points off each other and that became very apparent very early on and when *both* of us started to think, my God, this is stupid and what are we doing to the kids, then the aggression started to fade.

Nevertheless, it cannot be assumed that all that gets in the way of parents agreeing access arrangements is their own hurt or bitterness (in other words, their more or less 'selfish' preoccupation with the past marital history). In some instances, the mediators' reformulation was strongly resisted. The mother quoted below did not feel that the children's interests were as easily identified as the mediators implied. She regarded their approach as hectoring and simplistic:

A lady and a gentleman sat down with myself and [husband] and asked us what the problem was. And I think [husband] said I would not let him see the children and I said, 'That's not so. It's because he's so unreliable, that's why he won't see the children.' And the Conciliation Bureau went on explaining to me how important it is for the children to see their father and to keep contact and I thought, 'Don't you bloody tell me that. I know all that.' And that's more or less a summary.

Most custodial parents whom we interviewed at Bromley endorsed the principle that the children should enjoy regular 'access'. Several in fact complained that they did not need to be told this: they felt just as strongly on the point as did the mediators:

I'm sure they're very helpful people, but me, the person I am, I know that [about children needing to see their father]—that is something I know. I know more about family life than many people—it's something I desperately want in my whole life, even now. So for me, that didn't particularly apply . . .

The nub of these custodial parents' criticism was that whilst the mediators tried to represent the children's interests, they were committed to one particular standpoint (that access should take place) without fully understanding all the circumstances of the case. It is clear therefore that to identify a shared goal—the child's best interests— does not in itself take one very far. There is still the problem of agreeing what those interests are and how they should be pursued, and it is this which is likely to prove contentious.

The strongest challenge to the assumption that maintenance of contact with the non-custodial parent is necessarily in children's long term interests comes from the work of Goldstein, Freud, and Solnit. These authors, writing on the basis of extensive clinical experience, suggest that children have difficulty in profiting from and maintaining contact with two parents who are not in positive contact with one another. They argue that 'a visiting or visited parent has little chance to serve as a true object for love, trust and identification, since this role is based on his being available on an uninterrupted day-to-day basis' (Goldstein, Freud, and Solnit 1973, 38).

But it would appear that the commitment to 'access' has, for some mediators, become almost an article of faith—also espoused, it must be said, by judicial officers and the divorce court welfare service. The custodial parent who resists is often assumed to be acting in a spirit of vengeance; the children are assumed to be suffering as a result. Perhaps she is; perhaps they are. But this is an area which merits further study. Whatever one thinks of the arguments of Goldstein, Freud, and Solnit, the question of 'access' needs to be approached with a more open mind than some mediators appear to bring to the subject at present.

The Partisan

8

The Solicitor—More Than Just a Partisan

FOR all the current interest in mediation in divorce, there is no doubt that solicitors continue to dominate the scene. In the overwhelming majority of cases, both husband and wife will, at some point, consult a solicitor. Of the 299 people interviewed in the course of our study of contested applications, all but two had sought legal advice. Even in the earlier 'Special Procedure' study, 99 per cent of our sample of 230 petitioner parents had consulted a solicitor, as had 92 per cent of the 144 respondent parents interviewed. (Of 22 people who did not have dependent children, 6 had not sought legal advice at any stage, suggesting perhaps that 'do-it-yourself divorce' is more feasible for this group.) We also found that most people approached a solicitor at a comparatively early stage, perhaps before they were really sure whether their marriage was at an end.

As well as being the parties' legal advisers, solicitors play a vital role in negotiating the legal settlement of contested issues. Indeed, the current preoccupation with 'conciliation' has served to divert attention from what remains by far the dominant mode of dispute resolution, namely, bipartisan negotiation conducted either through or alongside legal advisers. The solicitor is likely to be as powerful a catalyst as any mediator, whilst also fulfilling a number of other roles, some of which, such as 'personal counsellor', are largely unacknowledged.

It is partly because of the solicitor's central role that critics of the 'adversarial' approach to family disputes have tended to focus on his or her part in the proceedings. This in turn has led to a marked ambivalence towards the development of legal services. On the one hand, there is a desire to improve the quality and availability of legal advice and representation (as seen, for example, in Section 64 of the 1975 Children's Act which introduced separate representation for parents and children in care proceedings). At the same time there are moves to cut down on the 'unnecessary' use of lawyers so that one often finds a plea for improved access to legal services set alongside equally vigorous arguments in support of 'participation' and consumer control over the litigation process (Amren and Macleod 1979).

General Impressions

In an earlier study of 102 divorce petitioners, Murch found that 56 per cent were 'very satisfied' with their solicitor. On the other hand, 12 per cent had changed solicitors, usually because they were unhappy with the solicitor's performance for some reason (Murch 1980, 17). Amongst our later sample of contested applications, the level of discontent was considerably greater, 26 per cent having moved to a new firm of solicitors at some stage in the divorce process. In some of these cases the period of legal advice covered several years; nevertheless, given that changing solicitors is a difficult step for most people to take, this degree of mobility suggests a disturbingly high level of dissatisfaction amongst matrimonial clients. Of those who had moved, the majority were relieved that they had done so. The performances of the two solicitors were presented as a striking contrast:

My second solicitor—oh, he was marvellous, you wouldn't think it would make such a difference. I think if I'd have gone to him in the first place things might have turned out a lot better.

He was the only one what done anything for me. The rest of them, they was a load of rubbish. But he was very good. He had time, didn't he? [to new partner]. He listened. He done things.

There seems to be such a discrepancy between solicitors. I went to [solicitor] first of all and if I'd carried on the way he wanted me to, then it would still be going on today. Then I went to [second solicitor] and things couldn't have been easier. He explained the easiest way to go about things.

These statements are all drawn from the accounts of parties to contested legal proceedings interviewed in the course of our 'Concili-ation in Divorce' research project. The analysis of solicitor role and performance which is developed in this and the succeeding chapter is largely based on this study.

In the course of this project we discovered that not only does the service provided by solicitors vary spectacularly in quality, but also that within the broad range of what might be regarded as appropriate (or at least, not negligent) work styles, there is a remarkable variety of approaches in response to (but not wholly matched with) an almost equally varied set of client expectations. Many of the problems arose in the area of the solicitor's approach to disputes (for which see Chapter 9), but there were other areas of incompatibility. Of these, one of the most interesting (and least discussed) was that of a clash of values related to gender. Several of the men whom we interviewed had been disconcerted to find that their case was to be handled by a woman solicitor, particularly where, as in one or two cases, it was discovered that this solicitor was a campaigner for women's rights. There was an equivalent problem from the woman's point of view, the following account providing one of several illustrations of this:

> I felt that there were attitudes that came across that made me feel that perhaps he was more sympathetic to my husband's side of it. I mentioned being a single parent and doing a course and he just seemed very unsympathetic about that and about women going out to work or doing any further education when they had children. The impression I got was that he thought that women should be at home and that I was going to be judged on the standard of care of my children as if there were two people looking after the children—it wasn't going to be taken into account that I was one person looking after them on very limited finances and I think possibly a woman solicitor with children herself might have been more sympathetic to my case.

There also appeared to be considerable differences between solicitors in terms of what might be regarded as more uniformly desirable attributes such as a willingness to give advice and to act promptly—in general, the kind of experience and 'grasp' which enabled some solicitors to perform efficiently, whilst others, it appeared to their clients, merely floundered around. As one husband remarked: 'If I could tell one thing to anybody getting divorced it would be to check around to make sure you get a bloody good solicitor.' But few of those we interviewed had taken such precautions. It was far more common to rue one's original choice.

We also noted a tendency for a positive view of the client's own solicitor to correlate with a negative view of the solicitor on the other side, and vice versa. For example, of 136 people who told us that their own solicitor had been 'very helpful', 62 (46 per cent) regarded the spouse's solicitor as having been either unduly aggressive, or incompetent; whereas of the 35 who said that their solicitor had been 'not at all helpful', only 6 (17 per cent) described their spouse's solicitor in these terms; the majority amongst this latter group considered that he or she had been 'very good'.

One possible inference to be drawn from the above relationship is that people's judgement was affected by their degree of satisfaction with the final outcome. However, it did not seem to us that this was a decisive factor, if only because, in the majority of cases, there was no clear 'winner' and 'loser'. An alternative explanation would be that since people lack experience of solicitors, they don't really know what to expect, in which case one possible yardstick is the performance of whoever is acting on the other side. In some cases we noted an explicit comparison being drawn, with one solicitor's virtues being used to highlight the other's shortcomings.

The Solicitor as Counsellor

Solicitors will say that at the point when they are first approached by a matrimonial client, he or she is likely to be completely depressed and demoralized. One woman solicitor told me that she had come to regard divorce as a constant round of bitterness and weeping—'like being in at the funeral'. Alternatively, there is the type of case in which, as another solicitor put it, 'the aggression and hostility are phenomenal'. In either of these circumstances, the emotional investment placed in solicitors is likely to be high. This was how one very experienced matrimonial lawyer explained it to me:

Divorce happens abruptly—particularly 1(2)(a) and 1(2)(b).[1] People miss out on the feeling of being divorced. They need guidance on the social problems involved—just as the Probation Officer provides in the criminal court. Divorce is traumatic—the equivalent of someone of good character going to court for the first time on a criminal charge.

It is not uncommon for solicitors to be faced with clients who are undecided about whether or not they wish their marriage to continue. It is difficult for this ambivalence to be reconciled with the view that the solicitor's responsibility is to act on her client's instructions. In many cases she is being used as a sounding board. This requires her to be forthright where necessary, but also to provide counselling and support. Such roles are difficult to define; they are seldom asked for directly by the client and they yield little in the way of tangible results—one is tempted to say, the very stuff of social work. It may be for this reason that some solicitors see a need for alternative sources of preliminary counselling and advice. As one explained:

'The mechanics of divorce are often secondary; the question is how to handle clients in an emotionally fraught state and the profession is very bad at this.'

---

[1] Divorce petitions based on 'adultery' and 'behaviour' respectively. These petitions may be filed whilst husband and wife are still living together.

Prior to April 1977, the Legal Aid Fund enabled some sympathetic solicitors to provide an undercover counselling sevice for their matrimonial clients. Since then, legal aid has not been available for uncontested decree proceedings. This has meant that solicitors' preliminary advice has had to be covered under the more limited 'Green Form' scheme (Davis, Macleod, and Murch 1982*b*). Many solicitors argue that as a result of this change they can no longer afford to provide the same level of care for their clients. Certainly there is pressure on them to limit their involvement at this preliminary stage; in many cases they do little more than carry out a series of straightforward administrative tasks. Our interviews confirmed that many people felt they were 'hurried through' by their solicitor:

She wouldn't go off at various tangents that I wanted to explore. She was very brisk. She didn't want to discuss any aspects which she felt were not strictly relevant to today's problem and this was one of my complaints in fact. I would have much preferred to have had some sort of broad policy and known what the devil the policy was, so there could have been more discussion.

This kind of experience would suggest that the decision to reduce the scope of matrimonial legal aid was based on a failure to recognize (or acknowledge) that the provision of more general advice, and perhaps even a measure of emotional support, is an important part of the divorce lawyer's role. It is also possible that the greater financial constraint exacerbated a problem which has its roots elsewhere— perhaps in the difficulty experienced by many lawyers (and, one might say, by 'law' in general) in coming to terms with the private and the personal. This in turn may be why a number of solicitors favour the introduction of independent mediation services. They see them less as a vehicle for resolving disputes, than as a source of emotional support. This is a reflection of the fact that even the most thoughtful solicitors do not welcome the ambivalence and uncertainty with which they are often faced; accordingly, they tend to exaggerate social workers' capacity to humanize the legal process. They also devalue their own ability to shoulder some of this emotional burden, believing that their legal training has not equipped them to cope with these aspects. This is despite the fact that the solicitor is well placed to offer non-stigmatic advice which need not be purely legal in character (Murch 1980, 35).

It is important to recognize that the solicitor's partisanship enables him to provide a different order of 'support' from that which may be offered by mediators or welfare officers. This was how one young custodial father summed up what his solicitor had done for him. The family circumstances in this case were desperate, with considerable risk of the three young children being taken into local authority care:

I'll tell you something, if it weren't for him, I'd be dead-loss. Definitely, because I would never have gone through it by myself. He advised not to stand down and take all of it, like. He said that I should get my part in as well as what she had. And that's what I've been doing—that's what I've been fighting for now over twelve months. I'm not going to give up now. But like I said, if it weren't for him, I'd be dead-loss. I reckon he's been excellent, A1 condition, I'd been lost if it weren't for him—for these last twelve months anyway.

When the parties are at their most vulnerable—in conflict with one another and confronted with legal machinery which they do not understand—the only 'support' worth having may be that which is unashamedly partisan. Qualities which do not in themselves imply partisanship, such as a willingness to listen, or being 'down to earth'— each of which is highly valued—need to be provided within a framework of unambiguous partisanship because partisanship is what many people feel they need when they are under threat. It is not possible to separate sensitivity and understanding on the one hand from partisanship on the other; in many people's minds the two things go together. Solicitors who understand this provide a haven of support for their clients throughout the divorce period:

He really takes things out of your hands. Basically I get agitated and worry a lot, but I found if I went down to see him—'oh, don't worry', you know, and I'd think 'Great'. He used to take everything away from me, every worry. I'd say, you know, I was frightened to death of my husband, really petrified, he used to hit me about and he used to threaten this and that. And . . . 'Let him try, just let him try'. I used to feel great. He was really good in both ways, professional and psychological.

An aspect of solicitors' 'support' which was particularly appreciated was that which was provided on court premises. For most people, going to court is an ordeal, even if it is only to attend the relatively innocuous Children's Appointment. We gathered, in the course of the 'Special Procedure' study, that some solicitors held strong views about the stress on parents which was associated with this judicial interview. The solicitor's attendance is not covered under the legal aid scheme; hence, most parents go on their own (Davis, Macleod, and Murch 1983). But some solicitors went along unpaid. As one young mother recalled:

He said he wouldn't let me go on my own. He thinks it's the most important part of the whole episode, because there are children involved. Most women have never been to court before. He took me down there and brought me home. I was very nervous. He helped me feel at ease. I wouldn't have known what to expect on my own. I know he did the same for my friend.

Such demonstrations of concern were most effective where the solicitor was regarded as being approachable or 'on a level' with the client. This was a key element in many laudatory accounts obtained in the course of the 'Conciliation in Divorce' study, as seen in the following case where a young woman recounts her solicitor's no-nonsense approach in court:

My solicitor made things better. She always made me feel comfortable with her, if you understand my meaning. She never acted the big 'I am', like a lot of solicitors. She used to drag me out of court. She'd say 'Sit there, have a cigarette, calm down and stop talking!' She's that type—she really took over, whereas I think I would have gone to pieces without her.

We found no obvious differences between the sexes in terms of their investment in their solicitor and reliance on him (or her) for emotional support as well as purely legal advice. It would be quite wrong to imagine that men, any more than women, were seeking purely technical competence. But in this, as in other areas, the service provided by solicitors varied spectacularly in quality. Many appeared to lack either the aptitude or the inclination to offer any kind of counselling or general advice service to their matrimonial clients. This point was made by several solicitors interviewed in the course of an earlier study of BCFCS. The following were two typical comments:

I only deal with the law—I'm not qualified to deal with people's personal problems. I'm not going to be used as a sounding board; I expect to implement their decision.

I think solicitors should confine themselves to legal problems and not become glorified social workers.

It is understandable that some solicitors shy away from a counselling role, but the failure of understanding which was perceived by some clients had consequences beyond this. It served to limit the solicitor's effectiveness even within the narrowest definition of his responsibilities as a legal adviser.

Solicitors' nervousness in this area has also encouraged an artificial dichotomy between issues relating to children (which some appear to think may safely be left to an independent mediation service) and disputes over money and property (which continue to be jealously guarded by the legal profession). An implicit assumption underlying such a division is that issues relating to children are 'emotional' and therefore come within the province of mediators trained in counselling or social work, whereas lawyers should confine themselves to matters of fact and clear conflicts of interest. Such a division reflects the interests of the professional groups involved in matrimonial breakdown, rather than any psychological reality. This is for two reasons: first, as already pointed out, 'emotional' support is inextricably bound up with the offer of partisanship; and secondly, emotional resistances, so-called, often arise through anger and resentment at what is perceived to be unfair treatment; in other words, the parties' 'emotional' needs cannot be separated from questions of justice.

Advice from the Partisan

It is through the solicitor that the client sees her experience translated for the first time into legal terms. She is advised of the limits within which she can operate in this framework and she may be introduced to a new set of assumptions which do not match her original expectations. It is difficult for her to question the way in which her situation is interpreted; she has no point of comparision. The solicitor therefore has considerable control over the route that is pursued. She has to find out what her client wants, what matters are in dispute, and whether these issues are negotiable. There is pressure on the solicitor to translate a complicated personal story into a plan of legal action. To some extent this applies to all litigation, but the problem is perhaps most acute in the context of divorce proceedings.

There are a number of specific issues relating to this one broad area of advice-giving and it is important to distinguish between them. The first concerns the extent to which legal advice needs to be given dispassionately. In the course of the 'Special Procedure' study, we asked the parties whether they had wanted their solicitor to be 'impartial' or to be firmly partisan. Quite rightly, it was pointed out by some that this question was based on a false dichotomy. Many people told us that they had simply wanted 'professional advice'. In some of these cases there was little or no dispute, so perhaps it is not surprising that what was being sought was sound advice, delivered in a neutral vein:

I just wanted information, impartiality. I felt that it was my divorce just as it had been my marriage and I wanted to make a decision about what was and wasn't done. I wanted to tell him what I wanted. Then, hopefully, he could tell me the right legal steps to get that.

As will become clear in Chapter 9, such an approach is not acceptable to the more embattled matrimonial clients, but others are content for their solicitor to remain emotionally neutral—provided, that is, that he succeeds in conveying to them that in the event of any dispute, their interests will be safeguarded.

There are also some couples who remain on friendly terms. Although not necessarily in agreement on all issues, many would welcome the opportunity to receive joint advice from a solicitor. They tend to find, however, that solicitors are reluctant to offer this. As one of our Bromley informants explained:

We're a very strange couple, Mike and I, really. Because he came to the first solicitor *with* me and what we wanted to do—it might sound weird—we wanted to see a solicitor together. We wanted him to explain all the pros and cons of the situation. But a solicitor will *not* see you together. He's got this thing, he must act in the best interests of his client, so it was very, very difficult.

It is interesting that the wish to secure joint advice is referred to rather apologetically, as being 'strange' and 'weird'. Perhaps that was the impression this woman was given, but I suspect that there is a small but by no means negligible group for whom joint advice might be perfectly feasible. On the other hand, it is not surprising that most solicitors are reluctant to place themselves in a position where they may face a conflict of interest. They are trained as partisans and are therefore sceptical of the possibility of giving neutral advice in a situation of actual or potential conflict. This was how one solicitor explained his reluctance:

I did it once and I was very worried. I was afraid of an allegation that I was misleading the client. It's very difficult to advise two sides of a dispute fairly—apart from anything else, you're given information in confidence.

Solicitors often find themselves advising one party to a divorce, whilst the spouse (usually the husband) is unrepresented. Apart from the problem of dealing with an untrained adversary who does not know the rules, the solicitor may fear that he will be accused of exploiting this imbalance. In *A Guide to the Professional Conduct of Solicitors*, published by The Law Society and sent to all newly admitted solicitors, it is said that:

Any conduct by a solicitor, whether or not in his professional capacity, towards members of the public which is fraudulent or contains any element of fraud or by which the solicitor uses his position to take an unfair advantage, either for himself or another person, over another party, especially where that party is not independently represented, constitutes unbefitting conduct.

An even more fraught situation arises where a client whom the solicitor may already be advising asks him to speak to his or her unrepresented spouse. As one woman recalled:

The solicitor did have my husband into the office and explain a few things to him. He asked me, could *I* explain to [husband] about the fact that the divorce still had to be filed, or would it be better coming from him? I said, 'Well, the way he is, it would be better coming from you.' And he said, 'Well, it's really against ethics, but for your sake, I'll do it.' Because he wanted to avoid a blow-up situation in the house. So he did do that, but it's unethical apparently, to meet with both.

The problem, clearly enough, is that on divorce the parties' interests are likely to be opposed. It is upon this central premiss that the adversarial system is based. The unsatisfactory corollary is that technical legal advice always comes in partisan wrapping, so failing to cater for those couples who *can* agree—and who perhaps set great store by their ability to maintain amicable relations in difficult circumstances. It is a pity that we have not yet developed a form of advice-giving which caters for them.

What Quality of Advice?

The question which I now want to address is whether, as partisans, solicitors are sufficiently knowledgeable and alert to give appropriate advice when it is most needed. The impression gained from some client interviews—and indeed from conversations with solicitors themselves—was that many felt uneasy unless presented with either an agreed package or, alternatively, a clear conflict of interest. One husband explained the criterion which he had adopted in choosing a solicitor in the first place:

I went to see—I can't remember if it was two or three local solicitors—just to see which one suited me best, one that I could identify most readily with. Actually the test I applied was, was he prepared to give me *advice*, rather than simply to listen and then act on what were—what appeared to be, my wishes. I mean, I wanted someone who could actually advise me rather than simply react to what I thought was the right thing to do.

Whilst few people appeared to exercise much care in their choice of solicitor, a willingness to give advice was amongst the foremost attributes which, with hindsight, they realized they should have been seeking. For despite what appears to be the dominant public image of solicitors' conduct in matrimonial cases, it was more common for us to be told that a solicitor had failed to give advice, than to hear complaints that he had been too controlling:

I'd get a sheaf of correspondence sometimes—say, three letters off my ex-wife's solicitors and a little covering letter saying, 'We have received these letters and we await your instructions', which was singularly unhelpful really, because one doesn't know—you know, it would be much better if . . . 'We've received these letters, can you come in, so we can have a chat about what steps we can take.' I mean, I didn't know if I could ignore the letters or whether I had to do something about them.

With [solicitor] I felt I would say things and then the conversation would always go, 'Well, what do you want to do, Mr S?' And I was saying, 'Well, I don't know what I can do. What *can* I do? I used to think, well, I'm paying this woman to tell me . . . I got quite resentful at times . . . I was very unhappy with what I thought was non-professional behaviour.

The parties may first approach a solicitor at the point when they feel they are facing some major decision, such as whether to vacate the matrimonial home, or whether to concede care and control to their spouse. The solicitor's failure to offer advice at this early stage, and in particular, his reluctance or inability to outline the various options which could be pursued, was seen by some clients as having seriously jeopardized any prospect of achieving a satisfactory final outcome. It was only some time later, when the case was finished, that they appreciated what might have been. This was one woman's account in a case where the husband secured care and control of the couple's only child:

Not being really aware of the legal system and what you can do and what you can't do, I wasn't very good at instructing my solicitor, and I found that he didn't really supply me with enough help and point me in a direction . . . he said that the choice was mine. Either we went to court and we fought it, or I gave in, basically. He never said to me what to do, or where to go, or how to act, or what was possible or what was not possible. I wasn't really in a state to know—didn't have enough commonsense at that time. I was too emotionally distraught to use my commonsense. All I wanted to do was to get away and sort out the situation as smooth as possible, as opposed to as well as possible. My solicitor did everything that I directed him to do, but he didn't offer any suggestion as to how things *could* happen. For example, I found out afterwards that joint custody was possible, and that would have been a really good idea, but at the time I didn't know about joint custody.

We came across several cases in which one or other party felt that they had lost out because they did not know the full legal position, their solicitor having failed to advise them correctly at an earlier stage. In the following case the husband felt that he had not been properly advised as to his financial liability:

He should have done a bit more fighting for me. We went to court to get the divorce so they [ex-wife and her new partner] could get married. He should have put me wise to the fact she might *not* get remarried and I would be paying for the next thirty to forty years. He didn't say that. I didn't realize at the time.

The most vital area of preliminary decision-making is probably that which concerns the matrimonial home. The period when a couple are deciding to separate is often a time of great uncertainty and the decision to quit the home can have unlooked-for consequences. Many people had reason to be grateful for their solicitor's advice at that point:

He gave me some free advice, right off from the very beginning over the telephone—because I was worried—should I move out completely? Will things get better if I go back again? And of course he advised me, 'get back in there and stay there, otherwise you're going to lose your home as well', and that was for free, before he'd even met me. When I first went to him I wasn't a lot of help to him because I was in a very emotional state at the time, I remember. He certainly put me at ease and more or less pulled me together.

On the other hand, there were those who suffered badly as a result of their solicitor's failure to warn them of the possible consequences of vacating the home. Most were women: at the time, they had been desperate to leave, but had they fully understood the consequences of doing so—particularly with regard to future contact with their children—they might well have opted to remain for another few months, until issues of custody and access were resolved.

From the solicitor's point of view, these problems may appear in a rather different light. For example, he may feel that the client's emotional state is such as to preclude any reasoned discussion of the legal options. This was how one solicitor explained the difficulty which he faced:

Clients, being human, are all different and most of them are so emotionally fired up that one doubts their ability to make any objective assessment about anything. I have one client, whom I am still seeing, who will sometimes sit through a long interview and I know very well not a word I have said has sunk in. I have taken to writing to her after the interview, repeating what I said.

One can see therefore that a degree of sensitivity to the client's emotional state (what some might characterize as the 'counselling' or 'social work' aspect of the solicitor's role) is essential if he is to discharge his more technical, or purely 'legal' responsibilities. A solicitor who lacks this understanding is likely to be ineffective in *all* aspects, including that of conveying sound legal advice.

Legal Costs

There is one area in particular where it would appear that solicitors do not provide their clients with sufficient information, or, alternatively, where they fail to convey this in such a way that it can be absorbed. In the words of one of our informants:

[Solicitor] is very helpful on giving you advice on what you can do on the legal side, but when it comes down to what it's going to cost you, that's a different matter—a load of flannel goes on.

In most of the cases we studied as part of the 'Conciliation in Divorce' project, the likely cost of the solicitor's services had simply not been discussed. Clients were reluctant to ask and their solicitors did not tell them. 59 per cent of our informants told us that their solicitor had not discussed costs with them at any stage. This is remarkable given that our sample was made up entirely of contested legal applications.

Even where the client was more than satisfied with the solicitor's conduct in other areas (and, as we have seen, there were many highly favourable accounts) the failure to give any prior information about costs was regarded as a very serious weakness:

I think that really is my only criticism—that I don't think I have been given sufficient guidance as we've gone along as to what everything is costing us. I mean, they've been enormously scrupulous to tell me what are the rights and wrongs and what I can and can't do. But I think had I known how much all this was going to cost, I would have acted differently. I would either have gone ahead initially with an application for the money to come out of source, or left it.

Many unassisted litigants own their own home and this may contribute to an unspoken assumption on the part of some solicitors that 'the house will pay the costs'. We were occasionally left wondering whether solicitors regard capital derived from the sale of the matrimonial home as somehow not real money, or at least, not to be regarded in the same light as other income. Even though it has to be used to buy other accommodation, there may still be a tendency to regard it as profit, rather as if the matrimonial home were a demented fruit machine, permanently on 'jackpot'. This was one woman's account:

I mentioned costs to him. I think at one stage I said 'How do I pay your bill?' and I was told not to worry about that. That would be sorted out at a later date. In fact it was more or less put to me I wasn't to worry about it. And then, in the end, it seemed to me that everybody had planned it that way: the house was going to be the way of paying for the costs.

It was not only unassisted litigants who experienced problems with regard to costs. Of those who had legal aid to cover at least some aspect of the divorce, many did not understand (or had not had it properly explained to them) that even if they were awarded legal aid, the solicitor might require payment for work done prior to the certificate being issued; nor did they always appreciate that the certificate is confined to specific issues, and furthermore, that if it is terminated, it will be necessary to reapply before embarking on further litigation. Of course, solicitors know all these things. But they do not alway succeed in communicating the information to their clients. The most dramatic example was the following, the speaker being a woman in her fifties:

Yes, I had to pay £900. It was a terrible shock. I thought it was all on legal aid, then I got this bill—right out of the blue. I could have collapsed—it seemed a terrifying amount. I was on my way to work when I saw this envelope lying on the mat. I wished I hadn't opened it. I think if I'd had a weak heart, I'd probably have had a heart attack there and then. I wish I'd left it till I got home because all that day I was trembling and weeping—I just didn't know what to do. I felt I could have collapsed. The next day, I tried to contact my solicitor but I discovered he'd left that firm by then and I had this letter from another man. He said that I'd only had legal aid for part of the costs, that when it came to the access I'd refused legal aid. Well, I ask you, I'd have had to be crazy, wouldn't I? I'd had legal aid for the divorce and I thought I was still on it. I'd have been stark, staring mad to refuse legal aid—it's just ridiculous to say such a thing. But this solicitor said I'd have to pay it, so I'm paying £40 a month. I feel it's going to take me a lifetime to pay it off and I wasn't even the guilty party, that's what gets me. It was him that left me and him that caused all the trouble over access. It made me very bitter. I thought I'd never pay it, although I've managed somehow. I finish paying next October.

The woman quoted above was a hospital cleaner (and head of a one-parent family) for whom £40 per month was a considerable sum.

Assisted clients were also faced with the problem of the Statutory Charge, a form of 'clawback' under which the Law Society is required to recoup the costs of litigation from any property 'recovered or preserved' in the course of the proceedings.[2] Its real impact is in respect of the matrimonial home. If the settlement includes a property or lump sum award, the parties may be required to repay the Legal Aid Fund out of the proceeds; only the first £2,500 is exempt.

We discovered that many people were totally ignorant (until too late) of the operation and effect of the charge:

I must confess that I was of the opinion that getting legal aid—that was it. This [the statutory charge] has only come to light recently. It's only since there's going to be some cash on the table that it's come to light. Only once I can remember I did ask him [solicitor]—I said, 'Who will be paying for all of this?' He said, 'The tax-payer'. That's the only time it was raised.

He [solicitor] was very good, really, except for the fact he misled me over the costs. He didn't mention the statutory costs at all, so it came as a big shock. The bill came after the custody hearing and when I rang him up, he told me about the statutory costs. He said, 'Oh, I forgot to mention that there will be statutory costs on this.' . . . I only got a £5,000 settlement and out of that I only ended up getting £3,500.

Why does there appear to be this general failure to inform clients of the likely cost of divorce proceedings? One obvious answer is that costs are difficult to predict. They will depend on the options pursued, the attitude of the other side, and the success of any negotiations. Whilst this is certainly true, it does not really explain the failure to discuss what the costs *might* be; to give an idea of the cost implications of various options (such as briefing a barrister); to indicate the solicitor's hourly rate; or to inform the client of any standard charges, such as for telephone calls, letters, etc. Even if the solicitor cannot give an 'estimate' in the way that a plumber or carpenter might be expected to do, this does not account for his failure to mention the subject at all.

---

[2] This arises under the Legal Aid Act 1974. In the legal aid year of 1983–4, charges under s. 9(6) of the Act, mainly concerned with sales of matrimonial homes, reaped £7,619,640 for the Legal Aid Fund.

A second possibility is that the failure to inform is a deliberate tactic on the part of solicitors, inducing the client to take steps which she would not have authorized had she known the cost, or else enabling the solicitor to overcharge at the end of the day. But whilst there is no doubt that for most ordinary people legal services are expensive, that is not the same as saying that solicitors deliberately inflate their charges, or that they travel to their destination by the most circuitous route. Indeed, the taxi-driver analogy is quite apt; these days, matrimonial solicitors have fares waiting on every corner; the last thing most of them want to do is spend their time driving one client round and round the block. Nevertheless, the lack of information about costs creates a climate in which overcharging, or imprecision in the calculation of bills, is likely to go undetected. In this respect, the following thoughtful comment from one of our informants is worthy of note:

Always with solicitors I find it necessary to watch them. Not that I think that they intentionally overcharge—I think possibly they don't overcharge at all—but I think that solicitors are in a profession which is too well protected and thus, the discipline of commerce doesn't touch them and therefore I think they can cheerfully write three letters where one will do without really being over-conscientious about the man who's actually paying for it.

A third factor—and one that solicitors have suggested to me—is that at the outset of matrimonial proceedings the client may be feeling very distressed, so that it would appear rather clumsy (not to say totally unavailing) were the solicitor to bring up the subject of payment. In many respects the first interview is probably the best time to do this, but one can see that it is also the worst. Solicitors may also feel that their client is too angry, or too preoccupied with the justice of their case, to take account of the likely cost of contested proceedings. This was confirmed by some of our informants:

I didn't think twice, I was so determined that I was going to go through with it. I had a letter from [solicitor]. He was almost begging me to let the job go—forget it. I weren't prepared to do that. I carried on. But he sent through to tell me what it was gonna cost. High Court Judge, he said, his fee is £2,000 a day. And I said, I don't care what it is—I'll sell the house first.

I didn't give a damn really, because one, you don't think straight, and secondly, all you care about is what is happening then—the money side of it don't matter. I mean, on reflection, I went to London with [solicitor] on a train and it was only a year or two later that I thought of how I was paying £30 an hour for that man to sit on a train and talk to me.

In several of these cases the question of payment was never tackled directly, so that an air of unreality pervaded the whole subject. But there is no getting away from the fact that the solicitor has a responsibility to ensure that his client is fully aware of the costs being incurred. As is clear from the first of the above extracts, some solicitors are at pains to do this. Others may do their best, only to find that their client is in no state to absorb such information, or regards it as of secondary importance. It was clear in one or two instances that the husband, in particular, had had no intention of paying—indeed, it seemed in keeping with the mood of embattled desperation which these men brought to their litigation that they were quite prepared to face imprisonment at the end of it.

Whilst acknowledging the above difficulties, one must still say that the message concerning solicitors' failure to inform was repeated too often for it to be entirely disregarded. It was almost as if solicitors wanted to give the impression that money was not important to them, rather in the manner of their nineteenth-century counterparts, some of whom may have practised for enjoyment, rather than pecuniary gain. Why should this be? One answer may lie in solicitors' view of themselves as members of a profession, one of the marks of a profession (as distinct from business) being that practitioners are embarrassed by the mention of money. The professional ideal is one of service to the client, and secondly, of adherence to a set of standards which they themselves define. Abel has explained this in terms of professionals' difficulty in controlling the market (this being because the 'need' for their services is not always readily perceived). In order to compensate for this, they invoke the ideology of a pre-capitalist tradition, emphasizing 'anti-market' principles such as opposition to competition, craftmanship. and the intrinsic value of work. Abel notes that this ideology remains influential, 'although its anachronistic features are increasingly apparent' (Abel 1979).

One might suppose that the most glaring anachronism is that solicitors operate a resolutely private service which is paid for, in large part, out of public funds. But whether their work is publicly or privately funded appears in one sense to make little difference: some solicitors display the same insouciance with regard to the cost implications of the different strategies which they might be inclined to pursue. As one husband recalled:

He told me that costs could be quite open-ended. In effect, that there was no limit . . . whatever bill was put in front of you, you just pay. They cannot give you an estimate.

In one or two cases there was an explicit endorsement of the solicitor's professional or 'gentlemanly' approach to the subject:

At first, like, he didn't mention the costs, which is the sign of a good solicitor, you might think. They naturally think the person's going to pay anyway. That's how a professional approach should be. You don't worry [about costs] if you're going to do something as important as that.

Such reticence may have been appropriate in an age when the professions were keen to play down their interest in monetary reward and drew their clientele from a class whose ideas on the subject were equally high-flown, but it seem ill-conceived as a response to today's principal one-off litigant, the poorly informed, strapped-for-cash matrimonial client.

I end this section with a revealing account of the way in which one man, having suffered an expensive divorce, determined, when he next encountered a solicitor, to ask for an estimate—in much the same way as if he were dealing with a practitioner of some less illustrious trade:

No, they never tell you. I had a situation that happened to me two years ago, where one of my employees was killed in a car crash and his wife, who I knew well—we went to see a solicitor that I recommended. She was frightened to death and he went all through it and I just sat there and said nothing because I was only there to hold her hand. In the end he said, 'Well, that'll be fine Mrs X, you can go now', and I said, 'No, hang on a minute, what's it going to cost?' And he really didn't like it. He said, 'It's nothing to do with you.' I said, 'I'm here on her behalf.' 'Well, Mrs X should ask.' I said, 'She's too upset to ask, can't you see that?' And he said, 'Well, it will be around £500.' And I said it out loud, 'About £500 then.' And she sort of looked as much as to say, 'You shouldn't have asked.' But I thought, 'No, dammit, I've been down that road in a different way.'

Efficiency and 'Backing'

Implicit in many of the favourable comments on other facets of solicitors' handling of these cases (supportiveness, willingness to advise, and so on) was the message that they had acted *efficiently*. There were several aspects to this, not the least of which was *continuity* of advice, rather than permitting the client to be passed from one solicitor to another within a firm. It is not uncommon in matrimonial work for the client to be interviewed initially by a fairly senior solicitor, perhaps a 'partner', and then to be passed to a junior solicitor or articled clerk who handles the case thereafter. The main reasons for this are, first, that matrimonial work does not pay as well as other areas of legal practice, so that it is difficult for senior members of a firm to meet their cost targets whilst doing this kind of work; and secondly, that matrimonial work is regarded, by some within the profession, as technically undemanding and therefore suitable for junior staff. But from the client's point of view, to be 'passed down the line' in this way did not inspire confidence:

I thought he himself was very good but I was getting a little fed up being passed on to all the others, his underlings. How can you work with five different people?

In some cases this arrangement contributed to the client's perception that he or she was not given authoritative advice:

I think [solicitor] was working for himself and took on all aspects: conveyancing, the whole lot, and I felt I was dealing, a hell of a lot of times, with clerks. I was telling *them* what they ought to do; I didn't feel they was giving *me* advice.

Just as unsatisfactory was the experience of being passed from solicitor to solicitor, or articled clerk to articled clerk, the acting solicitor being engaged on other, more pressing business:

I saw two or three solicitors [within the same firm] and on each occasion I had to go through the whole thing again until I knew it all by heart. I feel I could have conducted my case far better because I remembered the dates and I could remember lots of incidents that, being passed from one solicitor to another, they tended to forget what happened before.

In a few instances the original solicitor was leaving the firm, in which case nothing could be done. But more often, it appeared, decisions to transfer a client were taken either in order to save costs, or else for administrative reasons, such as to ease the pressure on a solicitor who suddenly found her time taken up by a few, very demanding cases. As far as the client was concerned, this might contribute to an impression of being just another case, slotted into the office routine:

They kept changing. I'd go a few times, the same one would be there, say, four times that I'd go and then I'd go again, 'Oh, I'm sorry, he's left. You'll have to see Mrs So and So, or Mr So and So.' And I thought, 'Well, they haven't seen me. How can they know what sort of person I am?' And then they'd say, 'Oh sorry. Have to look up your file', and they'd be reading it and you'd think—well—I only wish I could have found somebody else, a better solicitor, because I honestly thought they just didn't give a damn, couldn't care less, as though it's an everyday occurrence. Probably it is in their case but I didn't want to feel that. I mean, I didn't think that I was special, but I just wanted a little bit of—not sympathy—just concern, I think, to know what was best. I was going to them for help. I didn't know the legal position. I didn't know anything to do with the courts and maintenance and access. I expected them to inform me. I was getting no help there. I know that sounds ridiculous, but honestly it's true. You know, sometimes I'd have an appointment at half past two; it was half past three before they'd see me. And I was worrying about [child]. It was all that worry on top at that time. Sometimes I felt I was going out of my mind, as though nobody gave a damn. And, of course, I was silly enough not to go and find another solicitor, because you can if you're not satisfied, but being a bit stupid, I didn't. I kept going, thinking things would change, but they didn't.

It is clear from the above account that being passed from one solicitor to another may be just one factor contributing to a sense of being treated with a lack of care. This lackadaisical approach was in marked contrast to the impression of energy and 'grasp' which was conveyed by other solicitors. Many were relatively inexperienced, but they were so energetic and so obviously committed to their client's case that he or she was able to come through a potentially traumatic divorce relatively unscathed. It is evident, indeed, that experience does not in itself provide any clear pointer to the solicitor's competence. Some young solicitors obviously develop a 'feel' for matrimonial work and we noted that one or two of the younger Bristol solicitors were regularly the subject of enthusiastic praise from clients who had perhaps begun by imagining that all solicitors were middle-aged, only to discover that, like policemen, they were getting younger:

He's been absolutely marvellous. I'm gonna be truthful—the first time I met him, I thought, this is gonna be bloody useless 'cos from the look of him, he was fresh out of college, very, very young, very—what I thought was inexperienced. But after a short while I came to trust that man and I've got nothing but admiration for the way he handled the case—and even beyond that, there are several people I have come into contact with who seem to be running into similar problems, and I have recommended him.

This one solicitor had several such commendations, which suggests that although different clients may respond to different styles, there are one or two core attributes which excite general approval. First among these is the sense that the solicitor is giving his full backing; this need not mean that he is needlessly aggressive, but he has to be committed to his client's case and he has to be competent. Of course it may be difficult in certain respects for the client to judge technical competence, so one cannot always be sure that the solicitor is not being commended for the enthusiasm with which he runs around in circles.

Murch, for example, found that some petitioners' respect for their solicitor's abilities was based on his having secured them a divorce decree (1980, 34), a task which, in most cases, is no more complicated than completing an Income Tax form. But it would be quite wrong to dismiss clients' assessments entirely, as some commentators have sought to do (see, for example, Megarry 1962, 35–6). Several of our informants distinguished between the elements of emotional support, technical competence, and conspicuous activity for its own sake. The woman quoted below had been battling for care and control of her two children. In the early stages of the case she had been prepared to suspend judgement, but she concluded that her earlier misgivings about her solicitor's abilities had proved well-founded:

I'd say my solicitor was agreeing to everything as it came along. Whereas my husband was sending affidavits through left, right and centre, sworn by as many people as possible. When I suggested that I counteracted them, he said that it wasn't really necessary. But to me it seemed to be necessary because I was getting a character-assassination job done on me and I wasn't defending myself. But he considered it wasn't necessary. He was very willing to concede all the time and not try to play them at their own game. He did say that he'd never dealt with a case like mine before, and I can remember asking him whether he thought he could deal with the case, whether he would be able to fight it, and he said, 'Well, I'm sure I can do that', but I did query it all the time because to me he didn't seem like he was . . . I just thought, perhaps he'll pull through in the end, you know, perhaps on the big day, he'll be there, guns at the ready. Because I think sometimes people are slow to sort of move along and although they don't appear to be doing very much, they're doing a hell of a lot, and I think you've got to bear that in mind—they may come up trumps; but he didn't. I think he was just out of his depth. Afterwards, I felt that I'd been totally let down by him and that it was a complete and utter waste of time.

This woman was full of praise for her husband's solicitor. She considered that he had been 'underhanded', but she admired the way in which he had taken control of the case—making demands, gathering affidavits from neighbours and so on—whereas her own solicitor had been purely reactive. She was one of several people who regarded their spouse's solicitor as having been more demanding, more in control, and in every way 'stronger' than their own. In common with those others, she was less inclined to criticize this aggression than to feel rather envious, wishing that it had been exercised on her behalf.

Solicitors' approach to contested applications is a matter which I pursue in the next chapter, but before doing so I want to examine one other aspect of solicitors' conduct of these cases, that is, whether they acted reasonably promptly, so that the case was not allowed to remain on the books without any real progress being made.

Delay

One of the most common complaints made by parties interviewed in the 'Conciliation in Divorce' study was that their solicitor had moved too slowly. As one woman put it:

You never feel they're getting on fast enough. You've got to ring up and be a nuisance before anything seems to get done. I don't know, perhaps that is solicitors in general, everybody seems to say so.

It was not surprising that many people questioned the solicitor's motives in, as they saw it, prolonging matters unduly. Some concluded that this was his way of making more money out of their case:

It's all down to the solicitors, they slow it up time and time again. And then, when you write to the courts for a hearing, you can't get in for about three to four months—and then you've got to go through solicitors again. The whole system is so slow and dreary, it's just a game for solicitors and they drag it out. I wish I was a solicitor, I'd make pounds out of the divorce game.

Another, less cynical explanation for the way in which some solicitors appear to take no action for months on end is simply that this can be an effective means of achieving settlement. Indeed, it has been argued that it is 'very much a solicitor's duty to protect the client from himself or herself in these circumstances, by failing to litigate with the speed that the client expects or even demands' (Saint 1982). The particular circumstances referred to are the early stages of matrimonial litigation, when, according to the author, 'emotions are running high', 'the client is his or her own worst enemy', 'logical thought is non-existent', and 'the client is reckless as to outcome'.

Several solicitors with whom I have discussed this general point acknowledge that they use delaying tactics quite deliberately. Their experience is that it works, but the cost to the client (in terms of frustration and anxiety, if not financially) offers a strong argument against a such strategy. There is much to be said for not acting precipitately, but in some of the cases we studied it was tempting to ascribe the solicitor's conduct to sheer indolence:

It got to the stage, quite frankly, where I was so dissatisfied I made an appointment to see one of the partners and he basically apologized for the fact that really nothing had happened, that the treatment we'd had was not satisfactory and he took over the case. I felt that after two years we'd achieved absolutely nothing in terms of concrete proposals—nothing at all—and you know, it just wasn't good enough. All right, you allow a little bit of time, but two years for something as simple as working out access and various other bits and pieces! I've got a file of letters, one after another, which really did absolutely nothing. Their [solicitors'] argument was that the courts required us to sort out access. We could not come to an agreement—that was fairly obvious—in which case a definitive statement had to be made by somebody, but nobody was prepared to take it to the court.

The same problem arose in relation to finance and property disputes. As another husband explained:

My real complaint is that it's taken solicitors so long to come to an agreement in my case. Other people can get divorces and settlements inside a year, but this has gone on for five years and I just can't understand why. I would have sooner gone to court in the first year and had it all dealt with and finished . . . It's just dragged on and on and we've got nowhere; and every month it's gone on, it's gone more and more over to the wife's side; more money, half the house, more money, *all* the house—it's getting worse and worse. I feel like saying, 'Here, chuck it all in, you might as well have the lot, I'm not going to work any more.'

It would appear that some solicitors are reluctant to actually *do* anything. They behave as if, given time and a low-key approach on their part, the case will somehow wend its way to a satisfactory conclusion. It is almost as if legal advisers have lost all faith in the court as a forum for resolving disputes; either that or they have decided that the real problem with our system of family law is that judges and registrars are overworked.

Before accepting such an analysis, one would need to ask whether the interests of the courts and the legal profession are not both served by this strategy of 'diversion'. Courts want *apparently* high caseloads in order to justify their continued employment of the present number of very expensive personnel; but the fewer cases which actually have to be adjudicated, the better, because it means less work for everyone.

Solicitors likewise require high caseloads; every case represents chargeable work. But they also want a good proportion of chargeable work *within* each case; that is probably best achieved through minimal, routine involvment. This 'back burner' strategy enables solicitors to do quite well financially since many cases will 'settle' in the long run without requiring much effort on their part.

It might be thought that client dissatisfaction with this laid-back approach, reflected for example in solicitors' general reluctance to make open demands and open offers, would have led to increased pressure for structural change. But herein lies a paradox. Solicitors feel that they cannot afford to turn work away. So they take on cases without having the resources to deal with them. But, taken overall, there is no shortage of work for family lawyers: even if the number of divorce cases has reached a plateau, the graph of contested 'ancillary matters' continues to rise. It is this expanding workload which vitiates the pressure which would otherwise be placed on solicitors to modify their approach to matrimonial litigation. It is true that solicitors may fairly claim to have become more conciliatory—a matter which I explore in Chapter 9—but they also exert such a strong grip on the divorce 'market' that they can continue to garner all these cases without, in many instances, doing very much with them. One of the virtues of private practice is meant to be that it is responsive to demand and to customer dissatisfaction with what is on offer. But a profession which operates a publicly funded private practice, and which enjoys— despite the advent of the new mediators—a virtual monopoly position, can afford to be demand *un*responsive.

Fortunately, however, solicitors' approach to these matters is not uniform. The professional ideal of service to the client is not anachronistic in itself and it was clear that many solicitors *do* act; they *are* efficient; and some (a minority, it has to be said) display commendable speed off the mark:

It was only in the last five months that we had anything to do with him and he worked at the speed of light. He was marvellous. Within about three or four months it was all sorted out and it had gone to the court and been cleared up. I thing we got about four letters from him and that was it, it was done.

One final point: efficiency, in the sense of an effective handling of the legal aspects of the case, does not invariably go hand in hand with a kindly, sympathetic approach. But we were surprised at how often the two things did indeed go together. We were also given several accounts of solicitors who showed themselves to be brusquely incompetent. The most effective solicitors, technically speaking, appeared to be those who displayed an understanding of their clients' emotional state and were generous with their own time.

9

Negotiator and Champion

WHERE does the responsibility lie for the acrimony and misunder-
standing which so often appears to be a feature of divorce proceedings?
Can it be explained simply and solely in terms of the parties' need to
work out their feelings of anger and rejection; or should we look to
solicitors' needlessly aggressive conduct of these disputes; or, thirdly,
does the fault lie with the so-called 'adversarial system'? Take the
following case, drawn from the 'Conciliation in Divorce' study of
contested applications, as an illustration of the difficulties involved in
providing a clear answer to these questions.

Mr and Mrs X agreed to divorce on the basis of two years'
separation. However, when the wife consulted a solicitor, he advised
her to petition on the basis of adultery (citing her husband's cohabitee)
because this would be in her financial interests. When the husband
received this petition, he responded by applying for care and control of
the couple's teenage son. This was regarded by the wife as highly
provocative and the divorce became very unpleasant from that point.
The husband had not intended to consult a solicitor, but at this stage
felt bound to do so—a decision which eventually cost him £2000. Mr
and Mrs X both agree that matters got out of hand as a result of the
advice given to the wife by her solicitor. There is however a difference
between them in that whilst Mr X maintains that his wife's solicitor
advised her incorrectly, she is not so sure and regards Mr X's
emotional insecurity and guilt as the cause of his aggressive reaction to
the divorce petition. They are now on friendly terms and meet quite
often.

In this chapter I shall be exploring the question of how aggressive
solicitors are, or need to be, in their approach to negotiations with 'the
other side'. As indicated by the above outline, this question is more
complex than might at first appear, although as a general guide it is
worth noting that when we asked those interviewed in the course of
our study of contested applications whether their solicitor 'had tried to
keep the divorce as friendly as possible', 57 per cent replied that she

had done so; only 16 per cent said that she had not; whilst 22 per cent answered to the effect that their divorce could not possibly have been friendly, given the way husband and wife had come to regard one another. Most solicitors and barristers will say that they regard matrimonial disputes in a different light to other forms of litigation. One prominent barrister has referred to 'walking that extremely delicate tightrope, which is the daily lot of counsel who have to handle custody disputes' (Lincoln 1981). This 'tightrope' analogy suggests a balance between the client's short-term interests and the need to promote future co-operation. The writer went on to suggest that:

as often as not [the advocate] has to mitigate the strength of an argument in the hope that he will not accentuate or intensify the animosity between the parties, for it is his duty not to forget that the litigation process is an episode in the matrimonial history, sometimes a very crucial and hatred-generating episode.

This was also the view taken by many of the solicitors whom I interviewed in the course of an earlier study of the Bristol Courts Family Conciliation Service. As one very experienced practitioner put it: 'The prime function of the divorce solicitor is conciliation—to bury the marriage decently with muted trumpets.'

This kind of low-key approach is consistent with the view that divorce is characterized by ambivalence and the complex interplay of separate and mutual interests. But it is doubtful whether there is one 'right' way of responding to this complexity; different clients will expect, and approve, different styles. Some demand unquestioning partisanship:

You want him to be completely on your side. I mean, he's dealing with your case only . . . he's being employed by me to look after my interests, so he's bound to be biased. If he's not, he's a poor solicitor.

I wanted him to get the best deal possible as far as I was concerned. I don't want him standing up for the opposition—she's quite capable of that herself.

It is undeniable that the need for a champion can be very strong—and in some cases this may be amply justified. This was particularly apparent in our 'Conciliation in Divorce' study of contested applications, from which the customer accounts in this chapter are derived. The first priority, as far as most of this group were concerned, was that their solicitor should protect their interests. We should note, however, that this is not necessarily at odds with a conciliatory approach. Some solicitors have the happy knack (at least in relation to some clients) of supporting from the sideline, encouraging the parties to sort out as much as possible between themselves, whilst yet conveying that in the last resort their own client's interest would be safeguarded. As one woman explained:

> He was brilliant, absolutely brilliant. And he's also quite sort of sensible and fair—he will put the argument to you and try and make you see sense, even though sometimes it's difficult for you to do that. But at the same time, ultimately, he is there to back you and if you make that decision and that's what you want, then he'll go ahead and carry it through for you. He had to be quite forceful on occasions, but not without my prior knowledge and sometimes we both agreed that it was necessary to be quite forceful.

This solicitor's approach might be described as conciliatory, but within a framework of clear partisanship. Insofar as there is any standard approach which matrimonial clients are seeking, this would appear to be it. Although these couples had all been in dispute about some aspect of their divorce, the most enthusiastic testimonials were for solicitors who had been seen to be 'conciliatory'. Of the 136 people in Bristol who told us that their solicitors had been 'very helpful', 92 (67 per cent) thought that he had been conciliatory; amongst those who regarded their solicitor as 'not at all helpful', the fact that he had been over-aggressive towards the other side often contributed to this feeling of dissatisfaction. Conciliatory solicitors were actually *more* likely to be perceived as having protected their client's interests. The following is one illustration of a successful 'marriage' of these two elements:

> Well, there's only been one dispute which was over access and he was very fair. He could see my point but he could also see the other side's point, and in the end we came to an amicable compromise. I was aiming for something I knew I couldn't get and so was my husband, and we sort of met in the middle, and so I suppose we both got what we wanted really. It was all sorted out outside the court's time. That's the sort of thing he does, you see. He says, if we do it outside the court's time, then we can get it done quickly. All we have to do is go before a registrar and say, this is what we've decided, but if it's a hassle, it draws it all out, and this is what I didn't know, you see.

A conciliatory solicitor may also guide his client away from some of the pitfalls which are set for him by our present divorce law, as illustrated by the practice of those solicitors who, on receipt of a 'behaviour' petition, use the face-saving device of writing to the petitioner's solicitor setting out the respondent's views and obtaining an assurance that the allegations will not be raised in the course of ancillary proceedings. The parties' feelings of anger and resentment can easily be exacerbated in the course of such preliminary legal skirmishing. The trick which some solicitors appear to bring off is that of absorbing some of this animosity, whilst yet not appearing to run away from it. One man referred to his solicitor as a 'street-wise old matrimonial lawyer' who had advised him what the market would bear. He was an experienced negotiator who had reined him in where necessary. Another husband explained:

They were aggressive and I would say he only came back with like for like, you know. So whatever attitude they came to us with, we responded accordingly. There was no aggression from our side whatsoever; only from me personally, but it stopped at the solicitor. He mellowed the thing down, to put it in the right context, you know.

Some clients put the emphasis on the solicitor's conciliatory approach, others on his alertness and resolution in safeguarding their interests, but for the majority there was no incompatibility between these two elements. Both were associated with the solicitor's ability to respond to his client's frustration and anxiety:

I failed a couple of times to take his advice—which proved to be honest advice. And as far as I'm concerned, he's been very good to me—he's been very patient as well. There's been such a topsy-turvy—he's had a hard time really. And there's been a couple of times when I should have taken his advice and, being what I am, I haven't. I think he's been very patient. I can't express myself in words, like, to what I think he did. I don't understand the law whatsoever, because the jargon is not for me. But the way I see it, he's treated me with his best ability to a layman that doesn't understand anything. I feel as though he's been for my interests. Though we haven't won a lot of great things, he's stopped us from tearing each other apart. There's been times when I've been near to tears in his office, when we've had so much frustration and upset, and he's just sat there and let me ramble on—I've been there for about an hour—I do get a regular hour with him, explaining—we do seem to have so much trouble. And to get it down, he's wrote pages and pages of what's been going on. And if I pick up the phone and phone him, he's ever so good.

As is evident from the above account, it is possible for a client to regard his solicitor as being 'for my interests', and yet to acknowledge that he had 'stopped us from tearing each other apart'. The security and confidence which this solicitor, amongst others, seemed able to generate is a tribute to his interpersonal as well as technical skill. On the other hand, there were a great many cases in which the solicitor was regarded as having been insufficiently robust or wholehearted. This was reflected in the following criticisms:

He wasn't with me 100 per cent against all others. He and I weren't in a team that we were 100 per cent right against my wife. He just told me that certain things would happen if we took another course.

He was totally neutral. He hasn't fought for me one little bit. I think he should be fighting for me and he isn't.

Many clients found it difficult to comprehend their solicitor's willingness to accept a compromise settlement. They had no doubt as to the justice of their case and they expected their solicitor to pursue it without equivocation. Accordingly, they felt dissatisfied with the kind of professional distancing which was displayed. They interpreted this as a sign of weakness, perhaps suspecting that the solicitor was too concerned to maintain his own professional credibility.

The greatest dissatisfaction was expressed in relation to the solicitor's performance in the course of preliminary negotiation on court premises. The following is one example of a client who felt badly let down by her solicitor's willingness to make concessions at this stage:

You get down there and you're all . . . you know . . . you think he's going to say this, he's going to say that, he knows what the situation is, and you get there and it's, 'Well, we'll give him a few more weeks'; and, you know, you've geared yourself up to that one day in court, and then he agrees with the other one to prolong it a bit more. And you think, 'Never!' And to him, he's looking at his watch, to get back. You're out of court and you're all done in and he says, 'Cheerio Mrs T—as though, you know, you've been out on an outing! And you feels all drained and everything, and nothing really *happened*; and it's all prolonged again for another few weeks, or till the courts can fit in another date. And now I realize, it's all money, which is the court's time and money, and nothing is settled.

We came across many other cases in which, rather than the matter being adjourned, one side or the other was prevailed upon to accept a 'settlement' which was not remotely satisfactory as far as they were concerned. Some of those who expressed these reservations had considerable admiration for their solicitor as a person; they were just not sure, given the situation they were in, that a conciliatory stance was appropriate. One woman described her solicitor as 'a lovely man', but felt nevertheless that he had not been tough enough when faced with the much more 'dogmatic' solicitor on the other side. Another commented: 'I thought he was a gentleman and not the man to handle my case.'

This was a rather fuller account, from a respondent husband who had failed to secure what he regarded as sufficient access to his two children:

I think he was very helpful, very sympathetic. But I think at a later stage, when things developed, he wasn't sufficiently aggressive. He continued looking for a consensus-type solution to problems which I feel, with hindsight . . . we were looking for conciliation and the other party weren't, so I was the loser in the long run. . . . I think he could have been stronger in my interests. He tried very hard and I admire him for that and in normal circumstances, it might have been a better solution. But unless both parties are prepared to compromise, if one is always looking for a middle course, he suffers.

Many solicitors are only too well aware of these difficulties. As one explained:

It is very difficult, even if you are conciliation-minded, since the clients could well lose confidence in you and feel the solicitors are cooking things up.

Another commented:

I have to be careful; I must act on instructions. I did lose one client through being too forthright.

There are a number of possible explanations for this finding that, far from being regarded as unduly litigious, many solicitors were seen as having been too accommodating. One possibility is that, given solicitors' greater knowledge of the law and of the 'going rate' when it comes to all manner of divorce settlements, they are concerned not to allow their clients' sense of injustice—even of outrage—to draw them into litigation which is unlikely, in the end, to succeed. This was how one Bristol solicitor summed up the dilemma which he faced:

It is of course perfectly correct to say that the solicitor's job is to protect the client's interests, and, if necessary, to pursue those interests. However, the core of the problem is to identify what the client's real interests are. Very often, they are not what the client thinks they are. The most obvious case is the client who comes to the first interview angry and injured by the other spouse, with the one idea of getting their own back. Almost certainly it is not going to be in their best interests to have a stand up fight.

This solicitor questioned whether it was appropriate to give unqualified support in every case:

The real purpose is to give the client confidence that the solicitor has made a correct diagnosis of the problem, advised on the best solution, and supported the client through the process of trying to achieve that solution. Blind partisanship might not be in the best long term interests of the client. Detached objectivity is really what the client needs and should expect.

But this 'objectivity' can leave the client feeling frustrated and dissatisfied. A relatively minor illustration of this clash of expectations is to be found in the difficulty which some clients experience in coming to terms with the fact that the two solicitors are on friendly terms. Not familiar with the professional ethos of conducting work on one level and social life on another, this affability undermines the kind of close identification with their own case which they need in order to feel confident that they and their solicitor are pursuing a common cause. They talk in terms of 'partnership' or 'having his backing', thereby revealing the emotional component of the relationship. Where the client discovered that his solicitor, although acting like a partisan, did not really *feel* like one, the analogy which this brought to mind was that of the game, a term which was often employed when discussing the legal process, with clients in the role of pawns:

It was as though they [the two solicitors] knew each other and they were going for a beer afterwards. I felt as though I was a pawn. They tend to put you in a situation where *you* are the person they are disliking. They send all these nasty letters to and fro and then when they meet they say hello and are as nice as pie—and you are waiting for an outburst of some sort. They seem to put you in that frame of mind. I'm just a pawn in a chess game. I don't think they've really got people at heart—it's just a job to them, isn't it?

To lawyers the 'adversarial system' does not imply anger, aggression, or ill-feeling; it merely acknowledges the fact of separate and competing interests. Furthermore, by virtue of their familiarity with the pattern of settlement in similar cases, the eventual outcome may appear relatively predictable. But these professional understandings are generally not shared by the parties; their approach to the issues is very far from being objective. Thus we discovered several cases in which *both* sides felt that their respective solicitors had been too ready to make concessions.

As one would expect, some solicitors are more skilled than others at diverting their clients from what they regard as the perils of litigation. This was how one man recalled the advice which he was given:

I'll tell you what [solicitor] actually said. Before she knew anything about the situation, she said, 'There are all sorts of things you can do, but as far as any co-operation between you and your partner are concerned, if you take any legal action, it's guaranteed to wreck it.' My legal advice was that it is very, very difficult for men to get custody, but that under the circumstances, if I wanted to, and bearing in mind that it would put the lid on *any* co-operation between us at all—and that lack of co-operation is the most damaging thing you could do—that they were certainly prepared to try.

As a rallying cry to the troops on the eve of battle, this does not quite rank alongside 'England expects that every man shall do his duty'. One assumes that this solicitor did not want to fight because she thought her client would lose. Of course, if Lord Nelson had taken the same view, this book might have been written in French, but aside from the possibility that solicitors may on occasion be unduly pessimistic, few would quarrel with this general settlement orientation. The problem lies more with some solicitors' tendency to dismiss the client's own view of the problem. In each of the following two cases, the speaker having changed solicitor, the performance of two legal advisers is being compared. The focus is on these solicitors' approach to the client, rather than on any difference which their contrasting styles may have made to the final outcome:

Mrs L. I don't think he [first solicitor] understood. I felt very much like when you're interviewed by the police over something and you're trying to relate . . . and they're not really interested because that doesn't fit in with what *they* want to know. And in your mind it all goes together. That's how he came across to me. He didn't seem interested to know the details, so I didn't feel as though, if he couldn't see the picture clearly, then I couldn't see how anyone else could. Whereas [second solicitor] turned round to me when I first went to him and said, 'Write down things as you go along day to day and send them to me.' I mean it was pages and pages, you know, and I thought, 'You poor man!' but at least you felt as if someone was involved and someone was aware of what was happening. Whether he ever read it or not is another matter [laughs] but it made me feel better.

Mr S. I didn't seem to be getting any joy out of the first one. The first one didn't seem to help me at all. All he was concerned with was that I was going to lose no matter what, and I thought well, surely, I am at home with the children, my wife left me, surely I must have some standing. But he said, no, what will happen is, you'll have to go and she will have the children. And I thought that was totally wrong. So I went to another one and he explained a lot of things to me. He sat there for an *hour* and explained it and didn't charge me anything and he was very good about it. He said more than likely you will have to leave home, it depends on what your wife wants. And I found a great deal more comfort when he . . . he explained things a lot better. He took more time with it. He said there was a fair chance that I could end up having the children myself but I'd have to have very good grounds for it, which I expained to him I thought I had.

Lawyers operate in a highly normative world, one ruled by precedent and case law. It is their job to know this framework and, provided one accepts it, it is not difficult to negotiate a settlement within the guidelines which it provides. But the weakness of this approach is that it assumes a kind of standardized client to whom the solicitor assumes standardized ends (Simon 1978). The tendency therefore is to act for this hypothetical client, despite the fact that the solicitor's *real* client may desire a different outcome.

Underpinning this approach is the assumption that the client does not know what action is in his or her best interests. It has been pointed out, however, that just because the lawyer knows things which the client does not know, this need not lead to the conclusion that the lawyer generally knows what is best for the client. This legitimizes professional control and 'transforms the client into a child, with a problem to be solved' (Chang 1984).

Solicitors for their part might argue that their training and experience have indeed equipped them with knowledge which the client does not possess, and in particular, that they are better placed than their clients to identify *long-term* interests and thus to take decisions which will help them through the process of marriage breakdown with the minimum of psychological and financial damage. As it was put in the course of one revealing article (also referred to in the previous chapter):

What, then, is the solicitor's duty in the matrimonial dispute? It surely is that a concerted effort should be made by both solicitors to find the fair and proper answer within the limits offered by the law and the facts of each case, and it must be within their power in a very, very high proportion of cases for this to be achieved. The minority that do go to court should only be those where a complete failure to be reasoned and be reasonable on the part of the *client* causes negotiations to break down . . . If the parties accept a settlement, both can be said to be tolerably happy. If the court is asked to arbitrate, the order will mean that one client will be defeated, and in all probability both will be unhappy and dissatisfied. (Saint 1982)

We may note in this article, and in much recent discussion of the divorce lawyer's role, a beguiling slippage between two ideas. First, there is the assessment (now generally accepted) that prior to the new 'conciliation' climate making itself felt, many solicitors were needlessly aggressive and displayed a lamentable disinclination to engage in constructive negotiation. From this we move to an assertion that it is the solicitors' responsibility to secure *settlement* in virtually all cases, and furthermore, that these 'settlements' will render both parties tolerably happy. For solicitors to be conciliatory is one thing; to be determined to promote 'settlement' is quite another. A conciliatory approach is appropriate because the solicitor should seek not to aggravate the problem, and because it may be possible to demonstrate to the parties that there is something to be said for listening to the other person's point of view. But the pressure to 'settle' does not flow from any humanitarian motive; rather, it arises from the need to cut legal costs and limit the demands on judicial time.

I have already indicated that the 'conciliatory' solicitor met with general approval, but there were some cases, involving very bitter dispute, where one or other party felt that not enough had been done to counter the aggressive tactics of the other side. There was a sharp contrast in this respect between the 'Special Procedure' survey and our later study of contested applications. In the course of the earlier project we came across several cases where it appeared that the parties had felt very bitter at the outset of their divorce, but had since modified their view of their former partner and so, with hindsight, were grateful for the conciliatory advice proffered by their solicitor. But in our later study of legally contested cases we found much less evidence of this gradual coming to terms. There were many cases in which it appeared that the solicitor had acted in the conciliatory manner which is now generally approved, only for the client to conclude that his feelings were not being taken into account and that the strength of his case was being undermined from within:

I lost the case before I was even judged. Her solicitor had a way of wording things—making me out a right villian—and my solicitor would let him get away with it. I typed all my answers exactly as I wanted them put down and he changed them all around, so it wouldn't be as forceful a representation of myself as I hoped it would be. I think he let her get away—he was agreeing to what she said.

The moderately worded affidavit might be regarded as part of the stock in trade of the 'new breed of matrimonial lawyer',[1] but if the

---

[1] The perception that there *is* a new breed, and that this needs to be encouraged, was reflected in the formation of the *Solicitors' Family Law Association* in 1982. The Association's first objective was: 'To encourage solicitors to represent their clients in a manner which promotes the sensitive, efficient and economic handling of family disputes and assists individuals to reconcile their differences, and to seek solutions fair to all members of the family and to children in particular.' (*The Law Society's Gazette*, 12 January 1983, 66).

client is not persuaded of the wisdom of such a course, he or she is likely to feel very aggrieved. This was one of several aspects of solicitors' performance which, whilst consistent with current 'progressive' thinking within the profession, did not always find favour with the client. (I should perhaps distinguish between men and women in this respect since comparatively few wives appeared to regret the absence of aggressive, blaming statements and affidavits. On the other hand, both sexes were strongly critical of those solicitors who were regarded as making inappropriate concessions, thereby negotiating a 'settlement' which their client regarded as tantamount to a defeat.)

There has of course been considerable criticism levelled at overly aggressive solicitors, it being said that they take no account of the impact of their actions on the parties' future relationship, or upon the children of the marriage (Murch 1980, 38). However, as a corollary to the evidence presented in Chapter 3, some of the men whom we interviewed complained that their solicitor should not have allowed these considerations to enter in, since they tended to undermine partisan commitment:

I think he was trying to get access back on friendly terms, but, as far as I was concerned, it shouldn't have been that, because the way I was feeling at the time—you'd been without seeing your own son for a long time—all you want is to get back and see him, no matter what happens. He was trying to make it all nice and pally and it weren't going to work. What it should have been is: 'Right, you're allowed access, the court has allowed you access. You've got it. Go and get him.' That should have been the attitude to take.

I don't think he had my interests at heart; he was more concerned at the outset that I should support her and the kids and all this and that. You should do that even if you get divorced . . . that's what he believed.

I am not suggesting that the approach of either of these solicitors was 'wrong' in any general sense. But it is important to recognize that some divorcing couples have no sense of their having interests in common. They simply want the strongest possible case presented on their behalf, which, after all, is the premiss upon which the adversarial system has been built. Indeed, given that the state has virtually abandoned any attempt to sustain marriage through law (Davis and Murch 1988), this perception of separate and competing interests can be the only basis upon which divorce retains its identity as a legal process (rather than becoming a purely administrative matter, or, on the other hand, being taken over by some other professional group, such as marriage counsellors or child welfare experts). Once lawyers find it necessary to take account of the long-term interests of children, or of the parties' future relationship, then divorce as a legal process is called into question, because this is not legal knowledge. If lawyers' partisanship has to be tempered by considerations born of child psychology, or even family therapy, one is bound to ask why they (and in particular, why solicitors) should continue to occupy such a dominant position.

In fact, the evidence from the research studies on which I have been engaged suggests that many couples still prefer to operate within a framework of rights; far from indicating that law and the courts are no longer needed, this suggests that some solicitors are in rather too much of a hurry to compromise their one area of specialist expertise. This does not mean that vigorous pursuit of the client's separate interests needs to be expressed through the use of inflammatory language, or by means of provocative allegations which the other side are known not to accept and which are barely relevant in any event. But, as I have already suggested, it does call into question the present 'settlement' orientation of legal advisers and judicial officers. This is a reflection of the public, rather than any private interest; all too often it bears no relation to the parties' own concerns. It is probably best understood as a form of rationing and its 'success' should only be measured in these terms. From the parties' point of view it offers the worst of both worlds, an unsatisfactory outcome for which they bear notional responsibility. It also has implications for the organization and funding of legal services: if what is on offer is a form of joint arbitration by solicitors (or, at a later stage, by barristers) then one might suppose that a salaried service would offer this more efficiently than private practitioners operating within the adversarial tradition, with all the paraphernalia of separate legal aid applications and the like.

The Gladiators

It may seem surprising that I have yet to raise the spectre of the aggressively litigious solicitor, causing trouble where there was none before—or at least, aggravating disputes unnecessarily. I had previously gathered from conversations with solicitors that there is felt to be a relatively small group of 'difficult' or needlessly aggressive solicitors who are readily identified by their fellow practitioners.

Accordingly, we asked everyone interviewed as part of our study of contested applications whether their own solicitor had been 'unnecessarily forceful and aggressive'. Only 19 (7 per cent) of those interviewed in Bristol said that he had been, with a further 4 (1 per cent) uncertain.

Although this figure appears to be much smaller than folk-myth would suggest (and perhaps smaller than it was a few years ago), 7 per cent is not an insignificant proportion. The most telling criticisms centred on the wording of letters and affidavits. In several cases it appeared that the tone of the letters (and, in some cases, the exaggerations contained within them) was bound to engender bad feeling:

[Solicitor] wrote a letter saying that he would point out that in English law [husband] would have to pay the maintenance until the child was 17, which, first of all, I thought, well, that's not going to put him in a good mood, when you start immediately with, 'In English law you've got to pay'. All I wanted him was very informally to say, 'We think there's some mistake. We think you believe she's 17, when really, she's still 16.' And then he went on about my age and pension and putting up the maintenance. I mean, the whole tone of the letter, if I'd received it, I'd have been blazing mad. Of course, we never had a reply.

It would appear that an element of 'chivalry' enters into some solicitors' conduct of these cases, so that they are particularly inclined to adopt an aggressive posture when acting for the wife. This was another example:

[Husband] admitted that he'd been violent but he thought it was overplayed by my solicitor and to a certain extent I think it was. Where I'd say to my solicitor, when he wanted details, 'He pulled my hair', my solicitor would write down, 'He grabbed me by the hair'. He always made it sound more dramatic, and I think this is what my husband was complaining of, in some cases with just cause. I mean, none of the incidents were fictitious; they were all true, but they were painted in red, if you like, by my solicitor, to add weight to the case.

There were occasions where husband and wife tried, through communicating directly with one another, to limit the damage which they feared would flow from a destructively worded solicitor's letter. In a few instances there appeared to have been two sets of negotiations running in parallel: formal, written communication between solicitors; and informal (often secret) conversations between husband and wife, some of which served to undermine the positions taken up by their legal representatives. At the same time, it is important to acknowledge that by virtue of their position as intermediaries, solicitors may be used as scapegoats, disguising the parties' own responsibility for the stances being adopted. For example, there were cases in which the husband claimed he was acting on his solicitor's advice, but the wife suspected that he was concealing his own determination not to pay more maintenance. It appeared even more common for the wife's solicitor to be used in this way, perhaps because many women were under strong pressure to agree to their husband's proposals. This was one man's account:

When I spoke to my wife [about a letter received from her solicitor] she said, 'Where on earth did you get this from—I never said anything like that.' So I asked her, 'Why don't you put something down in writing so your solicitor can't ignore it?' But she wouldn't. That was the general impression I got—her solicitor was leading her on, to get her to try to get all she could out of me.

But when the wife was interviewed, she described her solicitor in terms which gave no hint of the aggressively partisan figure perceived by her husband. What appears to have happened, in this as in several other cases, was that the wife was determined to obtain a financial settlement which exceeded that which the husband was prepared to offer, but at the same time (perhaps for the sake of the children, but also to avoid unpleasantness or bullying) she preferred to remain on reasonable terms with him. The solicitor was then left to bear the brunt of the husband's anger. In the following case, the wife admitted that she had used her solicitor in this way:

Knowing [husband] as he was, there are certain things I wouldn't have said anyway, you know. I kept aside what I felt was best not mentioned. I got the money in the end because I said, okay, send the bailiffs round and let them calculate what there is. [Husband] said, 'That wasn't you, was it, that was your solicitor', and I didn't say anything because if I'd said it was me, we'd have had another ding-dong. You know what I mean—you learn to keep quiet. Of course, poor solicitors get it in the neck, don't they? But after all, that's their job.

Even without this element of duplicity, there were several cases in which the solicitor's robust approach had been welcomed by the wife, whereas from the husband's point of view it was perceived as needlessly aggressive:

Wife [of her solicitor]. I think he had to be [aggressive] because I'm soft. 'Cos I was a fool really, I was daft. He had the strength I needed. He was the right one for me.

Husband [of wife's solicitor in the same case]. A right bastard. I could show you some of the letters that were written and you'd see why—horrible letters, really vindictive—as though he had something personal against me.

Having described circumstances in which it is appropriate and necessary for solicitors to be firmly—perhaps even aggressively—partisan, it may be easier to identify those justifications for solicitors' aggression which are drawn from the realm of legal fiction, or myth. For example, we found no evidence that the aggressive pursuit of rival claims acts as a kind of safety valve, reducing the emotional temperature of disputes. Although it has been suggested that partisan support from a lawyer can help people work through dangerous and often violent feelings (Murch 1980, 36), we did not come across anyone who said this.

Nor did we uncover any evidence to support the suggestion that if these couples are not provided with the machinery to conduct an exhausting and expensive struggle, they will divert their conflict to other channels. This assumption of the cathartic effect of partisan support (and specifically of the courtroom battle) has long been cherished within the legal profession. To some extent it would appear to be supported by anthropological accounts of dispute resolution. Gulliver, for example, has characterized certain preliminary stages of the bargaining process as being marked by all the signs of fiercely antagonistic conflict (1979, 136 ff.). This pattern has also been noted by Douglas. She describes the early stages of negotiation as follows:

Each side shows prodigious zeal for exposing and discrediting its opposite; and sooner or later there almost invariably comes from each side a conscious, studied, hard-hitting critique of the other. These attacks are typically vigorous and spirited; not infrequently they are also derisive and venomous. (1962, 15)

Should we accept therefore that in despatching vituperative letters and affidavits, solicitors are echoing the working out of familial and other conflicts in primitive cultures (the implication of which might be that these performances, being universal, have some psychological aptness or utility)? Probably not. If parties to divorce proceedings are indeed seeking a public forum in which they can denounce the scandalous behaviour of their spouse to a receptive and sympathetic audience, it is very important to recognize that this is not what they get. The trial process is stylized and rigidly controlled; displays of emotion are frowned on and the occasion is dominated by professional partisans. Even more significant is the fact that most contested applications do not reach the point of an adjudication; they are 'settled' by legal advisers, perhaps following the exchange of aggressively worded affidavits, or letters which begin (as one solicitor characterized them to me) 'I am astonished . . . ' or 'I am appalled . . . '. So there is really very little basis for comparison with primitive cultures. In our present-day divorce disputes, the aggressive display is written rather than oral, protracted rather than immediate, expressed by professional actors rather than by the disputants, and effectively denied or unacknowledged in the final outcome.

Loss of Control

The evidence presented in this chapter is clearly at odds with some rather unconvincing arguments which have been advanced concerning the evils of the 'adversarial system', or the need to settle disputes through 'conciliation' rather than the courts. Whilst there is often scope for mediation in family disputes, some issues cannot be negotiated away. There is also the problem of unequal bargaining power, not to mention bullying of various kinds. So people need protection and they need support, which is why they seek the help of trained partisans.

But the conversion of a family dispute into a legal issue, justiciable by a court, is likely to involve considerable artificiality. Some responsibility for this must be laid at the door of solicitors, if only because the task of translation, enabling a private quarrel to be expressed in such a way that it becomes open to formal legal solution, falls largely to them. In many instances it appeared that the parties' own understandings and views of the justice of their case were regarded as comparatively unimportant; the 'translation', one might say, was only one way. Some solicitors do not even appreciate that there is a problem; as one commented to me rather ruefully: 'Clients do find it hard to believe that many claims put forward are by way of bargaining only.'

Why, one might ask, should claims be put forward 'by way of bargaining only'? The difficulties which then arise can be attributed to the client's failure to understand the processes in which she is involved, but one could equally point to solicitors' reluctance or inability to make these comprehensible. The end result is the same: the client's control over the conduct of her own case declines to vanishing point. Even the most independent characters find this hard to overcome. As one woman explained:

The legal system, I don't like it at all. I dread going to my solicitor. I come out with a hundred and one questions unanswered. I answer all the affidavits myself—I'm sure I could have fought the whole thing myself if I knew how the law works and what the law would request of me.

If either party feels that they need the court's protection, they have little option other than to seek professional legal advice. Thereafter, an issue which they may regard as essentially straightforward is transformed into a highly technical and inaccessible legal matter. The result is that they do not understand what is going on, and secondly, they are not allowed to contribute directly to the resolution of their quarrel. This is what is sometimes termed a 'double bind'. It was at the heart of much of the criticism of the legal process which we encountered.

The Welfare Investigator

10

The Welfare Investigator

PART mediator, part adjudicator, with a position of influence which can lead to his being perceived by the parties as unashamedly partisan, the court welfare officer occupies a central role in the resolution of divorce disputes. Although some welfare officers have of late been attracted by the possibility of taking on therapeutic or mediating roles, the majority continue to regard their prime responsibility as being the preparation of court reports. These reports are intended to assist the judge or registrar in cases where there is a dispute between the parents over custody or access arrangements, or where there is some doubt as to whether the proposals for the children are 'satisfactory'. At the same time, most welfare officers will attempt to 'conciliate' between parents in these circumstances, so that, in some cases at least, there will be no dispute left for the court to adjudicate. This conciliation role has been given greater prominence in recent years and many welfare officers derive great satisfaction from it, claiming that it is of greater benefit to the parties and their children than the traditional form of welfare enquiry (Howard and Shepherd 1982). The welfare officer's 'conciliator' role is considered in Chapter 11.

The Research Base

The research evidence upon which both this and the following chapter are based is drawn entirely from the 'Conciliation in Divorce' study of contested applications. It will be recalled that this involved our interviewing 299 parties to contested legal proceedings. There were 79 cases in which we interviewed both parties. Of a total of 220 cases, 164 had involved a dispute over custody or access. In the majority of these, the divorce court welfare service were involved at some stage.

It is important to acknowledge, however, that whilst the overall number of cases was more than sufficient for most purposes, we were principally concerned with the various forms of 'conciliation' being attempted in conjunction with legal proceedings. We did not seek to explore the welfare officer's investigative and reporting roles in any depth. This is a matter for some regret, although, as explained in Chapter 2, I attach greater weight to the parties' *unsolicited* accounts than I do to comments made in response to the interviewer's direct questions. All references to the welfare service were noted and subsequently transcribed along with the rest of our material. However, no more than a third of those interviewed contributed information in this area. It is possible, in these circumstances, that we have obtained a distorted view of 'consumer' reaction to the service as a whole. It may be, for example, that people who had critical things to say about the welfare service were the ones most inclined to bring the subject up.

Initial Reactions

It appeared that very few of the parents who had experienced a welfare report had resented it being ordered. Some did not think it was necessary, but most had been pleased, this being seen as a necessary stage which they would have to go through in order to resolve the issues in their case. For those who felt confident that they were going to 'win', the report was generally regarded as the means by which they would get their case across.

That said, the parties' views concerning the welfare officer in their case were, to say the least, mixed. The criticism most frequently expressed was that the welfare officer had seemed inexperienced, relying on theory rather than first-hand knowledge of families and children.

The Importance of First-hand Knowledge

As Murch also found (1980, 173–4), parents set considerable store by the welfare officer's own parenting experience. The following comment reflected the views of many: 'I told her she's got to have children of her own to understand them. If you don't have children of your own, you don't know what you're talking about.'

In the following case, both husband and wife were critical:

Wife. It was a woman, a very young girl. Though she was married, she had no children. I left her talking to my children and each time she went they kept saying, 'Mum, we don't like her, she doesn't understand', and then when I did speak to her, I could see what they meant. She may have training, but she didn't have the feeling of what was needed with children. She wouldn't see their point of view. All she kept repeating was that perhaps they ought to go out more with their father. They felt she was pushing them.

Husband. My impression was that she didn't know a single thing she was on about. She was too young to understand.

Several parents explicitly repudiated academic learning or 'theory' as a basis for effective practice. In their eyes this was associated with the use of jargon and other clichéd explanations which were foreign to their own experience. The following was one of the gentler assessments of such expertise:

I think he meant well, but I don't believe he understood half of the problems. You can go so far with books and rules and regulations but there comes a point when you leave them behind and it's got to be a more natural thing. Later on, he came out with a comment which was way off the mark—I think, there again, he was trying to help me—he suggested that I look at my divorce as if it was a death in the family—something that's very sad, but you can't get away from it, it's happened. I thought to myself—how remote from the real problem are you—because all right, what he said is true, a death in the family is sad and you've got to live with it, but divorce is entirely different because although it's happened, people are still involved with each other, so it's not dead. So although he meant well—odd remarks like that—as I say, I'm not knocking the man personally—but there again everybody's different, aren't they; everybody's problems must be different and everybody's divorce must be different. It must be difficult to be in a position like that.

The Costs of Investigation

One should not assume that the above criticisms (and others rather more trenchantly expressed) were simply a reflection of the welfare officer's youth, or of the fact that he or she was not married with a family. After all, several people had doubted their solicitor's abilities on first meeting, only to revise their opinion when they discovered how competent he really was. It is more credible to suppose that the welfare officer's relative youth, or the fact that he or she had no children, was seized upon by these parents as a focus for the indignation which they felt at the investigation which they were having to undergo, with their competence and authority as parents apparently being called into question.

Recently divorced people may have unresolved feelings about their marriage; they may feel that they have failed as parents and that they are on the point of losing their children; they may regard themselves as unsuccessful negotiators, since they have failed to secure an 'amicable' divorce; and they may be experiencing considerable anxiety about *new* parental roles and relationships. In short, they could probably do with some encouragement and support. But the welfare officer's role, as parents very quickly come to appreciate, is largely that of investigator on behalf of the court. Parents realize, in fact, that they are being placed under scrutiny. It is not surprising, therefore, that they should feel defensive. This was the reaction of one young mother in these circumstances:

I didn't get on very well with her [welfare officer]. She wanted to know the ins and outs of everything. If I remember rightly, the baby, he had a nappy rash and she wanted to know what I was going to do about it. So I told her if she waited 'til I took his dirty nappy off, washed him down, put cream on his bum and put a clean one on, she'd see for herself, you know.

This woman's reaction to the welfare officer may well reflect her vulnerability at the time, in which case one should not assume that it was the approach of the individual officer which made her feel that her status was being undermined. But the fact that there are these costs for parents makes it all the more imperative that the investigation be successful in meeting what one must take to be its primary objective, that of helping to determine the most appropriate arrangements for these children's future care.

Effectiveness of the Investigation as a Means of Safeguarding Children's Interests

If one imagines that *the court* determines which parent should have day to day care of their children, then this is obviously a momentous decision calling for the most painstaking investigation. It may appear surprising in these circumstances that the amount of time which the welfare officer actually spent with parents and children, prior to drafting a court report containing a firm recommendation, was in general extremely limited. Several parents expressed doubts as to whether, in the course of a few brief visits, the welfare officer could possibly come to terms with the family history, the personalities, and all the various issues involved in their case:

> It seems to me that they were so short of time—in fact, you know, I think I worked it out that he actually spent about two hours in total over three visits—and the decision was based on that—which affected my kids for the rest of their lives. I didn't feel that I had sufficient time with these people so that they could make *any* kind of judgement as to what I was like. And anybody who was rather clever and made a habit of telling lies could have fooled these people as regards character, as regards ability, as regards general attitude to life—could have fooled them completely.

This was the view of a non-custodial mother in a different case:

> I don't feel that anyone can come into someone's home and reach a verdict about who is the right person to bring up the child, you know, all in an hour's meeting. I feel very strongly about this. She used to go on about my husband's helpfulness, how well my daughter was getting on at school, you know, about how cosy everything had become. In fact, it just showed me how, when you're going through that period, if you want something enough, you become anything to get it. How someone can see through all that in a matter of an hour, I just do not know.

The two accounts presented here offer important clues as to why the welfare officer's investigations may appear somewhat perfunctory. In both instances there were grounds for supposing that the actual recommendation was not as centrally important as is often assumed. Close examination of these cases confirmed that it was parents and children, rather than the court, who were the ultimate decision-makers. Thus, in the first case, although the father refers to the welfare officer's recommendation affecting his children for the rest of their lives, the three children involved were all in their teens and two of them subsequently moved to live with him without the court being involved.

This 'private re-ordering' following a court adjudication was by no means exceptional. In the course of the 'Conciliation in Divorce' study of contested applications we came across 32 Bristol cases in which there had been a full hearing on the issue of care and control. Amongst these we noted a subsequent transfer of care in 12 (38 per cent). This was generally *agreed* between the parents and the court merely informed that the change had taken place. The transfer was sometimes effected as little as one week after the trial.

The divorce court is presented with a 'snapshot' of each family's circumstances. Decisions taken with regard to both access and care and control are inevitably tentative and provisional. Subsequent changes in living arrangements, of which there may be several, are likely to be undertaken without the court being involved in any way. Michael King (1987) puts it well:

The order is made, the file closed, but their lives continue. The adults make and break new relationships. More children are born. People grow older; they change. They change jobs, change schools, move home. They become ill; sometimes they die. Yet hardly ever do these important events in the lives of those children whose welfare the courts seek to promote result in the family returning to the court for judges or magistrates to decide what is now in the best interests of the child. (The only exception is when a previously divorced parent divorces again or separates from a new partner.) It seems, therefore, that everyone, or at least all the adults, be they social workers or parents and their partners, are quite content to arrange matters among themselves without any guidance (or interference) from the courts.

Even allowing for the fact that parents do sometimes adhere to the court's order (and it is not my intention to suggest that custody and access orders have *no* import, even when their terms are observed only for a brief period) it would still be unwise to assume that the welfare officer's views concerning the character and parenting skills of the applicants are likely to have more than a marginal impact upon her recommendation, or indeed upon the court's decision. There is a degree of standardization in these matters, not surprising given the invidiousness of the task and the fact that the issues raised are to a considerable extent 'beyond the reach of expert understanding' (Sutton 1981), requiring the application of 'that old fashioned quality termed "wisdom"' (Ormrod 1973). We know, for example, that welfare officers and courts are reluctant to remove children from whichever parent is currently exercising day to day care (Eekelaar *et al.* 1977); that it is assumed that very young children need to be in the care of their mother (Eekelaar 1984, 78 f.; Cretney 1984, 333); and that there is a presumption in favour of 'access' by the non-custodial parent.[1]

Some of these ideas may appear so 'natural' that they do not even need stating, never mind questioning. Underlying beliefs such as 'children need mothering' may be very important in helping to form the welfare officer's view of the family, although these may not be

---

[1] *M* v. *M* [1973] 2 All E. R. 81.

referred to directly (Sutton 1981). Nor is it only welfare officers who rely on articles of faith such as these. The same is true of judges and registrars, solicitors and barristers. One might say that this whole area of law rests on various ill-defined and ill-understood notions concerning the roots of psychological health (or 'disturbance') in children. This is despite the fact that there are enormous cultural and individual differences in matters of child care, whilst the social consensus, if any, may change quite rapidly (Murch 1980, 176).

It is understandable in these circumstances that welfare officers faced with parents' diametrically opposed views in relation to access, or care and control, will tend to 'pigeon-hole' issues, so that they give the impression of failing to recognize that the designated 'loser' might also have a case. These dissatisfied customers tend to be either non-custodial fathers, frustrated in their desire to assume care and control, or custodial mothers, having to grant access to the husband in circumstances which they believe cause their children additional distress. These are the classic losers in the present system; their case is seen by everyone to be weak and the welfare officer's intervention can appear designed to secure their reluctant compliance.

The three problems which I have outlined—lack of relevant personal experience, insufficient knowledge of the family, and an undue standardization of approach—are brought together in the following account of one custodial mother who had attempted (unsuccessfully) to resist the welfare officer's recommendation that her former husband be granted 'access':

She [welfare officer] can't have two kids walk in and know them and what they feel and how they are. I brought them up from birth. I know them. I gave birth to them. How has she got the right to make a decision for my children's future? She doesn't know them. She doesn't know me. She doesn't know (husband). It's wrong that they've got the powers they have to say, you will do this and you will do that. I know they've got to have rules because a lot of people—in a lot of cases it can be good for the children to see their father. The mother might not be all she could be. But they don't really know. I couldn't believe that a person who had never had children could come along and tell you how to bring them up and what to do, because although they've been trained, if they haven't been through the experiences or they don't really know the situation, how do they know how they'd react? It's like a nurse or a midwife. In the clinic I attended the midwife said that her attitude to expectant mothers in labour after she had her own baby was far different to what it was before. I think this is the problem with divorces. It's all right to say, have an amicable divorce and the father ought to see the children, because it's his children, but do they know what those kids feel like?

For all that I have said about the relative standardization of the welfare officer's approach, and despite the evidence that parents and children, rather than courts, are the ultimate decision-makers, there is no doubt that *at the time* the welfare officer's investigations assume tremendous importance in the eyes of most parents. Although it may not be the case in fact, they feel that their future as carers for their children is in doubt. This was demonstrated most acutely in parents' reactions to the welfare officer's attempt to interview the children. It appeared that their self-image as successful carers was severely threatened by this (a point also made by King 1987) and in some instances it appeared that the welfare officer failed to take account of this anxiety, perhaps even reinforcing parents' feeling that their own authority was being drained away. The man whose account is presented below is a custodial father, and therefore someone whom we might suppose especially vulnerable in these circumstances. The story presented is 'two stages removed' in that the child had given her account to the father, who then presented it to us. It would be most unwise, therefore, to use this or other similar accounts in order to form a judgement as to the welfare officer's skill, or lack of it, in eliciting children's views. But this is how vulnerable parents tend to react to this form of investigation. It is interesting to observe that the question of the officer's relative youth, and of her lack of parenting experience, was raised yet again.

She came half past five, six o'clock in the evening. She said, 'Well, can I speak to the children?' and I said, 'Well, of course, what do you want me to do, go out, like?' She said, 'Well, no, I'd like to speak to them one by one.' In the meantime they haven't seen their mother for eleven months, getting on for, call it a year. And so I said, 'Well, fair enough'. So she went up to the bedrooms and she was questioning them one by one. Well I think Pam [youngest child] went up. Well, she was only tiny then, obviously, so she was more confused. Then when our Iris [second eldest] came down, I said, 'What's she on about anyway?' 'Oh, she wants to know if we wants to go with our mother, telling us, by the sea and the sand, we could have them sort out school for us.' You know, I mean, well that was it, that was when I blew my top 'cos she had no rights in questioning the kids like that, you know. So that's when I told her, 'Get out . . . you want to find out more about the parents before you start talking to the children', I said, 'because all you're doing is confusing them'—which it was. Find out more about the parents before you start questioning the children, especially at young ages. I think Social Services does more damage . . . I mean, like, she turned round to me and she said, 'Ooh, I've done 4 years, 5 years training.' I said, 'If you haven't got kids, don't talk to me about kids', I said, "cos you haven't got a clue. All you work', I said, 'is nine 'til five. Bringing up kids is 24 hours a day', I said, 'not just nine 'til five. You can walk out from trouble, people can't.' I told her, 'Get out' in the end 'cos she was no help at all. Like I said, I found her more damaging than anything.'

A paradox has begun to emerge. On the one hand, most contested cases are 'settled' by legal advisers, without recourse to adjudication; such decisions as are made by the courts tend to be based on readily identifiable criteria, well understood by legal and welfare practitioners; custody and access orders are unenforceable without the co-operation of the parties in any event. But despite all this, the welfare investigation itself can be extremely stressful, exposing parents and children to levels of official scrutiny which are normally associated only with cases of child abuse or neglect. In order to understand why such a *powerful process* should be applied to such *limited effect* it is necessary to consider the symbolic meanings which are attached to welfare investigations on divorce.

Symbolism and Stigma

What is often missing from discussions of the role of the divorce court welfare service is any recognition that divorce is itself stigmatizing, and that this stigma may be reinforced through welfare investigation. Stigma is a product of the way in which *other people* view a particular status or condition (Scott 1970, 282). Divorce and its consequences are often compared (implicitly rather than explicitly) with an image of 'the whole family'—that is to say, a married couple and their minor children (Berger and Berger 1983, 60). Welfare officers can become the agents through which society's moral disapproval of this inferior condition is transmitted to parents. In other words, the requirement that parents submit to a humbling process of investigation may be seen as a form of punishment. This is especially effective since it concerns children who, given changing moral values, form the divorcing couples' Achilles' heel. There has undoubtedly been a switch in the court's attention away from the divorce decree towards the children of the family. This is explicable in terms of society's eye for the most telling punitive response, as well as in terms of the more traditional explanation based on the need to safeguard children's interests.

This is not intended as personal criticism of welfare officers, although I have seen enough of welfare officers in Bristol and South

East London to realize that they vary enormously in terms of the sensitivity and other necessary attributes which they bring to the task: they are not chosen with anything like enough care. In particular, there seems little attempt to rule out those probation officers whose own attitude to divorcing parents is ambivalent, or even frankly crtitical. It is not surprising in these circumstances that the 'punishment' aspect of the investigation can be more apparent (to parents) than any supposed child welfare safety net. Many of the accounts which we were given reflected the unease which parents felt at being judged in an area where (by virtue of their decision to separate, thus depriving their children of a 'normal' upbringing) their competence was already in doubt.

I don't think that a person in an adjudicative role should adopt such an almost patronizing manner. Her questions were very naïve too. Everybody knows, well, anyone honest who's had kids knows, that every now and again you feel you could strangle them. But when I told her this, you know, half joking, she looked at me amazed and all stern, as if I was beyond contempt. Well, I thought she was just mad, you can't adopt that kind of tone in her kind of job. People say things like I did, but I wouldn't actually have done it. She was just incredible . . . When she talked to me she made me feel almost criminal, as if I had done something wrong . . . and she was only about my age, anyway. That made me angry, so I asked her just what she thought she was doing—she didn't like that, of course—but I thought her manner totally unsuitable to her job. I think we both mentioned to our respective solicitors that we didn't think much of how the courts checked up on the children. It makes it all seem so sordid, so . . . improper.

Perhaps it is a reflection of the insecurity felt by someone new to a very difficult job that they should make bids for authority in this way. This was one of several cases in which the welfare officer was seen to have displayed none of the modesty or sense of personal fallibility which might be expected of someone venturing, all too briefly, on to new and difficult terrain:

They had to do a welfare report and the thing that really shook me was the woman who came down and introduced herself—youngish woman, mid 20s. I asked her if she had her own children and she replied, very sharply, 'No—and if I had any, I certainly wouldn't be doing this.' That was her very first remark and I thought, they should not have someone doing reports on children who hasn't had children . . . she really put me off. I don't really think she knew how to do her job. When I asked her about benefits and how to transfer a claim from my wife to myself, she said she didn't know what to do. I thought that was significant, you know, one of the really practical ways in which they could help you . . .

In considering what weight to attach to these accounts, one must bear in mind the possibility that parents' anxiety may have led them to magnify any hint of welfare officer disapprobation. But it is equally possible that welfare officers are themselves influenced by these negative perceptions which parents feel themselves to be struggling against. Training provides a badge of competence, but this is dangerously two-edged in the case of welfare officers who are working with a low status group, threatened with the withdrawal of their authority as parents. Some of the accounts which we were given suggested the kind of arrogance and assumption of moral superiority which is only affected by those who perceive themselves to be working with a low status clientele.

In this respect, it is reasonable to suppose that the probation connection is itself part of the problem. There is bound to be a risk that, as a result ot the organizational and staffing links with the criminal branch of the service, the stigma of deviance and inadequacy will rub off on divorcing couples. After all, the main job of probation is to regulate the poor and criminal classes. The service deals with a low status group—that of 'offender'—who, it may be argued, have behaved in a way which is careless of the interests of others; as a result, they have to suffer some encroachment on their own liberties. This is a view which is also held of divorcing parents, or at least, of that group of parents whose family circumstances are held to be sufficiently problematic as to merit outside investigation. The fact that this investigation is undertaken by probation officers is not the result of some strange mischance. It reflects these couples' social status.

In trying to understand some officers' authoritarian or judgemental approach, it is also important to bear in mind the fact that parents do not pay for the divorce court welfare service; there is not even a means test. The officer's first priority is to satisfy the court, rather than the parents. The latter find themselves in much the same position as clients of any other statutory welfare agency: that is, they have no power of patronage over the worker. Johnstone suggests that '[client] patronage tends to balance the professional's power which is derived from expertise and specialisation . . . patronage makes the professional accountable to the client' (1972, 80 f.). This is the position in a voluntary agency (such as the majority of mediation services in this country) or where fees are paid (as may be the case with a solicitor). As far as the latter is concerned, even if the client is in receipt of legal aid, he is still free to take his business (and the state's money) elsewhere. But when it comes to the welfare inquiry, the court is the client. Parents often ask that a different officer be assigned to their case; this request is almost invariably refused. Given such powerlessness, they may well feel bound to conform to the welfare officer's expectations, so they behave passively, 'normally', even abjectly. Only *afterwards* may they protest.

A Ray of Light

Despite the bleak picture which has been presented to date, I accept that many welfare officers worry greatly over the responsibilities which they carry. They are conscious of their fallibility and modest about their achievements. Some of this, although not nearly as much as those responsible for the service might wish, was reflected in our interviews. For example, one respondent father remarked of an officer who had recently joined the Bristol team:

To be quite frank, through all the legal jungle that I've been through up to now, I find that the divorce court welfare officer is the big ray of light in the whole system. I find that she's more unbiased and willing to sit down with people and just talk.

Other laudatory accounts drew attention to this officer's clear focus on the child. There were also one or two references to her determined and imaginative attempts to ease relationships within a reconstituted family. This was in marked contrast to the 'investigative' style of some colleagues. As one custodial mother recalled:

She [welfare officer] sort of grew on me. I thought, 'Well, you're in the right job'. She had Pat [child] really at the centre of things. She wanted her to talk to Alan [new partner], at least to get this chip off her shoulder, you know, for her to get it out of her system, because she didn't want her to grow up with this thing hanging over her. And one evening we were with her and she really worked hard, this woman. We were there ages and Pat finally agreed to see Alan in the room together with us, and all these emotions were coming out because [welfare officer] was really getting to the bottom of it and this was the first time she'd really cried. And you know, really it was what she needed. But Kevin [husband] used that against [welfare officer] to say Pat had been upset at this meeting and cried all the way through.

We can infer that the husband in this case would have been less approving of the welfare officer's efforts. That may be inevitable: the welfare officer is faced with the very difficult task of holding the ring between parents who are bitterly opposed; as we shall see in Chapter 11, the task of promoting genuine agreement (as distinct from legal settlement) is one that is seldom accomplished within an adversarial framework. Nevertheless, it appears that in these two cases the welfare officer made a positive contribution: her main virtue was that she did not appear to be sitting in judgement; secondly, her genuine concern for the child led her to get involved with this family, rather than simply observing from the sidelines; and thirdly, her own experience of family breakdown meant that she had some practical help to offer.

The Report

The welfare officer's written report to the court will usually contain a recommendation as to how the case should be decided. This is used by solicitors and barristers in the pre-trial bargaining which generally leads to a settlement of some kind. Failing that, it is likely to form the centrepiece of the trial. The welfare service's contribution to the settlement-seeking process is considered in Chapter 11.

The report is also likely to contain assessments of character and family relationships. This supporting material often proved as controversial as the recommendation itself, in that it appeared to confirm these parents' damaged status. For example, one man told us that the welfare officer referred to him as 'bitter and twisted'. He said it was the worst aspect of the whole case. As previously noted, the larding of character judgements which featured in so many welfare reports can be understood by reference to the ingrained habits developed through countless 'social inquiries' for the criminal courts. This in turn is a reflection of the unhappy linking of divorce court welfare work with criminality through the one joint agency of the probation service.

Even where the judgements were not so hurtful, parents often resented the way in which the welfare officer imposed his own interpretive gloss, rather than reporting accurately what had been said in the interview. As one woman remarked:

I thought the welfare officer was a neutral person who wouldn't form opinions about you particularly. She didn't write down faithfully what I said. When you're talking to someone, you think that they're so neutral that they will report what you say, even if they don't agree with it.

But it appears that few welfare officers are prepared simply to report what parents and children tell them, without interpretation of character, motive, or family dynamics. Such embellishments can be defended on the basis that this is what courts *expect* of the welfare officer, but it is an expectation that has grown through the court and welfare service becoming habituated to one another. For the most part, both sides appear comfortable with it, although, as we shall see in Chapter 11, some welfare officers are now struggling to develop new styles.

In these circumstances, it is important that welfare officers' reasoning be made explicit, and secondly, that their judgements be open to challenge. It is particularly disturbing therefore that some parents do not even see a copy of the final report. Whatever rationalizations are advanced, this can only be designed to protect the welfare service from scrutiny, challenge, and embarrassment. Most parents either feel too vulnerable to question this practice, or are simply ignorant of their rights:

She did [write a report], she bloody did, and I wasn't allowed to bloody read it and that is infuriating . . . that to me is part of the system that needs changing.

I didn't see the report. Are you allowed to? I *thought* she [welfare officer] was hiding something from me! Bugger! I had that feeling she was. I haven't seen that report, never seen it.

If the report is not seen, or seen only by the parties' solicitors, the welfare officer's influence is not subject to anything like as vigorous a check. It is indefensible that a document which can have such import, and which often contains sweeping assertions regarding the parties' parenting capacities, should not be read by them. It is no excuse to say that the report is the property of the court, or that is has been shown to the parties' solicitors. Indeed, the fact that the report will be read by both sets of solicitors only makes things worse; it suggests a cosy professional collusion—not so much a conspiracy against the laity as a subtle accommodation *between* conspiracies.

Conclusion

There is no doubt that our research findings present a somewhat unflattering image of the divorce court welfare service. Lack of understanding, use of jargon, the arrogant assumption of superior knowledge—these are painful criticisms for a service which is often thought of as representing the human face of our system of family law. From talking to welfare officers I have often gathered that they feel depressed and overburdened by their task. Subsequently, when interviewing parents, I have been struck by the discrepancy between officers' sense of powerlessness and the way in which they are perceived by parents—that is, as extremely powerful. This has implications for divorce court welfare practice, and indeed, certain of the approaches which I describe in the next chapter, whilst open to criticism in many respects, could be seen as an attempt to remedy parents' sense of powerlessness in the face of the court apparatus.

It is also important to acknowledge that this highly critical view of the court welfare service is not replicated in other studies. In a sense this is not surprising since the various research projects are not comparable. Eekelaar, for example, conducted a study based on interviews with welfare officers themselves (1982). He found that even where the report concerned only 'satisfaction', in 38 per cent of cases the officer considered that, as a result of his involvement, the parents would make voluntary adjustments which would be of benefit to the children; in a further 27 per cent the officer thought that his involvement would result in improved attitudes towards the children. Eekelaar concluded that 'despite the officers' brief simply to investigate and report to the court, the intervention can be used to improve attitudes within the family.' This only goes to confirm the point made in Chapter 2, that in research of this kind, everything depends on whom you ask.

Another, more recent study of divorce court welfare practice was conducted by Clulow and Vincent (1987). These researchers incorporated elements of participant observation into their research design. The welfare officers whose work was being investigated were operating a hybrid system which incorporated elements of marital and family therapy, 'conciliation', and welfare investigation (Clulow and Vincent 1987, 9). Having been engaged as co-workers on some of these cases, the researchers then conducted follow-up interviews with the parties. They encountered twice as many negative responses as they did positive ones, with men being especially critical (p. 151). This finding proved very distressing to the welfare officers concerned (pp. 181 ff.). The level of consumer satisfaction with welfare officers which is reported by Clulow and Vincent is similar to that encountered in the course of the 'Conciliation in Divorce' study. This is despite there being a new model under investigation, and despite the researchers having, in part, investigated their own practice.

A more directly comparable investigation is Murch's 1973 study of parents, in which a sample of 41 cases was obtained through welfare officers themselves (1980, 45 f.). The Murch findings reflect a broadly positive view of the welfare service. For example, in relation to parents becoming locked in entrenched positions, he comments as follows:

> Then, after this had been going on for months, the welfare officer arrives on the scene—he talks with both parents separately, he talks with the children, and gradually he opens up channels of communication which have become atrophied. The overwhelming message from these parents was: 'If only this impartial, family-minded person had come on the scene two years ago, before we got ourselves into this expensive log-jam.'

There is no escaping the fact that the balance of opinion in our survey was much more critical. We discovered that the welfare officer was often seen as anything but family-minded and impartial. When parents told us that the process had taken far too long, they usually meant that it took ages for the welfare officer to prepare his report, not that it was ages before he arrived on the scene.

Both studies have their limitations when it comes to research design. The numbers involved in the Murch survey were low and the fact that couples were referred through the welfare officer (who first asked permission of the parties) will almost certainly have contributed to a lack of representativeness in the sample. The number of cases eventually filtered through to the researchers formed only a small proportion of the welfare investigations undertaken within the research period. As far as my own work is concerned, it has already been explained that we did not ask parents directly about their experience of welfare reports; it is possible, in these circumstances, that critical judgements were over-represented. Nevertheless, in certain respects the Murch findings accord with our own. Common to both studies, for example, was the disillusionment with young, inexperienced welfare officers who attempted to impose their own viewpoint on parents. Murch suggested four key elements in the welfare officer's approach to his task: impartiality, family mindedness, avoidance of stigma, and openness (1980, 173 f.). These same messages were conveyed by the parents whom we interviewed.

11

Welfare and Conciliation

THE divorce court welfare service has, since the late 1970's, been preoccupied with 'conciliation'. Indeed, it has been suggested that it is 'crucial' that probation become 'the main provider for future conciliation services' (Guise 1983). For the most part, court welfare teams have responded to these promptings *either* by servicing 'in court' conciliation appointments, these being procedural experiments within the Magistrates or County Court, *or* by incorporating elements of 'conciliation' into their conduct of the welfare enquiry. The former activity will be discussed in Chapter 12, in the context of court procedure.

As far as the welfare enquiry is concerned, there are, I suggest, three models, or ideal types. Under the first of these, the welfare officer seeks to do two things: (a) to identify those children who are being inadequately cared for by their parents, perhaps because those parents are disabled by the emotional and material costs of divorce; and (b) to help determine the most appropriate child care arrangement in cases where parents themselves cannot agree. This model is therefore a combination of the *child protective* and the *quasi judicial*. It reflects welfare officers' traditional interpretation of their role and is what courts have come to expect. It is in keeping with the spirit of recent legislation, notably the Guardianship of Minors Act 1971, s. 1 and the Matrimonial Causes Act 1973, s. 41. It is clearly delineated in Wilkinson (1981) and Pugsley and Wilkinson (1984). It was explored in Chapter 10.

The remaining two models form the subject matter of this chapter. They are not, in fact, mutually exclusive. I shall characterise them as the *settlement-seeking* and the *therapeutic*. *Both* are commonly referred to as forms of 'conciliation'. Under the first of these, the welfare officer devotes her energies, first and foremost, to securing legal settlement of contested applications. In order to achieve this, she will utilize the authority which is derived partly from her position as acknowledged expert on child welfare matters, and partly from her role as trusted adviser to the court. Operating within a framework of child welfare legislation, and under the shadow of pending adjudication, she helps drive the settlement-seeking engine which ensures that most custody and access disputes never come to trial. She may be protecting parents from the pain, humiliation and ultimate futility of the trial process; or she may (in company with legal representatives and registrars) be performing a gatekeeping function, limiting access to judicial determination.

Turning to the style of welfare enquiry which I have characterised as *therapeutic*, there appears little research evidence to go on. It is possible, indeed, that this form of intervention assumes greater prominence in the literature than in the day to day practice of the court welfare service. Nevertheless, we are being offered a model which, even if idealized, is capable of judgement in its own terms. Welfare officers who seek to practise in this way are rather more wary of fulfilling the court's purposes. They are reluctant, for example, to place themselves in a position where they appear to be determining which is 'the better parent' (Howard and Shepherd 1982, Shepherd *et al.* 1984, Howard and Shepherd 1987, 6). They also tend to be sceptical about mediators' claims that 'rational, brief and focused negotiations (can) achieve workable settlements at a time when passions (are) inflamed' (Clulow and Vincent 1987, 5). Accordingly, these welfare officers will apply insights derived from the practice of family therapy in an attempt to modify parents' behaviour so that, ultimately, they achieve more satisfactory, less conflict-ridden relationships with one another and with their children. Just as with the settlement-seeking model, this may be seen as an entirely laudable attempt to help parents escape the delusion that there can be a satisfactory legal solution to their problems; or it may be construed as a bid for power of a subtler, 'therapeutic' kind—and, once again, as a denial of legal rights.

Model One: Settlement-Seeking

In the course of the 'Conciliation in Divorce' research project, we observed this model in operation at one of the courts within our study. It was often difficult to tell when conciliation ceased and the welfare investigation took over, but most of the parents whom we interviewed did not regard it as strange, or unacceptable, that the one officer should have performed both tasks. Only one complained, whereas six people told us that they were pleased that the same person had been involved throughout.

This finding will, presumably, give comfort to those who think that the two roles may be happily combined. But we also found that most people did not distinguish between the welfare officer's two 'hats'; or to be more precise, they had very little appreciation of his mediating role. They saw him as a *reporting officer*, whose function it was to advise the court. He was regarded as someone who was checking to see that the children were properly looked after, or else advising the judge as to which parent should exercise care and control. If anything, *solicitors* were more likely to be viewed as 'mediators', bringing the two sides together in order to negotiate.

This welfare officer's authoritative personal style left parents in no doubt that he was the court's representative. Accordingly, their eyes were firmly fixed on an eventual adjudication. One might say that 'the court' was present throughout the negotiations. As far as parents were concerned, the welfare officer's report-writing garb was not something which he was to slip on at some future date; they cast him in that role *immediately*; he was always potentially, if not actually sitting in judgement. This may explain the bickering and point-scoring which we observed in the course of the preliminary appointment on court premises (also dubbed a form of 'conciliation') as parents tried to impress this same welfare officer with the strength of their case.

It has to be remembered that 'conciliation', as far as these parents were concerned, would have been a totally unfamiliar model. They expected authority to manifest itself in one form or another and most were prepared to defer to the supposed expert. It is doubtful, therefore, whether the form of conciliation practised at this court offers any real advance over the old-style welfare investigation. Instead of offering informal mediation in the course of a court welfare enquiry, as Murch, among others, has indicated used to be the case (1980, 159 ff.), the process is reversed and the welfare officer prepares for adjudication within a supposedly 'conciliation' framework. It is hard to see that this entails any great step forward.

It so happens that of our sample of 20 cases at this court, at least three involved allegations of physical ill-treatment of children by their parents. In one of these, the welfare officer attended a Social Services 'case conference' before the court conciliation appointment. In the event, the case was adjourned for a further month, the registrar remarking that 'the whole thing is rather a mess'. A contributing factor in this 'mess', so it seemed to us, was the expectation that the welfare officer continue to 'conciliate' whilst simultaneously performing *two other roles*: (a) as linchpin in the social services child welfare safety-net; and (b) as adviser to the court when (as happened in due course) the case came for trial. Whilst this did not lead to as much confusion in the minds of parents as might have been expected, this was only because the 'child protection' and 'court advisory' roles predominated, to the virtual exclusion of 'conciliation'. There was little likelihood of this form of conciliation being rejected by parents: it simply went unrecognized by them.

Some might argue that such ambiguity in the welfare officer role serves a purpose in that it allows competing philosophies to be held in suspension without forcing the issue. But there are almost certainly costs involved for parents; apart from anything else, they will not be sure of what is going on, and that is bound to make them less powerful. There may also be costs in terms of the development of mediation practice. If, in the welfare service's hands, it takes this authoritarian form, then it becomes more difficult to believe in the possibility of a genuinely non-coercive dispute resolution service.

When welfare officers lend themselves to the settlement-seeking process in this way, their practice becomes not very different from that of solicitors or registrars. As indicated in Chapter 10, there is a tendency to develop a standardized view of the likely outcome in each case. One typical circumstance is that in which the custodial mother claims that the children do not want to see their father. The welfare officer in these circumstances is likely to be suspicious, a fairly standard assumption being that the mother has influenced the children in this direction. This, of course, will be very irritating for those parents who feel that they have conscientiously tried *not* to do this.

Another aspect of this 'pigeon-holing' could be seen in a general reluctance to disturb the status quo. This was the account of one non-custodial father who had tried in vain to persuade the welfare officer that it might be worth considering his rival claim for care and control:

She made us [self and new partner] feel that no way were we going to have a say in anything. We were very disappointed. We were told by the solicitor and the court that the welfare would present a completely unbiased view, but what was the first thing she said when she came down here? I could have strangled her, I really could and, okay, so the lady who came was obviously inexperienced, but she offered us nothing. She said, 'I see no reason why the children should be disturbed', and she said that before she'd even talked to us. We thought they had to talk to both sides and then bring the decision to the court. I can honestly say I've never been so frustrated in my life. Talking to the welfare at the time was as bad as talking to my ex-wife—I was banging my head against a brick wall. I was on the verge of making this monumental decision [to abandon all contact with his children] and all they did was push me further towards doing it rather than say, well, let's look at your problems and see if we can sort them out. It was terrible. She went to great lengths to say that however bad it was with their mother, it wouldn't do them any good to be moved, and she did everything possible to talk me out of it when all I wanted to do was say, 'Well, here's my side of it.' I never had a chance to do that. I was the big, bad ogre that wanted to take the kids away from their mother. That's how she made me feel. I was very upset. We [self and new partner] saw a marriage guidance counsellor and she was very helpful—the situation was tearing us apart. We wished we'd gone to see her sooner really—I can't sing her praises enough.

In fairness to the welfare officer in this case, she should not be criticized for her reluctance to contemplate moving the children from an environment in which they were happily established. It could be said, indeed, that she demonstrated her professional integrity by refusing to raise false hopes. The comparison with the marriage guidance counsellor to whom this man referred so positively may also be a little unjust. She was not under the same pressure as the welfare officer, having no direct influence on the outcome of the case. Nor was she placed in a mediating role, being expected somehow to try to reconcile these parents' competing aspirations. As discussed in Chapter 7, this is an extremely complex task. It is perhaps not surprising, therefore, that this welfare officer, as with so many of her colleagues, had not looked beyond what seemed to her to be the inevitable outcome of the case. In terms of Merry and Silbey's (1986) account of mediator settlement strategies, she was operating very much at the 'bargaining' end.

Given that one party to the dispute is being given a strong message that he or she would have little chance of success if the case were to come to trial, one can see that this kind of standardized approach may well be effective in achieving a high proportion of 'settlements'. Some parents suggested that this was the welfare officer's prime objective. As one father explained:

I think he's a fair guy, so I think he probably thinks I ought to see them. But again, he still wants a result either way, whether I do or I don't. I don't think he'd be that worried if I don't see my children, put it that way . . . which could still be the outcome at the end of it.

Other parents suggested that the welfare officer's concern to secure agreement had overridden his responsibility to protect the children's interests:

I think that I've seen a lot of welfare officers—five altogether—and not one of them has considered the children. All they've considered is cutting this case and finishing with it. In other words, they've got loads of cases. 'If you can come to an agreement, all the better for us.' Not what's best for the children.

It was only very occasionally that we were able to infer that the welfare officer had successfully won over a parent whose starting position was seen to be untenable. It was more common for parents to gain the impression that all the welfare officer wanted was 'a result'. This suggests that the activities of the welfare service cannot be understood simply by reference to a 'justice' or 'welfare' model; this settlement-seeking approach is primarily *administrative*. Welfare officers find themselves at the heart of the court's rationing, deflecting strategy. The number of cases which 'settle' does not find a place in the Judicial Statistics, but on the basis of our own investigations it is safe to conclude that the number of 'trials' in relation to custody or access is but a small fraction of the number of initially contested applications.

From the divorce court welfare service's point of view, there is some question as to whether this should be regarded as a matter for congratulation or disquiet. Apart from the implication that the service operates, in large measure, as a rationing device, our evidence suggests that welfare officers who become too wedded to the court's purposes may no longer be dispassionate and even-handed in their treatment of parents. For example, we noted that of those parents whose case was dealt with in the most determinedly 'settlement-seeking' court within our study, 75 per cent expressed a broadly favourable view of the welfare officer, but there were only two cases in which both parties agreed that he had been 'impartial'.

Of course, welfare officers are not partisan in the same sense as solicitors, whose task it is to advance the interests of one party to the conflict: if the welfare officer arrives at a judgement in favour of one parent, this would not normally reflect 'partisanship' in the sense of prior allegiance; the judgement could be a fair one in the light of all the evidence, due weight having been given to the arguments advanced on each side. But welfare officers operate in the rather murky waters of child care theory; what is more, their judgements reflect a value base, elements of which may not be shared by all parents. The most that can be claimed therefore is that welfare officers arrive at an *interpretation* of the child's best interests: they are not dealing with 'facts' or even seeking to balance competing arguments, with one side's case being weighed against that of the other. Parents often experience this as the officer developing an allegiance with one or other of them, based essentially on personal liking and value identification. As far as they are concerned, the welfare officer *becomes* partisan.

This approach—which might be characterized as 'partisanship waiting to happen'—is characteristic of the probation officer's performance of other tasks. Probation officers function, for much of their time, as partisans on behalf of their clients. They also aim at a kind of objectivity which is meant to be rooted in their knowledge of the personal and social circumstances of offenders. The service therefore tends to recruit those who are attracted and tantalized by this tension between partisanship and objective understanding; or, as it often appears in practice, between authority and support for the underdog. I use the word 'tantalized' quite deliberately because part of the attraction of such a complex role lies in its ambiguity and internal contradictions. That may help to explain why probation officers who regard themselves as 'anti-authority' continue to behave in very authoritarian ways, whilst welfare officers attracted to 'conciliation' may adopt a stance which can only be described as partisan.

In response to this, it is fair to say that many parents do not look for impartiality; the object, as far as they are concerned, is to get the welfare officer on their side. As we have seen, even those officers who try to resist being cast in the role of 'judge' are faced with the fact that many of the parents whom they see are bitterly at odds. To that extent the investigation in its present form virtually *demands* partisanship; it is taken for granted on all sides that the welfare officer will arrive at a judgement which favours one parent. Nevertheless, it would appear, on the basis both of our interviews and of the limited opportunity which we had for direct observation, that the welfare officer's actual practice only served to reinforce this expectation. For example, it seems that in the following case he allowed himself to become totally identified with the views of one parent, so abandoning the middle ground which one might expect a disinterested investigator to inhabit, not just temporarily, as might have been necessary in order to support one or other parent at a specific point in the negotiation, but finally and absolutely:

Wife I think he's been very helpful to me. He was somebody I felt I could turn to if my solicitor wasn't there. I could turn to [welfare officer] and get a helpful word.
Interviewer. Was he impartial?
Wife. No, I think he's been more supportive of me.

Husband. I've got no respect for him whatsoever. He's a family man himself, so he should respect another family man when he meets one. I put this point to him. I said, 'When you played football, you took your boy along. What is the difference between you and me? We're both fathers', I said, 'why can't I have my son on his own and take him to a sports? He's got a totally different outlook on life from his sisters', I said, 'you've got to appreciate that.' He said, 'That's splitting the family up.' 'What's the difference between you and me?' I said. 'You split your family up when you take your boy playing football.' He couldn't answer me. His reply was, 'I think you get ample access.' I was getting one Sunday a month. I didn't think it was ample access. I applied to the court then, after [welfare officer] saying to me, 'I think you've got more than enough access.' 'In fact', he said, 'when it goes to court, you might even lose what you've got now.' He said to me, 'I think your ex-wife is beautiful—I think she'd make a lovely witness in court', and all that sort of crap. I was standing there on the path when he was walking away and he said, 'I think you've got more than you're entitled to now. You could lose what you've got.' 'Well,' I said to him, 'I'm prepared to take the risk.' So we went to court and I got staying access with my children every other weekend—and the weekend they don't stay, I have them on the Sunday.

One factor which may contribute to these allegations of bias is the welfare officer's practice of seeing the parties separately. The main purpose of the joint interview is to get both parents to accept that it is *their* responsibility to make a decision. But it also, incidentally, discourages the welfare officer from becoming too closely identified with either parent. For someone who is naturally inclined to adopt a partisan stance, separate interviews do not provide the same check. Indeed, this may be why the separate interview format is strongly adhered to, despite protestations to the contrary. Many welfare officers will claim that they are engaged in a form of 'conciliation', which might be taken to imply that, as far as they are concerned, joint interviews are the norm. However, it would seem that their actual practice is more equivocal: like a fractious horse approaching a rather formidable obstacle labelled 'joint interview', the welfare officer gallops forward confidently enough, but at the last minute he veers to one side, dumping his rider in the ditch. This is unfortunate, because the joint interview is the only effective means of placing the onus upon parents to find a solution to their common problem. Otherwise, they are almost bound to devote their energies to persuading the welfare officer to take a favourable view of their own case. (I should stress that, unlike the model of divorce court welfare practice investigated by Clulow and Vincent (1987, 154 ff.), or practised by Shepherd et al (1984), I am not suggesting that children be present on these occasions. That would almost certainly incline the proceedings towards the therapeutic mode, with power reverting to the therapist.

A reluctance to engage in joint meetings suggests that the welfare officer's brand of 'conciliation' is directed not so much at achieving a resolution of the conflict (Davis 1983), as it is at the less ambitious project of securing legal settlement. The 'pigeon-holing' of disputes, referred to earlier, is another manifestation of this. So is the tendency for welfare officers to allow the investigation to proceed at a snail's pace. Many of the reports in the cases we studied had taken an inordinate length of time to prepare—over twelve months in some instances. This caused a great deal of anxiety and many parents considered it to be scandalous treatment:

It just dragged on and on and on—that was the most inhuman aspect. The application had gone in in July, the welfare officer made an appointment to come and see me in October. She didn't turn up—she came in November and we appeared before the judge in April. And quite honestly, if we were talking about sacks of potatoes, or if we were talking about money, I wouldn't worry in the slightest if it had gone on for months or even a year or so. But it was affecting my son. He knew what was going on. How do you live with that?

Delays such as this make it more difficult to alter the existing arrangements for the children's care. This was a considerable problem for those parents (mainly women, it appeared) who had left the matrimonial home when at their wits' end, only to find that any prospect of having the children return to live with them was receding as each day passed. Several of these cases were 'settled' on the recommendation of the welfare officer. In a few instances the non-custodial parent had come to accept the situation and to regard it as being for the best, but in other cases fatigue was clearly a factor. The following was one of several cases in which the non-custodial parent eventually withdrew her application:

It took ages. The time lapse was so great that I honestly believe that those children had more time to settle in with their father. They'd settled down, gone to school . . . why disrupt it again by having father move out in a terrible fuss and row and then me move in again and have to face them after they'd been, not exactly indoctrinated, but influenced, by seeing their father so upset. That is why I feel it's very, very important that decisions are made as quickly as possible so that you know exactly where you are and the family can be rehabilitated and get back to normal living.

It should not be assumed from this that delays are entirely—or even primarily—the responsibility of the court welfare service: solicitor inaction and problems of court listing also contribute. Furthermore, in Bristol, following a welfare service initiative, the court has now begun to fix return dates for the final hearing, these being scheduled for some ten weeks after the report is ordered. The situation may therefore have improved since our interviews were conducted.

Postscript to Model One: The Distinction Between Welfare Officer Conciliation and Report Preparation.

No discussion of the welfare officer's role in securing legal settlement would be complete without some reference to the debate concerning whether or not a welfare officer should be permitted both to 'conciliate' and to prepare a court report in the one case. This is a matter which has attracted a great deal of attention of late. The President of the Family Division has become 'increasingly disturbed' by the practice of allowing reports to be prepared by welfare officers who had previously attempted to 'conciliate' in the same case.[1] This is on the basis that conciliation needs to be conducted under conditions of confidentiality, such confidentiality being undermined by the possibility that a subsequent welfare report may be prepared by the same officer. His concern was amplified in a subsequent edition of *Family Law* in which he argued that:

Conciliation cannot be as effective and useful as it should be unless the participants are completely frank and forthcoming. Unless they can be assured that what passes during conciliation will not adversely affect their interest should the matter come to a conflict, it is not at all likely that they will feel able to participate without reserve in conciliation. It is for that reason ... that privilege is an essential feature of a successful conciliation system.[2]

In order that 'privilege' be maintained, it is the President's view that:

---

[1] Letter to Mr Tony Wells, published in *Family Law*, 16, 197.
[2] *Family Law*, 17, 181.

There should be a distinction of personality between a welfare officer who participates in a conciliation effort and the welfare officer who subsequently writes a welfare report if such should prove necessary.

This was also the line taken by Mr Justice Ewbank, in the leading case of Re H, when he is reported to have said that:

> Conciliation and reporting as a welfare officer are different functions. Conciliation is the helping of parties to resolve their disputes. The duty of a court welfare officer is to help the court to resolve disputes that the parties are unable to resolve. Both functions are of great value but they are not functions which are to be mixed up. Probation officers who are involved in conciliation are not subsequently to investigate and write welfare officer's reports.[3]

I would not like to suggest that this distinction is of no importance, but I nevertheless regard the separation of conciliation from report preparation *within a legal context* as something of a red herring. I doubt whether the distinction means much to parents and I have some sympathy with those welfare officers who believe that the issue of 'privilege' in the kind of conciliation which they, as welfare officers, are likely to undertake, has been given undue prominence (Pugsley *et al.* 1986). This is because any negotiation conducted within the framework of legal proceedings is likely to have a coercive feel to it. I suspect that it matters little whether this negotiation is labelled 'conciliation' or 'welfare report preparation'. Professional understandings and 'the shadow of the court' are likely to dominate in each case. For example, at one of the courts within our study, the welfare officer's preliminary interviews with the parties were given a 'conciliation' label; in Bristol, on the other hand, these same discussions were regarded as part of the welfare enquiry. The substance was the same in each case: the welfare officer did his best to secure agreement; failing that, he prepared a report for the court.

The really important distinction, in my view, is that between (a) intervention by professional third parties in the context of legal proceedings; and (b) non-statutory mediation *offered* to the parties as a service quite independent of any litigation which they may be contemplating. The welfare service's failure to distinguish between conciliation and report-writing in the context of legal proceedings is of marginal interest because the issue of privilege is marginal. Privilege matters little in circumstances where all the professional actors are gearing their efforts towards one end, namely, the securing of legal

---

[3] Re H., Ewbank J., 19 December 1985, *Family Law*, 16, 193.

settlement. The real issue concerns authority, rather than privilege. Once the parties enter the legal arena, they lose control over the conduct of their own case. This is partly because they feel out of their depth, but it also reflects the fact that they are no longer engaged in a private quarrel. This is revealed in the telling acknowledgement, by proponents of the 'privilege' argument, that if one parent makes allegations of child abuse, 'privilege' may have to be waived (Parkinson and Parker 1987). This in turn is a reflection of the court's broader responsibility to safeguard the interests of children.[4] It means that there can be no fundamental distinction between welfare officer 'conciliation' (in the context of legal proceedings) and the preliminary stages of report preparation. Such differences as do emerge will be a reflection of each welfare officer's personal style. Because legal proceedings are dominated by the rationing motif, conciliation within that context will be devoted to the pursuit of legal settlement. It is bound, therefore, to be coercive. One cannot escape from this unpalatable fact by juggling the personnel.

Model Two: Therapeutic and Interpretive

I now turn to a rather more sophisticated and 'therapeutic' form of enquiry, expounded by some welfare officers in their professional journal (Howard and Shepherd 1982; Shepherd *et al.* 1984). Lacking any research evidence, I must rely on these practitioners' own accounts of what they do. It is possible that these approaches are being given undue prominence; I do not believe that they feature nearly as prominently as the bargaining style referred to earlier. But on the other hand, it is evident from the content of both pre- and post-professional training courses that these therapeutic aspirations are central to the probation service's conception of its role.

Shepherd *et al.* describe a new approach to divorce court welfare work which is again termed 'conciliation'. Their focus, so they tell us, has switched from the court report to securing agreement between parents. They only exclude those cases in which there is seen to be a risk to the child, since for this group the view that the child's interests would necessarily be advanced through parental agreement seems less

---

[4] This responsibility is expressed in the *Guardianship of Minors Act, 1971, s.1,* and the *Matrimonial Causes Act, 1973, s.41.*

tenable. This 'conciliation' takes place in the context of an inquiry ordered by the court and the writers do not deny that in some cases they make *assessments*; however, they claim that such assessments are of the whole family, rather than of individuals. In line with this, they favour a joint meeting involving the co-workers, the parents and the children (the latter's contribution to be mainly 'non-verbal'). Where no agreement is reached, the welfare officer prepares a report in which he 'identifies the key issues and problems and assesses the factors in the family which may be blocking a resolution'. This report is not judgemental; it doesn't select out the better parent; it is, instead, insightful and interpretive.

Although termed 'conciliation', this model derives its inspiration from 'the systemic school of family therapy', said to involve 'an alternative way of conceptualizing and understanding human be-haviour' (Howard and Shepherd 1987, 30). These same authors had earlier observed that, under this model, the welfare officer does not commit himself to a particular outcome—or, as they put it, he does not make 'pseudo-professional judgements' (Shepherd *et al.* 1984). However, it was clear from the detailed accounts which they gave that whilst Howard and Shepherd may eschew pseudo-professional judgements in one area, they are quite prepared to make assessments of family relationships which some might regard as highly speculative. The following was offered as an example of their approach. It is an extract from the welfare report in a case which had apparently involved a series of contested applications over a period of eight years:

It is not insignificant that in one form or another this case has come before the courts many times since the divorce. Based on previous court documents and reports I would observe that the underlying theme of Mr F's application is to have due recognition that he is G's father and that he ought not to have to argue for, or demand paternal rights, which he believes others, including some courts and Welfare Services, describe as privileges. During the time they were married it is probable that Mr and Mrs F learned a lot about each other's strengths, weaknesses and needs in relation to the children. Mr F knows just how much Mrs F needs to show the protective aspect of her personality and his applications to the Court enable her to demonstrate just that. It is also possible that G, a bright and sensitive child, has learned that in expressing discontent to his father, his mother will become all the more protective of him. At the same time Mrs F, knowing how much Mr F wishes to be recognised as a father, gives him the opportunity to declare his feelings with intelligence and articulation by resisting his applications . . . This suggests that Mr F and Mrs

F have achieved a balance, albeit through court hearings, which has the effect of maintaining their son in a state of continual awareness of the attributes and qualities of both parents. (Shepherd *et al.* 1984)

Now this may be an extemely perceptive comment. But it is unlikely to bear much resemblance to the way in which Mr and Mrs F would describe their circumstances, or to the reason why Mr F felt it necessary to apply to the court for access to his son. There seems no good reason why parents should accept these assessments of family dynamics any more readily than they accept the kind of judgement of character and parental competence which one finds in other welfare reports.

In another case reported by Howard and Shepherd (1987, 93), they attribute the parents' quarrel over access to the concern felt on both sides that the former spouse's new marriage should prove successful. This opinion was conveyed to the parties in writing. One couple failed to keep their next appointment with the welfare officers, telephoning on the morning to say that one of them had a dental appointment. The other couple turned up, but informed the officers that their letter was wholly ridiculous; however, the access arrangements were now being managed without argument and the boy was much happier; they did not feel it necessary to pursue their application.

One can respect these welfare officers' attempts to develop a new approach to the welfare enquiry; there is not a great deal to be said for the standard form of investigation. In many respects it resembles a funeral: solemn, slow-moving, delivering itself of weighty judgements, by no means all of them true. But this new 'family therapy' type investigation has problems of its own. One is that the explanations employed are confined to a small professional coterie, which means that these understandings cannot easily advance the cause of party control. There is also the difficulty that these insights are essentially contestable. They do not rest on a secure knowledge base. Sutton's view of professional training as, in some cases at least, little more than a socialization into a particular ideology (Sutton 1981, 88) needs constantly to be borne in mind when confronting welfare officers' interpretation of family dynamics, or their accounts of individual character and motivation. I share Sutton's view that these matters are, for the most part, 'beyond the present reach of expert understanding' (1981, 48). It is curious that officers who espouse this 'therapeutic' approach to the welfare inquiry seem well aware of the limitations of professional judgement when it comes to advising the court as to which parent should exercise care and control, but they are only too willing to deliver their interpretations of behaviour within the family. Howard and Shepherd suggest that if their interpretation happens to be awry, nothing is lost (1987, 94). But this is surely too sanguine. If parents are confronted by explanations of motive and behaviour which they regard as fanciful, or even bizarre, it may well add to the stress which they experience.

But perhaps the main concern about this 'therapeutic' model of conciliation, placed in the hands of welfare officers, is that they seem to believe that this is the *only* way to resolve disputes. Parents who find it necessary to apply to a court are either misguided, or lacking proper help. It seems that the *offer* of conciliation is not enough: according to Shepherd and his colleagues, an attempt to mediate, followed (where the mediation is unsuccessful) by an application to the court 'pays only lip service to the principles of conciliation'. If conciliation is unsuccessful in resolving the dispute, this is only because 'the conciliators have not been skilful enough in stimulating the self-healing mechanisms of the family group' *or* 'because the system allows all concerned too readily to resort to the adversarial system' (Shepherd *et al.* 1984). This view is endorsed by the National Association of Probation Officers' consultation paper on this subject, in which it is argued that 'an unresolved dispute does not indicate that conciliation has failed, rather that the process is not as yet complete.'[5]

I believe this to be dangerous. There is no doubt that courts are not in a position finally to resolve family disputes: a decision may be taken, but unless it is an order for complete severance, the onus remains with the parties to make it work; this is made all the more difficult because the legal process tends to encourage the adoption of an aggressive, antagonistic stance on both sides. Nevertheless, parents have a right to adjudication. For many, that is the only protection which they have against bullying, or other forms of coercion. They also, as part of that process, have a right to painstaking, sensitively handled preliminary enquiry (Pugsley and Wilkinson 1984).

Howard and Shepherd are innovative practitioners, and no doubt highly skilled. Their refusal to pass critical judgements on individual parents is wholly commendable. Despite this, I hope that the divorce court welfare service as a whole does not seek to copy their method: first, because I remain sceptical of the knowledge base; and secondly,

---

[5] NAPO Discussion Paper on 'Conciliation', May 1984.

because I fear that their approach is bound to be ill-understood by parents and therefore likely to confer too much power on the conciliator/therapist. As previously noted, the roots of their practice lie in the systemic school of family therapy (Howard and Shepherd 1987, 30), which is presumably why they think it may be applied to everyone. Mediation, by contrast, has modest goals, and most mediation schemes are content that their clientele select themselves. Given the level of criticism of the divorce court welfare service which we encountered, there is much to be said for having modest goals.

The Possibility of an Independent Mediation Service, Run by Divorce Court Welfare

Although my task in this chapter has been to examine the conjunction of welfare investigation and conciliation, I have done so within the context of the welfare service's performance of its statutory responsibilities. I have therefore explored two practice experiments through which welfare officers attempt to apply some elements of the conciliation idea to their traditional investigative task. I have not gone beyond this, to ask whether divorce court welfare might provide the organizational umbrella under which *independent* conciliation schemes, not beholden to any court, could offer a mediation service to parents. That is a question which can be considered quite independently of the welfare service's attempts to modify its approach to court-inspired investigation. Much of the evidence upon which I relied in the discussion of mediation in Chapters 6 and 7 was based on a service of just this type, at Bromley in London. (For a more detailed examination of mediation in this context, see Davis and Roberts 1988). I merely note it here because this is an alternative direction in which some welfare officers have chosen to pursue their interest in 'conciliation'. Although operating under the aegis of divorce court welfare, mediation at the Bromley Bureau is a discrete activity. This is not simply a matter of the one officer not performing the mediating and report-writing tasks; it is rather that the mediators operate within a non-statutory framework. They are not servants of the court. The only 'settlements' which they feel under an obligation to pursue are those which make sense to the parties.

To date, little serious consideration has been given to the possibility that divorce court welfare might, on the Bromley model, provide the organizational framework within which independent mediation services could be developed. The Inter-departmental Committee was notably blinkered in its approach to this question. All the Committee's cost calculations, which led them to conclude that independent mediation services had to be left to local sponsors and volunteer effort, were based on the assumption that a network of entirely new services would have to be developed. This enabled them to arrive at a figure for funding out of court mediation which was far in excess of any legal aid savings which these services were likely to achieve.[6]

Some might argue that for a statutory service to promote 'conciliation' as something entirely separate from legal proceedings would be to create a false dichotomy between dispute resolution on the one hand and considerations of child welfare on the other. However, as should be clear from Chapter 7, this is to misrepresent the nature of mediation in this context. In many instances the only reason that parents are prepared to modify their position is that they recognize that it is in the children's interests for them to do so. It is clear therefore that the children's needs will be central to any discussion concerning custody or access arrangements. But there remains the quite separate question of who exercises authority (the court or the parents) within each negotiation. If parents are enabled to retain authority for any decisions which are taken, their prestige is enhanced. They cannot very readily retain this authority in the context of conciliation undertaken as an adjunct to legal proceedings.

Provision of what is in effect a dual service in South-East London reflects a sensitivity to the issue of authority and a recognition that, for some parents, the ability to resolve these issues without submitting themselves to professional experts is something to be valued in its own right. The essential point, which some sections of the court welfare service have yet to grasp, is that the best way to advance the welfare of children is to minimize the damage to the self-esteem of parents.

Postscript: Children's Rights

The present debate concerning the means by which we should protect the interests of children on their parents' divorce is sometimes framed in terms of 'children's rights', it being argued that recognition of such

[6] *Report of the Inter-departmental Committee on Conciliation*, Lord Chancellor's Department, 1983, paras. 4. 1 to 4. 26.

rights necessarily entails some loss of parental autonomy (Freeman 1983, 244 f.). It has been suggested that 'the practical problem is that of designing social institutions capable of enforcing children's rights under the equality principle without degenerating into a moral tyranny' (Eekelaar and Dingwall 1984, 109). These authors conclude that 'the present system is reasonably successful in these terms.'

In fact, the notion of children's rights has limited practical utility. In any child-care dispute, the conflict is over whose conception of the child's needs should prevail; in certain circumstances (such as care proceedings) the struggle may be between parents on the one hand and welfare professionals on the other, with everyone claiming to represent the best interests of the child. On divorce, the position is more complicated since parents' views may well differ, but it remains the case that *everyone* will argue on the basis of the children's interests; to invoke the notion of children's 'rights' does not provide any kind of answer.

But in much of the writing about divorce (and in the legislation, notably The Matrimonial Causes Act, 1973, s. 41) there is the idea that children need to be protected *against their parents*. Freeman, for example, says of the decision-making process in divorce that 'there can be few areas of life where the treatment of children as property rather than as persons is better exemplified' (1983, 192). He goes on to argue that 'this has been accentuated by the growing trend towards private ordering of divorce which reduces further the already minimal reviewing capacity of courts.' He suggests that 'private ordering may in fact be a mirage, an aspiration of liberals' (199) and asserts that 'firmer, not looser controls are required on private ordering of custody arrangements.' Not only that, 'decisions as to access are too important to be left to the custodial parent' (218).

But our interviews suggest that whatever doubts there may be about some parents' care-giving capacities, these are as nothing compared with the inability of experts to provide adequate alternative care, or even worthwhile assistance. Freeman has been led down this road by his adherence to the concept of children's rights. As Michael King (1987) has trenchantly observed:

[The idea that] children suddenly have rights to be respected and, where necessary, enforced by state intervention, is another example of simplistic, symbolic solutions being offered as a cure for complex relational problems, to which they are largely irrelevant.

Freeman's willingness to endorse an extension of the state's supervisory role is surprising in someone who has identified the currently fashionable idea of the Family Court with a 'triumph of the therapeutic' and warned that 'this century has witnessed a continual expansion of surveillance by professionals over family life' (1983, 232). Presumably this represents a change of mind, although, since these opposing sets of arguments appeared in the one volume, one cannot be sure in which direction.

I would not wish to deny that parental decisions may at times be selfish or ill-considered. All manner of oppression may exist within families. It has been noted that 'the case against intervention in family life often rests on the freedom of more powerful members (usually husbands in relation to wives and parents in relation to children) to exercise their power without restriction' (Jordan 1981, 45). But one must also recognize that, on the whole, parents are likely to have a better understanding of their children's needs and be more motivated by love of the child, than are professional interveners. This point has been well made by Brigitte and Peter Berger, writing with reference to teenage sexuality:

We feel strongly that parents' rights should take precedence—*not* over children's rights, which are usually not the real issue, but over the claims of various professionals to represent the best interests of children. Our general maxim here remains: in general, trust parents over against experts; the burden of proof against individual parents should be very strong indeed before the opposite choice is made. (1983, 213)

These writers are critical of the way in which private choices (such as divorce) become 'problematized' as public issues, and one can see that the dramatic increase in the scale of divorce over the past twenty years or so has been an absolute gift for the bureaucratic and professional welfare classes with all their expansionist tendencies. In the Bergers' terms, these groups 'inflate the definitions both of weakness and of need'. Current enthusiasm for 'conciliation'—which might be taken to imply support for *parental* decision-making—could be seen as heralding a move in the opposite direction. It is clear, however, that this idea can take many forms: it may, for example, be employed as a rationing device; or to add lustre to existing professional practice. Underlying the disagreement over the use of the *word* (a quarrel which, to many, must appear arid and self-indulgent) is the question of whether it is feasible and worthwhile to offer a new service to divorcing couples—one which they may patronize or ignore, as they wish. At the moment, the countervailing tendency would appear the stronger, that is, to employ conciliation either as a means of restricting access to judicial determination, or as a vehicle for therapeutic intervention. The rationing may be necessary; the therapist may be highly skilled; but it is worth reminding ourselves of the central aspiration which gave life to the conciliation movement. As I understand it, this was that couples who would otherwise have to submit to outside decision-making should be enabled to retain a greater measure of autonomy, and perhaps dignity, than is normally possible within the legal arena. This aspiration can easily be lost sight of in the midst of professional enthusiasm for applying some (but not all) of the principles of conciliation in the service of their own practice.

The Court

12

Preliminary Hearings and the Search for Settlement

CONCILIATION appointments which are held on court premises, as an integral part of contested legal proceedings, were first introduced in Bristol County Court in April 1977 (Parmiter 1981). Initially limited to decree proceedings, the system was extended in 1979 to cover contested custody and access applications. Most county court registrars have since followed suit and, in January 1983, a similar scheme was introduced in the Principal Divorce Registry. Some two-thirds of those interviewed in Bristol as part of our 'Conciliation in Divorce' study of contested applications had experienced a preliminary appointment. In 75 per cent of these cases the dispute was over custody or access, whilst in the remainder it concerned the divorce decree.

These attempts to introduce a forum for negotiation on court premises are experimental; precise arrangements vary from court to court. At the time of writing, there has been no rule introduced to make the procedure mandatory, although in practice, once the appointment system has been introduced in a particular court, it tends to become mandatory for all parties (and legal advisers) using that court. The position may well change following the report of the Matrimonial Causes Procedure Committee (Booth Committee). Booth was evidently impressed with the idea of preliminary appointments, recommending that there be an 'initial hearing' in most categories of divorce case.[1] This procedure might serve a variety of purposes and it is my intention in this chapter to draw what lessons I can from the parties' experience of the Bristol preliminary appointment system. Given the interest which this experiment has aroused, I should like to ask: what are the objectives underlying the introduction of conciliation on court premises? Much of the research evidence upon which I rely has appeared in Davis and Bader (1985) and Davis (1988).

---

[1] Report of the Matrimonial Causes Procedure Committee, July 1985, HMSO. See, in particular, paras. 4. 53 to 4. 90.

Conduct of the Appointments

The first point to emphasize, certainly in relation to Bristol County Court, is that much of the work involved in these appointments takes place in the court waiting area. On the mornings when the conciliation appointments are held, the Bristol court can be a hot-bed of negotiation with solicitors and welfare officers dashing to and fro. Two private interviewing rooms are generally available, but much of the 'nitty-gritty' of negotiation takes place out in the open, including, sometimes, that involving the welfare officers.

We asked our Bristol informants what they thought of the waiting area. 52 per cent were critical, their criticisms centring on the two related areas of overcrowding and lack of privacy:

We waited about an hour and a half . . . it's rather like Heathrow with a strike on—it's embarrassing for all concerned.

Terrible. All I was aware of was all the seats were occupied—all people, all problems—and it's all around you. It's like you can feel the atmosphere, the anxiety.

Appointments were listed for every half hour. It is impossible to devise a precise timetable since one cannot tell beforehand which cases will be adjourned immediately and which will take all morning. But there can obviously be delays and given the tension which many people are feeling, these can be particularly nerve-racking:

I was sitting there for a good half hour on my own. (Husband) there with his solicitor . . . me sitting there all on my own with nobody. It was awful. He [solicitor] turned up eventually. He was actually in the building somewhere with another case. But I was there for a good half hour on my own, thinking, which way to look, what to do with my hands. I felt quite lost and alone watching all these other transactions going on and I thought 'How can human beings come to this?'

Apart from feeling that they had to display their personal life in front of strangers, another reason for the stress which many people experienced was that they had to share the waiting area with their spouse. In some instances they had not seen one another for months (or even years in a few cases). They had been building themselves up for this moment and then there they were, the object of all this emotion, facing them across the room:

The only time I went to court, I had an appointment at half past ten and I had to stay from half past ten until quarter past two. My husband and his wife—or girlfriend as it was then—hanging around; you standing in one place and him standing somewhere else and it's an awful feeling. You're so emotionally taut, you're already at the stage where you can snap and you're going into this formal court with all these people around and you've got one set over here and one set over there—it's a terrible feeling. I honestly can't see why there can't be some system devised where you're not stuck there looking at your husband with his girlfriend.

Most people do not feel comfortable in a court. The strength of their reaction to this period in the waiting area no doubt reflects the way they felt about the whole business of getting a divorce. This may have been the only time they had to go to court and whilst some were able to cope with it reasonably well, it was common to find that the waiting period and the build-up of tension crystallized all their negative feelings:

It frightened me to death, to be quite honest with you, you know, with all the men sat round and just me sat there. It was just all men. I felt small.

Given the anxiety which many people experienced when having to confront their spouse, how did they manage to negotiate together? The answer is that in most cases they did not do so. In 56 per cent of cases in Bristol (excluding those in which only one party was present at the appointment) we were told that husband and wife had not talked together. Some had been anxious to avoid this, with the result that solicitors were driven to act as intermediaries. But it was more common for us to be told that solicitors had not *wanted* the parties to negotiate directly with one another:

His solicitor was one side and my solicitor was the other and we were about 12 feet apart. His wife [new partner] was there and my husband [new partner] and I were here. And they just kept swapping over. He'd go back and say, 'What about 7 o'clock?', and I'd say 'no' and he'd go back and say, 'What about half past seven?' It got a bit pathetic. It got ridiculous. I almost stood up and said, 'Look, can we stop this game?', because it just seemed childish to me. I could talk to him, he was only 12 feet away from me. He [wife's solicitor] told me I couldn't. I said to him, 'Surely we could sit by a table?' Oh no, we must do it like this—and they [solicitors] kept going off in a corner, having a little discussion and coming back and I just found it very stupid. It cost me £160 which absolutely flabbergasted me. I couldn't see any necessity for it at all. I went up to his solicitor afterwards and gave him a piece of my mind. That happened all the way through really. I don't think anyone encouraged you to communicate—you were told not to communicate. Everything had to go through your solicitors.

In these circumstances it was possible to arrive at 'settlements' for which the parties themselves felt no responsibility. In several cases it was evident that the 'agreement' had in fact amounted to a defeat. One woman, asked whether she and her husband had been able to resolve their dispute over access arrangements, replied: 'I think my solicitor did. All I remember was my solicitor saying, "we've lost."'

Some of the parents who remarked on their solicitors' having taken over the negotiations acknowledged that it was their own inability to resolve matters amicably in the first place that had got them in this position. Nevertheless, they were taken aback at the almost complete loss of authority and loss of control which they experienced once having embarked upon their litigation. It is one of the key messages of our research that this form of court-based conciliation did not succeed in rectifying this:

It was very busy that morning, absolutely packed down there. We had a fairly long wait—it was a good couple of hours I was there at least. It's very segregated [in the waiting area], isn't it? If your solicitor's there, you're grabbed, more or less. It's all a bit silly 'cos you and I are sat here now, and I'm talking to you—and there's a man I've lived with for 7 years sat on the other side—you could feel that you don't really know him—'Who's that?'—like you're sat on a bus, looking at a stranger. To me, it was ridiculous. I'd have gone across and spoken to him. But it seems not to be the done thing. I don't think my solicitor would have liked it if I'd done that. Neither do I think his solicitor would. I think they'd have been astounded if we'd talked to one another. There were other occasions when it was more acceptable, when there weren't so many people about, that we did actually talk to one another. It seems crazy, but you'd be surprised how many people think that way. I noticed all the other couples, and the solicitors were conferring, but there were the two people—really the ones who should have been . . . although then, why was I there? If we could have conferred and got on, then we wouldn't have been where we were.

Of course, not everyone wants or feels able to remain in control in these circumstances. For those who have tried and failed to reach an agreement, there may be a kind of tyranny in the expectation that, even when they have got as far as a courtroom, the matter is thrown back in their lap and they are required to exercise a responsibility which they have come to regard as beyond them:

If you have to rely on solicitors and the welfare they put pressure on you to come to an opinion and that's difficult. Ideally it should have gone to the solicitors and been left at that. I don't see that a lot of good comes out of the mediation—you are left with tremendous guilt if you haven't done enough yourself. It is so informal as to provide no guide-lines at all and it is rather hard to expect two people who do not talk, or cannot talk because their relationship has broken down so completely, to start talking again. You accept that there has to be a mediation appointment because that's the way it's done here, but my immediate thoughts [at having to go back a third time] were 'Oh gosh, not again.' Nothing is achieved by them to my mind. You see a welfare officer who, in my opinion, has read a book and has read your notes and that's the end of it. You're under pressure of time and a tremendous pressure to reach a decision—which you do, and it's only after that you wonder if it was the right decision. And because you're given the impression that it's *your* decision you have to live with your guilt. That's another aspect of it. You already have enough guilt without having more to add to it. I suppose, really, you need a scapegoat. If you have solicitors, you can always turn round and blame them . . . To have come face-to-face with your ex-husband and to know that people expect you to come to an opinion together on it is asking too much when the very reason that you're there is because you have broken down. It's a contradiction. I would definitely prefer a welfare officer right from the very beginning, somebody that *both* parties can talk to and produce a realistic opinion.

The woman quoted here had experienced three preliminary appointments, it being a feature of this procedure in the Bristol court that more than one appointment may be held on the same issue in the one case. This reluctance to allow cases to proceed to trial was quite striking. It suggests that in the absence of anything more constructive, conciliation becomes synonymous with delay. Having become used to the idea that the 'Special Procedure' has taken us into the realm of administrative divorce (in other words, that courts exercise only minimal supervision where both parties say they want a decree) we seem to be observing a parallel movement, some ten years later, in which courts seek to respond even to *disputes* between the parties in administrative rather than judicial terms.

The Solicitor at the Conciliation Appointment

As has already been implied, it is the normal practice in Bristol for solicitors to attend the conciliation appointment with their client. In most cases, legal aid will by that stage have been obtained. Parents' accounts of these waiting-room negotiations indicate that they regarded solicitors as being comfortable in this enviroment, whilst they themselves were not:

You put yourself in his hands. He knows the procedure—it's his game. I didn't know what to expect. I didn't know what to say. I've never been to any courts at all. And I felt they were much more formal than I expected.

The phrase 'it's his game' pretty well sums up what people had to tell us about this stage of the proceedings. Nevertheless, it was clear that in anticipating the appointment, they had wanted their solicitor to be present, and were glad, after the event, that he or she had been there. It is not surprising, given the present tendency for solicitors to negotiate *on behalf of* their clients, that the parties found it difficult to conceive that they could have managed on their own. Indeed, the strongest criticism of solicitors came from those parents who felt that they had been insufficiently protected. Some women, in particular, experienced a lack of support from their solicitor at the appointment. In some of the cases which we observed the solicitor appeared unfamiliar with the procedure, in which case one can understand that it would have been difficult for him (or her) to stand firm in the face of what can be a rather formidable settlement-seeking momentum. This was even more of a problem where, as often happened, the solicitor responsible for the case sent along a junior colleague in her stead.

The Welfare Officer at the Conciliation Appointment

Of the two non-aligned, potential mediating figures who are present at the appointments—the welfare officer and the registrar—it is the welfare officer who, at present, is regarded as the principal negotiator. For the most part, he or she will work directly with the parties (rather than with their solicitors), the discussion taking place either in the waiting area or in one of two interviewing rooms.

Whilst there was considerable criticism of the performance of the welfare officers at the appointment, this may be a reflection of the pressures associated with the court environment. These place the welfare officer in a kind of 'double bind', theoretically committed to enabling the parties to control the outcome of the proceedings, whilst nevertheless anxious to obtain an agreement. As one father recalled:

I got the distinct impression that I was behaving unreasonably in trying to prevent my wife from seeing my son. We were sat for hours. [Welfare officer] would come in and say a few words to us and ask me all over again—I imagine similar to police interviewing a suspect—just by sheer length of time and frustration the suspect will say, 'All right, I smashed the window'—that's the sort of frustration I felt. I would agree to anything just to get out of the place. At 2 o'clock he said, 'Now you've got to see a registrar and agree to something or come back in the morning.' I would agree to anything just to be released. My feelings at the time bore no relation to what the court said . . . no rights at all.

One can appreciate the welfare officer's dilemma in many of these cases. She must often feel that one parent is being unreasonable, or that she can anticipate the eventual outcome. But it is all too easy to assume in these circumstances that parents 'ought' to agree. The Bristol welfare officers have acknowledged to me that they have reservations on this point, but in practice it seems that they are caught up in the general assumption that success at the appointments is to be equated with the achievement of 'settlement'. As social workers, their role in legal proceedings has been conceived (by lawyers) as softening the rough edges of the legal process, offering time and an interest in the private and the personal. But it seems that if welfare officers are involved *too* closely with the court machinery, they become identified with it, so that they are transformed into Action Man, as preoccupied with the search for legal settlement as any lawyer.

Children's Attendance at the Conciliation Appointment

Of the 93 Bristol cases in our sample which had involved a mediation appointment concerning custody or access, the children attended the appointment in 25 (27 per cent). (There would often be more than one appointment in such cases, but the children, in our experience, would only be asked to attend once.) The reason for wanting the children to be present is fairly obvious; the dispute often centres on different interpretations of the children's wishes. What could be more sensible, therefore, than to let them speak for themselves? The problem is that the children will, in some cases, feel very ambivalent; they may not have a fixed view at all. On the other hand, they are likely to be heavily influenced by the custodial parent and to have strong feelings of loyalty towards him or her. So it is likely to be *one* parent (rather than both) who favours the children's attendance.

This is confirmed by the findings from the ten cases in our sample in which children attended the mediation appointment and we managed to interview both parents. Of the 10 women interviewed, 7 thought it right that their children be questioned at the court. But when the husbands were questioned, only 2 agreed with this judgement, whilst the former husbands of the 3 women who did *not* agree with the children's attendance all thought it right that they be present. So we get an almost complete 'misfit' between the two sides—not surprising in view of the fact that the children's evidence in these circumstances is so powerful.

Furthermore, the welfare officer is placed in a very weak position once the child (perhaps under considerable pressure) has expressed a view. All the welfare officer's negotiating strength has gone, with the result that he or she tends to be roundly criticized by both parents. In these circumstances, the child has become the adjudicator. Aside from the question of whether this is an appropriate burden for a child to bear, particularly one aged nine or ten,[2] it limits the scope of any subsequent negotiation. Once the child has spoken, there can often seem very little left to negotiate about; into the harbour of conciliation has come sailing the QE2, with the result that the welfare officer is left spluttering on the shore.

The Registrar's Chambers

Of the parents in our Bristol sample who had attended a mediation appointment, 84 per cent had, at some stage, entered the registrar's chambers. Whilst several people commented on the registrar's kindness towards them, it is fair to say that we came across major problems associated with this stage of the proceedings. The main drawbacks from the parties' point of view were, first, that they themselves seldom participated to any great extent; and secondly, that they often felt that they had little control over the final outcome. Fewer than a third of those interviewed recalled contributing to the chambers discussion; 38 per cent of men told us that they had said something to the registrar; only 23 per cent of women recalled having done so.

Solicitors' tendency to act as the parents' mouthpiece reflects the

[2] It is now the practice at the Principle Divorce Registry for children as young as this to be asked to attend the preliminary appointment.

rather uncomfortable blurring of the distinction between conciliation and more traditional forms of court hearing. The same point has been made in relation to negotiations conducted in the waiting area, but at this final stage of the proceedings, the message was unmistakable:

My husband's solicitor talked about him; my solicitor talked about my case. But as people, we were talked *about*, but not talked *to*, as I remember it. Really, I felt the case was taken away from us and they were deciding what *they* was going to do, and all we had to do was say 'yes' or 'no'.

I said, 'Can't I say anything to the registrar? It's all been going on what *they've* said.' There they are discussing something that's been going on in my house and I couldn't say anything and that made me mad. I was really mad all the way back in the car, saying, 'Why did he bring that up? Why didn't he let me explain?'

Another aspect of the excluding nature of the proceedings is the practice of asking parents to sit at the back of the room, usually a few yards apart from one another. Their solicitors meanwhile are at the front, facing the registrar across his desk:

[Husband] went without a solicitor and I went with my solicitor. So I was sat there at the end of the room by the wall and they were talking about me and I must have been getting red in the face, I was so fed up with it. And eventually the registrar went, 'Oh, Mrs T, would you like to sit up here with us? You seem rather left out of it.' And I looked at him and I thought 'Shall I say something?' I thought, 'No, I better not.' But even when I was moved up to the desk with everyone else, I still wasn't consulted about anything or asked anything. And it just seemed . . . I thought, 'Well, it's because my solicitor's here and his isn't.'

If the seating arrangements are as described above, it is almost inevitable that the registrar will address himself to the solicitors, rather than to the parties directly. Despite this, we were sometimes told that the registrar had indicated his willingness to listen—indeed, had encouraged those people who made the effort to speak up for themselves. But for the most part, it was only the more articulate and confident parties who succeeded in breaching the professional cocoon within which the proceedings were conducted.

It is hardly surprising in these circumstances that some people gained the impression that they were experiencing an adjudication. We were given a number of accounts which suggested that, subtly or not so subtly, the registrar had imposed his will on the proceedings. There will be those who persist in regarding this as a perfectly acceptable thing for the registrar to do. But whilst I would agree that judges and registrars should be more willing to adjudicate than they are at present, adjudication is not what is on offer at the appointments. This form of lawyer driven, lawyer dominated conciliation is all about securing *settlement*. Decisions are imposed, but they are presented as agreements. At its worst, the procedure is a thoroughly unsatisfactory hybrid: a cross between mediation without party-control and adjudication without the right to give evidence. The following case, in which we interviewed both parties, provides one graphic illustration of this:

Husband. [Registrar] didn't really have much to say, to be quite honest. I was shocked, I was expecting one side to say this, one side to say the other, one side to retaliate, and him [registrar] to listen, and he suddenly just picked up the file and said, 'Right, what's all the fuss about? All he's asking for is once a fortnight. I can see no reason why not and it will be from . . . And to her solicitor, [registrar] looked round and said, 'What do you feel, Mr R?', and he said, 'Well, in theory . . . ' 'I'm not on about theoretical, in practice it *will* be . . . ', and he looked up to mine and said, 'What do you think?' 'Fine, that suits us.' Bingo! And it was over. To be honest, we were in there for—what—a minute, it was very quick, slightly informal, but with a formal attitude to it . . . He was very positive, the registrar, and that was it. OK, I could just as easily have been on the receiving end of it and walked out of there with a ton weight on my shoulders. But I walked out of there quite happy, in fact, that something, as I thought at the time, had finally been decided. It was just cut and dried. Even my solicitor was surprised.

Wife. It seemed a sell-out. The impression I got was that the solicitors had sorted it all out beforehand, and I thought, what am I doing here? The children's welfare didn't come into it. Ralph [husband] was on his best behaviour. I felt I was a guilty party being taken to court for an offence. It was just like watching a film—Ralph coming the great daddy. I was just bewildered because it wasn't the man I knew, it was an actor stood there. It was a sell-out. I nudged my solicitor on one occasion to say something. He didn't—so I did. The registrar was saying, 'That sounds reasonable', and it was annoying me, because he didn't know the children. I got the feeling that I was like a rotten woman, stopping their father from seeing the children, but I wasn't. Ralph was sat there, playing a part, along with his solicitor, along with mine. They'd all discussed it. The registrar had looked at Ralph and he seemed a fantastic fellow—but to me, it didn't get near the truth.

The 'agreement' in this case lasted for precisely one access visit. The children no longer speak to their father, although he lives only a few doors away.

Accounts such as this demonstrate the non-mediatory character of 'in court conciliation'. This is not just a matter of registrars' inability to modify their traditional role. It is also necessary to take account of the parties' expectations: the fact that they are attending something called a conciliation appointment will mean little to them. Many had expected that their hazy notions of courtroom drama would be acted out before their eyes. In the event, these expectations were often realized—the appointment did indeed feel very like a trial. Some couples, having experienced the procedure, thought it *was* a trial. They 'agreed' without even realizing they were agreeing.

But it also has to be recognized that, as a form of trial, this procedure lacks almost all the safeguards traditionally associated with judicial determination. A reasonable expectation of any legal system is that it protect the vulnerable against undue pressure or manipulation; after all, what are courts for? At the time of divorce there are many who need that protection, just as there are those who have already suffered grave injustice. It would seem that this is not always recognized by the procedural reformers, just as it may be neglected by what appears to be a new breed of partisan.[3] The latter appear to have parted company with the knights of old: they no longer believe in righting wrongs. The development of a form of conciliation on court premises, coupled with the emergence of solicitors committed to the new settlement-seeking orthodoxy, has promoted legal settlement to the point where it has become a guiding principle.

Take the following case, in which the man arrived home from work one day to find his house stripped of all furniture. There was a note from his wife saying that she could no longer live with him; he subsequently discovered that their joint savings account had been cleared. In due course, the wife petitioned for divorce, citing her husband's unreasonable behaviour; he filed an 'Answer' to the petition, claiming that her allegations were lies; as far as he was concerned, *she* should be brought to account (publicly if possible) for what she had done to him. A conciliation appointment was held, at which his solicitor tried to persuade him to allow the divorce to proceed undefended:

What she [solicitor] was looking for was a compromise—she said we got to find a compromise, but the things she [wife] done was too bad for compromise. I think it should go through the court for a court to decide. Because I do not think that no law will uphold such things as what she done to me. Because she

[3] The Solicitors' Family Law Association has produced a Code of Practice (October 1983), the whole tenor of which is to encourage a conciliatory rather than a litigious approach to family disputes.

made my life for three years now a complete misery. I went through hunger, deficiency, the whole lot—God, them times was ever so bad. Many a night I got up here and I'd walk this house and I'd think about what she done. So I think something should learn her—you know, to tell her, for her to see—more than to compromise with her. I think that there should be something more in this than to compromise with her.

But in the end he gave in. Accounts such as this may serve as a warning to those who worship uncritically at the altar of administrative efficiency and 'savings'. We have to remember why we bothered to create a legal system in the first place. There is nothing to be proud of in simply diverting as many people as possible from the adjudicatory process. But it is in this light that 'conciliation' is increasingly being viewed. It is easy to forget that the case for mediation in family disputes rests on the premise that a neutral third party may be able to bring parents to the point where they will make concessions *without* arm-twisting, either out of a sense of fair play, or because they feel that it is in their children's interests for them to do so. In other words, the mediation case rests upon parents' presumed ambivalence. There is very little opportunity to explore such ambivalence in a courtroom, during an appointment scheduled to last half an hour. More fundamentally, there is little *inclination* to do this in the context of professionally dominated negotiations geared to the achievement of legal settlement.

The kind of pressure which is imposed in many of these cases does not help parents to find within their own definition of the problem any strand which is compatible with the case being put forward by the other side; in other words, it does not encourage them to be 'reasonable'. If any element of common ground exists, this is not the way to locate it—it may, instead, succeed in mobilizing all the 'fight' within that person's make-up. The following case provides one clear illustration of this. The speaker is a young woman who had care and control of her two children:

We went over overnight access. I was totally adamant, totally stubborn—no. I don't care what anyone says—no. And I walked into that courtroom saying 'no'. It's like 'I'll have a Guinness'. I was going in there saying 'no', 'no'— building up my courage, you see—I will not be intimidated this time. And I came out agreeing to it! And I felt totally shattered all over again. But the following ones—it's a shame really—I was going in getting nastier and nastier because it seemed to be the only way to cope with battling with everyone—that I'm going to be nasty, I'm going to be horrible and I'm going to say 'no' whether you like me or not. Which, I suppose, is failing to see what you're there for in the first place.

By way of contrast, a tentative agreement arrived at in the course of the appointment, provided it was entered into voluntarily, might provide a useful 'marker' which could then be modified at a later date:

The registrar said, 'Let's see what happens, see how it goes and if it works okay, come back in a month; we'll see how it's worked and if it's okay, or if you need any amendments, we'll sort them out then.' When we went back, [husband] did ask for a little more access and I gave it to him.

We were not given many accounts of a successful negotiation, satisfactory to both parties, but the following is one example. The wife's account was much fuller, but the husband also clearly endorsed the final agreement:

Wife. I think out of the whole divorce that was the most fantastic thing I've ever seen. She [solicitor] did work well. I was on one side of the room with her, he was on the other side with his solicitor. We went into a room with a social worker—court welfare officer—who explained to him why I was concerned about access times and him bringing them home late and she suggested to him the reasons behind what I was feeling. That woman was marvellous. She seemed to understand how we both felt and she *told* us she could understand how we both felt and why I was so concerned about the children and the times of access. She said to him that if I said they had to be home at a certain time, would he make sure he would bring them home at that time because young children shouldn't be out late at night and they also need a certain amount of time to readjust when they get home from being out with the other parent. None of that he had seemed to comprehend at all. It was a very short interview but she said what she needed to. She was very good.

Then we went back into the main waiting-room and my solicitor went backwards and forwards, backwards and forwards, and she sorted it out within a very short space of time, and by the time we got in to see the registrar . . . he was a marvellous man and he reduced my ex-husband and his solicitor from two grown men to *that* big. It was incredible. And the pair of them were still arguing about how I ought to have a welfare report done on me and I ought to have a supervision order. They kept on and on. He [registrar] kept saying, no, there's no need, it was a waste of the country's money. He was like a grandad. He said he understood why I needed those exact times because of how he's been bringing them home. He said, 'You get any trouble and you come back to me.'

Husband. A very nice man; extremely pleasant. It was his office, he controlled it; everything was done in a cool, calm, collected manner. He was very pleasant, but it was his show; he was a man it would be difficult to get one over on.

I have deliberately focused on the parties' response to these appointments—that is, on what the procedure meant to them, rather than on whether they reached agreement in the eyes of the court. But one must also take account of the formal 'settlement rate': in the Bristol court this appeared to be in the region of 58 per cent (although in some of these cases the substantive negotiations had been completed *prior* to the appointment). This relatively high figure may be compared with the parties' 'subjective' response to the conciliation procedure: 55 per cent told us that they had felt 'upset', 'angry' or 'disappointed' when they left the court. These replies lend support to one of the dominant themes to emerge from our study of these appointments, namely, that judged 'objectively' (that is, from the standpoint of the courts), they make a significant contribution to the efficient processing of disputes; but judged from the standpoint of the parties, the procedure often appears coercive, or somewhat removed from their real concerns.

Other Research

The only comparable research study of 'in-court mediation' which I have been able to unearth is that conducted by Pearson and Thoennes (1984*b*) who investigated the 'mediation experience' in the three courts of Los Angeles, Connecticut and Minnesota. These researchers report that 'at all locations, mediation was associated with a high degree of user satisfaction'. Even amongst those who failed to reach agreements, 'a clear majority . . . would encourage others to try'.

These results appear to have been arrived at on the basis of quantification of responses to the researchers' direct questions. The limitations of this approach are reflected in Pearson and Thoennes's own figures. For example, 70-80 per cent of their informants appreciated (on being asked, presumably) the benefit of an opportunity to share grievances. But 30–40 per cent complained of not being heard or understood. One third of those who reported reaching an agreement also informed the researchers that 'little or no progress' had been made in their case. The latter finding is described as 'intriguing' and as revealing that 'mediation is a complex process'. The researchers make the laconic observation that 'an agreement is not synonymous with a solution', but do not go on to draw any conclusions about the true nature of 'mediation' on court premises.

Some Concluding Thoughts

In order to obtain any form of outside help, it is usually necessary to pay a price in terms of loss of privacy, or loss of control. It is generally the weaker party to a dispute who will seek help, but in doing so, he or she may well discover that it is necessary to 'go public', whereupon decision-making power is passed to professional experts. But when it comes to mediation, this equation—appeal for help equals loss of power—is meant not to apply. Unfortunately, as far as the 'in court' model is concerned, it applies all too well. The tactics employed in some (although not all) cases seemed to boil down to: (a) adjournment and delay—preliminary appointment after preliminary appointment, so that one or other party eventually gave up the ghost; or (b) a rather crude arm-twisting, generally taking the form of persuading one or other party (often the less resolute) that they had little or no chance of winning their case; or (c) a search for compromise, almost regardless of the justice of the case or of the long-term viability of the proposed arrangement. As a result, one parent (and sometimes both) experienced frustration and even despair; 'agreements' were arrived at through weariness; and the quality of the justice administered was diminished rather than enhanced.

The first and most obvious question in any negotiation is 'where does the power lie?' In the course of preliminary appointments on court premises, as these are conducted at present, authority cannot be said to reside with the parties. They do not *feel* as if they are in control. So the element of coercion—the threat (for example) of an unfavourable recommendation in a welfare report—is used as the main negotiating weapon. I am not forgetting that in *any* negotiation the parties may judge it best to agree to a settlement which they are not completely happy with. Recourse to the legal process may be seen as the final option, to be avoided if possible. But when negotiations are conducted on court premises, there is a kind of concertina effect, so that 'the shadow of the court', which is bound to be there in the background, suddenly leaps into prominence, completely blocking out the parties' own perceptions and definitions of the problem. The task of the mediator is to promote agreement based on these private meanings. The evidence of this study would suggest that when it comes to preliminary appointments on court premises, the 'public' standards employed by solicitors, welfare officer, and registrar are allowed to do the job instead.

This brings me back to the question with which I started this chapter: what are the objectives of 'in court' conciliation? If one talks to judges or registrars about these matters it is apparent that they consider themselves to be part of a rather blunt instrument which cannot hope to grapple with the complexity and the rival versions of 'truth' which characterize custody or access disputes. So what is the court's response? The answer is simple, if unpalatable: it is to avoid tackling these issues at all unless forced to do so. To this end, the *cost* and above all the *delay* associated with the legal process act as rationing devices. This is central to my understanding of the reasons underlying the introduction of conciliation on court premises—and also, of the form which that conciliation may take. These appointments do not reflect any desire on the part of the court to become more accessible to divorcing couples at the time when outside intervention is most needed, or to engage in a deeper examination of complex family matters; on the contrary, the hope is that in some rather ill-defined way, the proportion of disputes which 'survive' to the stage where they have to be adjudicated will be yet further reduced.

13

The Trial

It has been remarked that, of available dispute-resolution mechanisms, 'it is quite extraordinary . . . that the most familiar by far is that remote long-stop, court adjudication' (Galanter 1985). My subject has been negotiation, rather than adjudication, but it is now time that I turned to the long-stop. None of the research studies on which I have been engaged involved a detailed study of the trial process, but of the 200 cases in which we interviewed one or both parties in the course of our 'Conciliation in Divorce' study of contested applications, 78 (39 per cent) had been listed for trial concerning custody, access, or the divorce decree. In fact, of 83 cases in which an 'answer' was filed to the divorce petition, only 7 (8 per cent) were fully tried. But when it came to contested custody or access applications, the 'settlement rate' was not nearly so high, 54 cases being listed for trial and some 35 or so being the subject of a full hearing. (There was an element of doubt in some instances, with neither the parties nor the documentary evidence conveying with absolute clarity that the issue had in fact been adjudicated.)

Pre-trial Negotiation

Cases listed for trial do not provide a reliable indicator of the number of trials actually held, for the simple reason that 'settlement' is the norm even at this late stage. From the lawyer's point of view there may appear no essential difference between settlements arrived at in these circumstances and those which are agreed by the parties between themselves, or negotiated with the aid of an independent mediator. Indeed, one prominent barrister has referred to this bargaining at the door of the court as a form of 'conciliation'.[1] It might be argued that these discussions are the natural culmination of a settlement-seeking

[1] Robert Johnson QC, then vice-chairman of the Family Law Bar Association, in a letter in LAG Bulletin, Jan. 1983

momentum which develops almost inevitably as the trial approaches. This is how lawyers generally prefer to regard them. But from the parties' point of view it may appear that, having resisted the various 'cooling out' mechanisms employed by welfare officers, registrars, and even their own legal representatives, they *still* find themselves unable (or denied the opportunity) to present their case to the court. It is inaccurate, therefore, to equate the parties' experience of pre-trial negotiation with that of conciliation under the auspices of an independent mediation service, such as the Bromley Bureau. The most significant difference is that the parties' direct involvement in pre-trial negotiation on court premises is likely to be minimal. The following case, in which the respondent had filed an 'answer' to the divorce petition, provides one illustration of this. This was the experience of the wife petitioner, a woman in her sixties, who was relieved to discover that her husband withdrew, at the last minute, his 'answer' to her divorce petition:

I still wasn't aware that it was sorted out, until I went in. That's why they [barristers and solicitors] were upstairs, I think. I think his barrister told [husband] there's no good carrying on—it's finished. Because solicitors have talks together, don't they? I know, on several occasions, it went on—they had a talk together. Of course, they know one another, don't they? They're friends. But I was surprised. I'd got all worked up—and two minutes and it was over. Thank goodness!

In the preceding chapter I described how the parties might be denied the opportunity to participate directly in the course of 'in court conciliation'. Hearing such accounts of negotiation conducted on the morning of the trial, this pattern becomes much more understandable; legal advisers are used to taking responsibility for negotiation on court premises. Furthermore, the parties appear to accept this: the woman quoted above had felt intimidated by her husband and so had not wanted to be involved directly; she was simply relieved to be spared the ordeal of a trial. As with most of our informants who had pushed matters to this point, she considered that she was unable to discuss the problem with her spouse in any constructive way.

The very fact of the parties being geared up for battle—an expectation which the flurry of activity in the days preceding the trial would have done nothing to vitiate—contributed to their feeling bewildered and insecure when suddenly ushered into an atmosphere of lawyer negotiation and bonhomie. In some cases it was not so much the 'settling' that people objected to, as the fact that opposing solicitors and barristers chatted together in a relaxed, even jocular fashion—which from the parties' point of view made the whole process seem rather collusive. But whilst that might be dismissed as a matter of 'form'—or good manners—there remains the much more serious problem of the parties coming under pressure from their own legal advisers. One woman recalled that her solicitor and barrister had each attempted to convince her that unless she agreed to some access visits taking place, she would lose care and control of her children. Both she and her (second) husband were infuriated by this 'blackmail'. It was only after her legal advisers had spoken to other members of her family (and they, in turn, had spoken to her) *and* after the barrister had managed to speak to her alone, out of her new husband's presence, that her agreement was secured. She was disappointed at her family's 'betrayal' and still believes that she was tricked into an agreement.

In relation to disputes over care and control, it was more likely to be the husband who was persuaded to withdraw his application. As one man recalled:

[Barrister] dealing with my case said to me, 'It seems your wife is stable in the house now, she's got a steady relationship with her boyfriend; the children seem quite happy; they're living in the house okay; their mother picks them up from school—it's just round the corner from where she works.' It was all planned. She said to me, 'You'll have to try for custody later on, if she still gives you trouble, not getting access to the child, then you'll have to appeal again.' If I'd gone for custody, she told me I wouldn't have a second chance, so she told me to wait until my case was stronger. I thought it *was* strong, but she said it wasn't. So I went into that court, sat down, the judge—who months before, when he stopped me going near to the house, had told me that he would get to the root of the matter, to see who was lying—he walked up onto that little box and said, 'Is the welfare report okay? Are you all agreed she should have the children? Fair enough then, bang; custody for the wife.' That barrister—who was she to tell me I shouldn't go in for custody? She didn't understand; they're my children; they're everything I ever worked for, everything I ever dreamed of.

One can well imagine that this man did not have a strong case in law, so that he might well have felt similar anger towards the judge, when, in due course, care and control would have been awarded to his wife. Nevertheless, this may have been a case where it would have been better to allow 'the designated loser' to have his say. It is judges who are meant to decide these cases, not legal representatives.

This is not to suggest that this strong settlement orientation is the responsibility of solicitors and barristers alone: it also reflects the attitude of adjudicators. We were given some accounts which suggested that judges and registrars are not above displaying impatience at having to adjudicate disputes which they regard as no more than petty squabbles. This rather dismissive attitude was picked up by parents, the following account (where the dispute concerned access to children in school holidays) being one of several examples:

When I went back to the court [registrar]'s attitude was, 'Why've you got to come back to court, it's such a stupid little thing', you know, regardless of all I'd done to try and sort it out. I reckoned it was a bleeding stupid idea too, but that's what it ended up as, you know, just to sort it out. I came out of there thinking he was speaking down to me . . . it might be daft to him, but it was important for me and the kids.

If this is how judges and registrars respond to disputes brought before them, they are sending a clear signal to legal representatives that they would do well to settle the case, thus enabling all those professionally involved to turn their attention to more weighty matters.

The Hearing

Most people know what to expect of a trial: they have seen it on television. The dominant image which is presented in these fictional accounts is that of justice triumphant thanks to the forensic skill of a silver-tongued advocate. The image is sustained to the extent that, in a dispute over care and control, or on a more complicated financial matter, it is usual for a barrister ('counsel') to be 'briefed' to act as advocate. This, as far as the parties were concerned, was the 'champion' who would present their case to the court.

But in other respects, this image of the way barristers behave was subject to immediate challenge. The first challenge, as we have seen, lay in the barrister proving more interested in 'settlement' than he was in winning the case in court. A second lay in his relative lack of familiarity with the case. In the 'Conciliation in Divorce' study, of 72 parties who had been represented by a barrister, 48 (67 per cent) had met him or her for the first time on the morning of the trial. This gave rise to considerable unease; it was advanced by some informants as the reason why their barrister had given a less than stirring performance in court:

I reckon I could have done as good a job. I reckon I could have asked the same questions what that woman asked. You've only got about a quarter of an hour before you go in the court and she's got to glean out what she thinks is our strong arguments out of a huge list of things, and try and pick out things to avoid. I got the impression that she didn't know enough, she didn't know enough about the case. I'm not saying she was inefficient—that would be unfair to the lady. But she certainly never had enough information.

It was more of a disadvantage having him there. He didn't get given the papers until an hour and a half before the hearing. He just didn't have a clue about what he was doing. He didn't know the case. He didn't know me. And the man was lost.

In most of these cases the hearing was the culmination of months of worry and uncertainty; the parties' relationship with one another may well have deteriorated in that time. In these circumstances the barrister was expected to be a doughty fighter who would advance their arguments (and nullify those of their spouse) with all the skill and vigour at his disposal. It was a bitter disappointment, therefore, to discover that he or she was not in full command of the facts of the case.

But whilst some people were disappointed in the performance of their champion, others reported that the barrister had displayed the kind of verbal fluency which we can all, in our mind's eye, bring to our impassioned pleas for justice (sadly, this seldom occurs whilst in a waking state). The following was one case in which the husband recalled his barrister's performance in court with obvious relish:

I thought he was very relaxed—so relaxed. I couldn't get over it. You know, these professional people—they rate words off just like, oh, I don't know— just like counting a couple of pound notes in your hand, you know. It's so relaxed, so easy-going, I can't understand it. Honest to God, I was amazed—I thought, you're doing very well here.

This was one of several cases in which the client was delighted to discover that his barrister's ease and general command of the situation made him (or her) the acknowledged expert in the courtroom. This was most evident in the magistrates' court, where barristers attend relatively infrequently. They may thus appear a somewhat exotic species, comfortably outshining not only the lay adjudicators, but also the other 'professionals' present—solicitors and magistrates' clerk— these being birds of duller plumage:

He was brilliant. I had a job to keep a straight face. I don't think I shall ever forget it. The lady who was sat up in the middle on the back—the magistrate I presume she was—looked down and asked the clerk of the court some query over something or another and with that the chappie (barrister) who was representing me got up and said, 'Excuse me, your honour, would you mind if I . . . and then he started quoting some paragraph, some chapter of this and verse of something else. And the clerk said, 'Well, I don't know anything about that.' With that the chappie said, 'Well, would you like to borrow my book on it?' So with that the clerk sat down and he [barrister] got on with telling him how to run the procedure of the court. He certainly knew his job. He proved it when he even tied the clerk of the court up in knots. It got to the stage then at the very end where the magistrate, instead of referring to the clerk of the court, was referring to my barrister. It was so incredible it was hard to sit there and keep a straight face.

The corollary of this delight in the strength of one's own advocate was a corresponding cheerfulness at the ineffectual performance of the barrister or solicitor on the other side. The same man remarked of his wife's solicitor:

Well, after my barrister questioned me, it was like a trainee getting up and questioning me after a fully experienced chappie had had a go.

One can well understand the importance, in these highly fraught situations, of having 'a fully experienced chappie' in one's corner. For the most part, this is what people appear to be looking for from their barrister: a competent, tough-minded fighter, respected by the court and ready to do battle on their behalf.

It is still open to question, however, whether our 'family courts' should encourage such gladiatorial encounters. As we shall see, they are extremely difficult to justify in terms of *outcome*, in which case one is left to reflect on their symbolic significance—or, as Michael King (1987) puts it, on 'the image that parents will take away from the proceedings about themselves and their relationship with their children'. If this is what trials are about, then the stylized legal encounter is an extremely chancy business. It may do wonders for the morale of one party to the conflict, but be thoroughly destructive from the point of view of their spouse. This was most apparent in relation to cross-examination: several of our informants considered that they had 'performed' disastrously. The image of themselves which they took away from the proceedings was by no means a flattering one:

I'd had to wait for months before I was actually allowed to say anything at all and I felt very nervous and I forgot to look at the judge and say 'Your Honour'. I wasn't used to being in a court and I found it very trying. Every time I would say something, my husband would be waiting and flapping his arms about, poking the barrister in the back and saying, 'Look, I think you should ask her this, that's not true', and that was going on the whole of the time through the questioning and when the judge summed up at the end, she said, 'Oh, I thought Mrs Y seemed rather nervous and under some strain', and I thought, well, really, it's not surprising after waiting for three or four months and having your children snatched away—I would have thought that she would have understood that—being in that situation and being questioned like that in a very formal way.

This account demonstrates just how contrived these exchanges may appear to be from the parties' point of view. In order to compete on equal terms with the 'professionals', they need to adapt to this strange environment. For most people, this is not a realistic possibility; hence the advice given by some legal advisers that their clients should give abrupt, limited answers when in the witness box in order not to give anything away:

My solicitor had explained it all. He said, when you get in there, there's only one way to do it and that's 'No sir, yes sir, three bags full sir.' You don't add anything on, basically, because they make a dog's dinner out of it all. He said, 'You've seen it on Crown Court, well, that's just what you've got to do.'

The woman in the above case was pleased that, thanks partly to her assiduous viewing habits, she had been able to master the occasion. But it was more common for the people we interviewed to complain that they had been led by the nose, or duped into giving misleading and damaging answers:

I wouldn't say I did myself justice in the box. I let the situation get to me; I didn't keep a cool enough head. These questions are so loaded—you can't get away with a straight 'yes' or 'no'. They can drag it out of you—they latch on—because they're professionals, aren't they, and you find you're saying something different to what you meant. And afterwards . . . you've said it, but you think, I didn't *mean* that.

The contest between professional advocate and novice litigant can appear so grossly unfair that the 'cross-examinee' may feel bound to resort to desperate strategies in order to strengthen her position. The following was one such case, by no means typical of the general run, but instructive nevertheless:

Robert [husband] had had this man [barrister] before for business—for not paying up—and he told me what a horrible man he was and a crafty one, and he'd tie me up in a knot to make me feel really small. So by the time I got there I was terrified of him, and when he started on me, I couldn't talk to him. The judge asked me what was wrong and I stood there and repeated all what my husband had said about him. I was so angry and so afraid, I thought, well, I just haven't got a chance because, you know, he's going to twist me up and everything. But I think I really embarrassed that man. He was a great big bloke, he was. I remember he went all red . . . once I got that out of my head, I felt a lot better.

The fact of there being this professionally dominated adjudicative process is a reflection of the highly developed rules and procedure governing the trial. These rules are intended to safeguard litigants, but they also act as a barrier, preventing direct communication with the court. On the whole, lawyers do not question their dominance of these proceedings: they advise their clients, with evident sincerity, to avoid the delays, expense and potential humiliation of a formal hearing. 'Be sensible—let us settle it for you' is the message that goes out. But they tend not to question the nature of the trial itself—whether it has to be quite so alienating, and whether the litigants need be in such a subservient position. This is in tune with the rationing motif, explored in Chapter 12. One way to limit demand is to emphasize the unappetizing nature of the final product: this renders litigants less resistant to 'cooling out', but it sidesteps the question of whether it might be possible to change the nature of the hearing—for example, by encouraging more direct communication between the parties and the judge.

This particular issue—the frustrations associated with being able to communicate with the court only through a 'front' man—was mentioned to us several times. It did not mean that our informants would have preferred to be entirely responsible for the presentation of their own case; for one thing, they suffered the handicap of not knowing which features of that case were relevant to the determination of a legal issue; nor, for the most part, did they feel that they could marshal and present this information in a coherent way. Nevertheless, they paid a high price for the lawyer's conversion of the dispute into legal terms. 'Topping and tailing' the issue in order to make it fit for legal consumption sometimes left the parties feeling that the key points as far as they were concerned had not been properly explained to the court. One of our informants remarked on the way in which her own barrister had 'used words without saying the right thing'; the picture presented was 'removed from how things are'. Unfortunately, using words so as not to say the right thing is, to some extent, what courts require. The conflict must be expressed in such a way as to make a legal determination possible. Since lawyers are the experts at doing this, it may appear inevitable that court proceedings be professionally dominated.

If, on the other hand, the final judicial determination is *not* the most important aspect of the trial, then the case for 'legal formal rationality' (Silbey 1981) is considerably undermined. The evidence of continuing, post-trial adjustments in both access arrangements and day to day care suggest that this is indeed the case. As previously noted, of the 32 Bristol cases in our 'Conciliation in Divorce' sample in which there had been a full hearing on care and control, there was a subsequent transfer of care (agreed between the parents) in 12 (38 per cent). This is not to suggest that the judge in these cases had made 'a mistake', but it certainly demonstrates that the decisions with which judges are faced, particularly in relation to care and control, can be extremely difficult (Ormrod 1973).

This was well understood by most of the parents we interviewed; indeed, some of them did not believe that the judge could possibly know enough about them and their children to be able to resolve the various competing claims. It appeared that what the judge had usually done was to play safe, as in awarding care and control to the mother, or in declining to disturb the children's present living arrangements. After all, what firm ground is there? These are welfare questions and barely justiciable. Where the above guidelines are in conflict, the judge will usually fall back on the recommendation contained in the welfare officer's report. It is the existence of these three basic ground-rules— presumption in favour of the mother; do not disturb the status quo; accept the welfare officer's recommendation—which enables legal advisers to 'settle' a good many otherwise intractable child care disputes.

Enforcement

Apart from the indications which we had of an agreed alteration, post-trial, of the custody or access arrangements, there was considerable evidence of one party's *defiance* of a court order, in which case it often appeared that their former spouse had no effective remedy. Orders for 'access' and maintenance are subject to massive levels of non-compliance.[2] This was why, when we asked people whether an

---

[2] The level of non-compliance cannot be measured simply by taking the number of subsequent applications aimed at securing enforcement of an earlier order. In practice, many people simply give up. Our interviews suggest that the level of non-compliance following a court order for *access* is in the region of 50 per cent.

agreement reached in their case had been 'fair', they often distinguished between the formal outcome, generally enshrined in a court
order, and its actual implementation.

As far as access is concerned, we found that the terms of the court
order (whether following an adjudication or 'by consent') were not
being adhered to in some 50 per cent of cases. In some of these, the
new arrangement had been agreed between the parties, but this was
often a matter of interpretation, with nearly half of the 'couples' whom
we interviewed giving contradictory accounts. The following were
typical of the views of the many non-custodial parents who no longer
saw their children and who had lost faith in the court process:

Every time I goes to court, it's the same. The court makes an order and I sees
him two or three times and then she stops it. I only seen him twice this last
time 'fore she stopped it. I can't take the strain of it, going back and fore to
court. So after the last time, I said, 'Bugger it, I won't see him no more.'

I don't think I'll ever go back [to court]. I've tried to talk to her [former wife],
either through her or through somebody else, but I won't go back down there
again because, again, I'll get what I want—and then what happens? . . . I'm
back to square one.

The problem for the court, faced with an apparent refusal to comply
with an access order, is that the sanctions available might have an even
more damaging effect on the children of the family. Some of the same
problems arise in relation to maintenance. In these circumstances,
imprisonment is seen as a more feasible option, but it is clear
nevertheless that judges defer taking this step for as long as possible.
As one woman explained:

You can go by the law all the way down the line and you don't get anywhere.
He can ignore it and do what he wants and cause as much problem as he likes
and just get away with it, like not paying maintenance for three years. He's not
worried about it. He can ignore my solicitor's letters until he's actually faced
with going to prison.

If not quite so distasteful as sending a custodial parent to prison for
refusing access, imprisoning the man for non-payment may seem
equally pointless, at least as far as that particular family is concerned.
This appears to be the view taken by some ex-wives, for many woman
do not persist with their application to the point where the husband
would be at serious risk of imprisonment. There is also the fact that
the cost of making repeated applications is so high—if not financially,
then in terms of energy expanded and, possibly, in the risk of further

alienating the man who may have it in his power to create difficulties in other ways.

All this serves to underline one rather uncomfortable message of this chapter, namely, that in relation to divorce disputes, the authority of the court can seldom be regarded as absolute; for all the apparent certainty and finality of the adjudicative process, the parties may, if they so wish, continue to make life difficult for one another. As Michael King has observed, if attempts by courts to impose their authority on parents' future behaviour actually work, it is largely because parents agree to let them work. Contrary to the impression given by statute, by case law, and by the Law Commision,[3]

it is not the future welfare of the child that is at stake in custody and access cases, but something very different, which can perhaps be described as the symbolic representation of parenthood, past, present and future. In other words, parents are arguing about, and judges and magistrates are determining, not the interests of the child, but rather the image that parents will take away from the proceedings about themselves and their relationship with their children. (King 1987)

Although I have not made a detailed study of the trial process, my experience of Children's Appointments conducted under s. 41 of the Matrimonial Causes Act 1973 (Davis, Macleod, and Murch 1983), plus the accounts of parents interviewed as part of the 'Conciliation in Divorce' study, lead me to conclude that King's analysis is substantially correct. Accepting this to be the case, what, one might ask, is the image of themselves which parents take away from contested custody and access proceedings? In many respects it is not a flattering one. For example, in recalling and making sense of their experience of cross-examination, the parties' key reference point was that of the criminal trial. Their sole preparation for the experience had often been in the form of repeated viewings of the TV series 'Crown Court' (which the author confesses to not having seen, but which is presumably about *criminal* trials). This identification was reinforced by their own feelings of distress or shame; they interpreted their experience in such a way as to support a conception of themselves as occupying a stigmatized role:

I felt dreadful because I'd only been there a few months before on jury service for a murder trial. And now I was standing in the same place as this fellow

[3] Law Commission Working Paper No. 96, *Family Law Review of Child Law: Custody*, HMSO 1986

who'd stabbed this man to death. I thought it was dreadful, absolutely dreadful. I thought: what am I doing standing here—just where he'd been standing just a few months before. Terrible.
Terrified. Absolutely terrified. Well, it's the unknown, I suppose. You wouldn't believe the state I was in, but I think it's all the unknown. You see these criminals and people you think have done things, they just seem to walk in and don't give a toss, but not knowing, not ever having had any dealings with courts . . . as soon as I saw him in his black gown, well, you think he might as well put a black hankie on his head as well—gives you an awful feeling.

Such accounts might lead one to question the *ritualistic* elements which are involved in the trial process, such as the use of the witness-box, the judge's elevation above the courtroom, and his wearing robes. One can see that these elements may be functional from the court's point of view, drawing attention to the judge's authority and perhaps assisting him in controlling the proceedings. One Australian prac-titioner, referring to the Family Court in his country (where the use of robes has been abolished) suggests that

the absence of any symbols of judicial office has led the public to be less ready to accept the judgements, the foibles and opinions of the bench than when they were delivered by a wigged and gowned figure of anonymous judicial authority. (Broun 1983)

One might well ask: for whom is that a problem? Certainly the symbolism of the court is functional from the point of view of the professionals involved. But what does it do for the parties? Do they feel more secure as a result? Are they any more likely to view the outcome as fair and just? In our present sceptical, less reverant age, such displays may well alienate 'consumers', rather than bolster the authority of decision-makers. But to say this, of course, is to beg the question of whether divorcing couples are to be regarded as consumers of a service. If, on the contrary, they are to be viewed as transgressors, it may be appropriate that they undergo a solemn ceremony which inspires, not just awe, but a little fear and humiliation as well.

Key Elements in a Family Court

Much has been written on the subject of a future 'Family Court', most of it concerned with subsidiary matters of organization and personnel. Two notable exceptions are Hoggett 1986 and McGregor 1987, but their contributions aside, there has been very little that examines the true nature of the present family jurisdiction in Magistrates' and County Court in order to ask just what it is that we hope to achieve in creating this new structure. There are very few models upon which to build, but I shall attempt, in the remainder of this chapter, to identify some criteria by which one might evaluate both our current 'family courts' and any future 'Family Court'.

The key question, in my view, is that of how to provide readily accessible judicial authority in the context of a court procedure which is sufficiently informal to enable the parties to state their views. This is known to be a difficult enterprise. Silbey (1981) refers to the distance between the litigant's conception of his trouble and the judge's ability, within the law, to deal with it. She suggests that 'the desire to "do justice", but have it done in a regular, procedurally correct way, according to the known, general, clear, consistent rules of law, characterizes the dilemma of western legal systems.' Or to put this another way, an ethic of responsive justice is inconsistent with adversarial due process.

Silbey suggests that, in the USA, *the lower courts* go some way towards promoting a dialogue between the various interested parties (professionals and litigants) concerning the nature of the problem and what might constitute a reasonable solution:

It appears that they go beyond narrowly assigned powers, beyond procedures and restraints which define their role . . . in fashioning individualized solutions to cases of grievance, trouble, or differences of interests and values. But it is not a chaotic enterprise. People come to court because the courts respond to their trouble and respond by providing compulsory, often final, resolutions. (1981, 24)

This is an attractive image, and one that may be thought especially appealing in the context of matrimonial disputes. However, one should be wary of assuming that this is the kind of service which 'lower courts' actually provide. It is not only the due process rights of the parties which may be compromised: as Silbey herself acknowledges, the lower courts tend to emphasize rapid case processing and volume control— in other words, a form of rationing which operates not by restricting access, but by limiting the service that is offered and imposing rapid termination. This, it could be argued, is precisely what the preliminary appointment system in the County Court offers us at the moment.

I have no experience of lower courts in the USA, but the accounts which we were given in the 'Conciliation in Divorce' study certainly cast doubt on any suggestion that Magistrates' Courts, simply by virtue of their being 'lower courts', are more responsive to the parties than single professional adjudicators. In general there appeared to have been even less opportunity to contribute directly to the proceedings than was offered in the County Court. This means that whilst I accept Silbey's analysis of the problem, I am rather more sceptical of her solution, particularly if this is assumed, by other writers, to apply to the English equivalent of the lower courts (Dingwall and Eekelaar 1984).

Another possible model is that of the French *juge des enfants* (King 1984). In the French courts, King suggests, 'the inquisitorial system and a disregard for the superficial trappings of procedural justice have allowed the development of a system much fairer for parents and families without detracting from the protection of the child' (1984, 147). This is King's account of some of the features of a typical hearing under the French system:

> Hearings before the judge, it must be emphasized, are not lengthy formal affairs—they can be over in ten minutes and usually last no longer than an hour—yet nor are they the mechanical rubber stamping of social workers' decisions. They take the form of informal discussions between judge, social worker and parents with the judge controlling the sequence of such discussions. The child will be brought to the court and the judge will in the case of older children talk to the child, either to seek his or her views on possible solutions to the problem or to explain what has been decided. (1984, 148)

It is important to acknowledge that the system which King describes operates in a different country and in relation to a different area of judicial responsibility. There may nevertheless be lessons to be learnt, particularly with regard to the court's attitude towards involving the parties in its decision-making. According to King, family rights in France do not depend on procedural protection and legal representation to the degree which one finds in English courts. They rely instead on 'an ideological approach to child protection that sees the family, including the extended family, as central to the child's future welfare' (149). This means that court hearings are less alienating for the parents. It is not that they are being offered some sort of beefed-up conciliation: the decisions taken are clearly judicial. But because the French system attaches greater importance to the maintenance of the family unit, parents are accorded higher status within legal proceedings.

On the basis of the above analysis, and utilizing the findings of the 'Conciliation in Divorce' research study, it is possible to identify a number of key elements which *ought* to find a place within a family court. These might be characterized as: judicial empathy; fairness; parental involvement; and judicial authority.

Judicial Empathy

Most litigants are novices in terms of their experience of the court environment. But their sense of alienation may be sharply diminished through the sympathetic approach of the judge or registrar. This was one woman's recollection of the judge in her case:

It was quite nice after all the questions that were being put to me by my lawyer and [husband's], the one thing that the judge asked—he turned to me and he said, 'How's the baby?', and I thought that was ever so nice. And I said, 'Well, actually, she's not very well.' 'Oh, what's the matter with her?' Which, after being pumped with all these different questions about us, it was nice for him to turn round and actually come out with something like that—it was the last thing I expected him to ask me.

Many of our informants had appeared before more than one judge; several remarked on the contrast in style:

There was a lady judge who seemed very understanding and very nice. She seemed to appreciate that these things weren't pleasant for you—but it may be purely because she was a woman—that she seemed to be able to get this over to you ... without actually saying anything, she seemed to give you this impression. Then there was another judge—he didn't seem as though he was quite—well, he seemed [spoken abruptly], 'Well, fine ... well, yes, here ... well, haven't we? ... shouldn't we have? ... yes, here it is.' He was sharp, short and knew the system—knew the legal system in and out—but again, he didn't seem to have much feeling for the case, if you know what I mean.

One might simply conclude from this that some judges can communicate with the men and women who appear before them, whilst others cannot. But not all judges *want* to communicate with litigants: they prefer, both literally and metaphorically, to remain sitting on high. This should not surprise us unduly: after all, it is in keeping with our conception of the nature of courts. But family disputes require something different, a closing of the gap between adjudicators and litigants. This is largely a matter of personal style, of judges feeling that they have enough confidence in their own authority not to need to impose this on the parties. It should not be assumed, therefore, that judges having lay status renders them any less distant from litigants, nor any more skilled at overcoming that distance.

Fairness

Judicial sympathy and understanding, which are noted and appreciated by parents quite independently of the outcome of their case, need to be displayed even-handedly if they are not to arouse resentment and distrust. Some judges manage this balancing act remarkably well. In approximately one-third of the 'Conciliation in Divorce' cases in which we interviewed both husband and wife, they each considered the judge to have been 'fair'—which implies, of course, that these positive (and spontaneous) assessments cut across gender lines:

Mr S. I was a bit shocked when I went into the court because it was a lady judge. My first impression, after all the trouble I'd had in the magistrates court, was, 'That's it, it's finished.' But as it turned out she was very, very fair.

Mrs T. He was probably a very nice man, but all I've got is this picture of this tall gaunt figure, terribly thin, more like an undertaker, and I was in fear and trembling—well, he was just doing his job. I made him smile once. He was very, very fair.

These tributes to the judge's evenhandedness were volunteered by both 'winners' and 'losers'. This was partly a response to the way in which some judges attempted to cushion disappointment, giving reasons for their decision and stressing the merits of the losing applicant; and it was partly a reflection of these same judges' manner of questioning the parties; of the way in which they responded to the respective barristers; and of the comments which they passed on the evidence presented. In short, it reflected their conduct of the whole case.

Parental Involvement

Not all trials conform to the ideal type, with the judge or registrar hearing the evidence and then making a pronouncement at the end. The distinction between adjudication on the one hand and negotiation (or 'conciliation') on the other can become blurred at times. I am not referring to the kind of settlement-seeking that takes place at the door of the court. This largely reflects professional interest in preventing the case coming to trial and is wholly dominated by lawyers. But in the course of the 'Special Procedure' research we observed some judges (they were the exception, rather than the rule) who went out of their way to encourage the parties to come to an agreement between themselves. We referred to this, perhaps inadvisedly, as a form of 'mediation' (Davis, Macleod, and Murch 1983). We were attempting to describe an occasional feature of the s. 41 'Children's Appointment' at which parents are asked about the proposed arrangements for their children's future care. These appointments are not intended to tackle disputes (it was common to find twenty to thirty appointments listed before one judge in a single morning), but despite the supposed absence of an issue, it emerged that many parents were still locked in conflict. In these circumstances, a few judges, as much by force of personality as through the use of their judicial powers, attempted to mediate between the two sides. The appointments had rather a conveyor-belt feel to them and so did not provide an ideal setting for this kind of judicial mediation. Nevertheless, it emerged that they *could* be employed for that purpose, the essential conditions appearing to be: (a) the presence of both parties; (b) an informal setting and flexibility in the timing of appointments; (c) a judge who is instrumental and authoritative but who has a conversational style and skill in developing rapport; and (d) imaginative use of ancillary services.

Solicitors seldom attended these appointments and it may well be that the presence of legal representatives makes it rather more difficult for the parties to be involved directly. It is not impossible, however, and in the course of our 'Conciliation in Divorce' study we gathered that some adjudicators had displayed considerable flexibility in the course of 'trying' a custody or access dispute. Take the following account of a defined access hearing. Despite what was in this instance an avowedly adjudicatory framework, it appears that the registrar did all he could to encourage the parties to work out their own solutions:

[Registrar] did actually suggest that we were very close to agreeing and maybe we ought to just try and sit down somewhere and have a cup of coffee and talk about it. And [husband] said, 'Absolutely not', and I said, 'Well, I wouldn't mind', and so it was actually arranged there and then. I think he was quite fair not to make a decision when he could have done—that's what it was for. He was just there to make a decision. And I thought that was quite good of him really—he seemed human.

The above should not be taken to imply that a framework for adjudication is unnecessary. There are times when one parent behaves quite ruthlessly towards the other, so that it is essential that someone in authority grasp what is going on. The following case provides a remarkable illustration of this—remarkable also for the frankness with which the husband recounted the way in which he had manipulated his wife and son:

Right up to the period that I got custody there was no way that I was prepared to talk about access, because what I tried to do was completely alienate Mary [wife] from Dave [son]. As far as I was concerned she was no longer his mother for this period of time and I would shelve him under my wing, or bring him closer to me—become more friendly. By keeping her away I felt I had a better chance of consolidating my position so far as going into that court was concerned and being cross-examined, or whatever. I felt that if Dave went to his mother for any period of time, then he might start swaying that way, or Mary could start swaying him that way and saying, 'Well, look, why don't you come and do this?—although she said she would never do it. But at the time the conflict was quite bitter and I wasn't prepared to trust her, so I made sure that Dave stayed here with me and he was completely and utterly alienated from his mother for what must have been over two years. I wanted this house and I wanted my son, and the only way I felt that I could do it was alienate Mary completely—get her right off the scene. As far as Dave was concerned, she never bloody existed.

Not surprisingly, the wife in this case had been in despair at her husband's behaviour. She had attended two conciliation appointments on court premises, but still she was getting nowhere. Finally, eighteen months after her initial application, the case came to trial. Her one piece of good fortune may have been that the hearing took place before a woman judge:

Wife. [Judge] sort of took over [husband] when he was in the witness box—she absolutely tore him to shreds. I thought she was great. I think we should have gone there in the first place. We should have forgotten about those conciliation appointments and gone straight to her. She got the access in the end and it had taken two years for me to get proper access and she did it in a couple of months.

Interviewer. How did she do that?

Wife. [Husband] was on the witness stand. He was saying lies and I couldn't stand it any longer and I just stood up and shouted and then she sort of took over. She literally got out of him what I'd been saying all along—that he'd turned [son] against me and things like that. She sort of really tore him to shreds. Everything he come back with, she come back with an answer and in the end he just give up, I think, and agreed access. She had so much fight behind her, it was unbelievable. It was the first time somebody had literally sat there and told him what he had to do, whereas those others [registrars], they didn't say anything really. She really stood up to him.

It is rare to come across a corroborated account which provides such powerful confirmation of the need for judicial authority in this type of dispute. The woman in this case had been manipulated to the point where her relationship with her son was almost destroyed. Accepting King's point that courts are seldom in a position to impose solutions unacceptable to parents, and that what they offer, in fact, is some redefinition of parents' image of themselves and of their relationship with one another, that redefinition can still be very important. The father in this case *might* have continued to obstruct his wife's access to their son, but he did not in fact do so. It seems reasonable to suppose that it took a powerful judicial voice to achieve that transformation.

14

Conclusion

DIVORCE is characterized by a heightened perception of separate and competing interests, although elements of mutuality may still persist. It can also be a period of intense emotional vulnerability as the parties contemplate their reversion to an unplanned single state. In these circumstances, most people experience a pressing need for well-informed partisan support. Unfortunately, the seemingly inevitable decision to involve professional third parties does bring problems in its train, principally through the loss of control which this entails.

It is salutary to note that many couples appear to have their own schedule for coming to terms both with marriage breakdown and with the issues arising from it. Their relationship continues to change in the period following separation, as does their attitude to such matters as access arrangements—and even to the question of which parent should exercise care and control. Some of the couples whom we interviewed regretted the way in which, having embarked upon the legal process, they found themselves locked into a seemingly inevitable escalation of hostility. As one husband recalled:

It was sad—although it was our fault perhaps—that it had to get all so legal and so involved with the authorities. I was so emotionally involved—I was like in a forest when it all started happening—I had to find someone to help me, because when it come at first, the documents and that, it was like a book coming at me. Receiving that sort of thing, I thought, well, she means business. I had to give back what was being chucked at me. But on reflection it was sad that it got that way.

There can be little worse than to reflect, in the light of a relatively harmonious relationship with one's former spouse, that years were spent fighting battles which have since lost all significance. This is especially poignant where the battle was largely concerned with *symbols*, such as 'joint custody'. As King (1987) observed, 'the more symbols you give parents to fight over, the more they will fight'. But for others whom we interviewed, it was not so much the quarrelling they regretted, as the eventual accommodation. They were bemused by the transition from an unmanageable private quarrel to a neatly cut and dried professional solution. In many cases there appeared to be a mismatch between the problem (subjective, individual, fluctuating) and the remedy (objective, generalized and seemingly final).

This arises in part because lawyers recognize the limitations of due process when it comes to grappling with the complexity and rival versions of truth which characterize custody or access disputes. Their response, unfortunately, is to avoid tackling these issues at all unless forced to do so. As a result, we find that the rationing motif increasingly dominates our system of family law. This is evident, for example, in the Booth Committee's proposals (paras. 3. 1 to 3. 16). The net effect may well be to further restrict access to judicial determination, rather than, as I would like to see, making judges and registrars *more* accessible—not as mediators, but as adjudicators.

This is an aspiration quite at odds with that which Dingwall (1986) had identified as being at the heart of the mediation movement, namely, a withering away of state power as people take more responsibility upon themselves. But in all the enthusiasm for conciliation, it is still necessary to consider the plight of those divorcing couples who have no confidence in their capacity to negotiate together. Many feel bound to soldier on without help (Davis, Macleod, and Murch 1982*a*). Others may apply to the court, only to find that their dispute is not fully aired, or that it is 'settled' without there being any real solution. It was clear from accounts which we were given of these couples' experience from the point of separation onwards that, at the time when all the really important decisions were being taken, one party (if not both) had felt totally unprotected. This in turn reflects what I believe to be an exclusively professional preoccupation with the need to terminate contested applications without resort to trial. The accent is not on the service being offered to the parties: the objective, on the contrary, is to restrict access to a service, the service in question being that of judicial determination. It is inevitable that a procedure which is concocted as a form of rationing, rather than as a means of expressing valued principles of justice, will serve the interests of courts and professional personnel, rather than litigants. 'Settlements' arrived at in these circumstances may make not the slightest contribution to a resolution of the problem as this is experienced by the parties.

Critics of the general trend towards mediation and arbitration have suggested that these services will come to replace genuine dispute resolution. In Abel's words (1982*b*), they represent 'a neutralisation of conflict that presents itself as a new and better mode of expressing conflict'. Bottomley (1984) has taken up this theme and emphasized the role of due process in protecting the rights of adults and children affected by divorce. But one can have no confidence that these rights will be protected during the highly pragmatic bargaining (or shabby horse-trading) in which legal advisers engage as they attempt to 'settle' cases without resort to adjudication. As Auerbach has noted, the concept of 'justice' loses its clarity in these circumstances:

> Justice becomes a compromise that gives the least offence to the most people ... lawyers and judges usually are satisfied with whatever results bargaining and negotiation produce; the process, not the result, is their primary concern. (1983, 11)

The hope is that conciliation will provide a new and better way of responding to family conflict. It undoubtedly has that potential for some couples, but conciliation cannot solve the problem of courts. We are still left with what, to repeat myself, I regard as the key question, namely, how to provide readily accessible judicial authority in the context of a court procedure which is sufficiently informal to enable the parties to state their views.

It has been observed that the policy of modern divorce law is towards a model of private ordering (Hoggett 1986). Certainly 'settlement' is now encouraged in relation to all substantive issues—decree, money, and children—but it is doubtful whether we should apply the term 'private ordering' to negotiations over which the parties exercise such limited control. It is limited for two reasons: first, as Hoggett herself observes, the state retains vestigial monitoring and control in all three areas; second, and more important, what is really on offer is a form of joint arbitration by legal representatives, with the parties having little option but to accept the solutions advanced. This is 'private' only in the sense of being hidden from public view. It is intended as a form of rationing, such rationing being an inevitable consequence of our commitment to due process within an adversarial (or accusatorial) framework. The latter is reliant upon a few very expensive professional advocates and its anachronistic features are all too apparent. Recognizing this, legal representatives (especially barristers) have turned themselves into expert 'settlers', thereby continuing to justify their existence—or, as some would see it, performing an essential service to the system. I would draw the opposite conclusion: I don't think we have nearly enough trials. I think that the nature of the trial process needs to be transformed, so that trials are made less alienating, less expensive—and we can have more of them.[1]

But unfortunately, little thought is currently being devoted to the core of the family law system, by which I mean judicial determination of contested applications. Suggestions for procedural reform are dominated by the rationing motif. One even finds extra-legal conciliation services being co-opted by courts as a further element in their diversion strategy.[2] This is precisely the kind of development which critics of conciliation in family disputes have warned against. The aggrandizing tendency of the conciliation movement, coupled with the rationing, deflecting strategies employed by courts, could lead to adjudication becoming so much a last resort that it is stigmatized as the refuge of the obsessive and the intransigent.

The tendency meanwhile is to assess the value of extra-legal services largely in terms of their impact on contested applications to the court, and secondly, on any savings which may accrue to the Legal Aid Fund. Apart from the innate implausibility of the savings argument, those who make such claims tend to forget that the legal profession has grown, if not fat, then at least numerous on the strength of legal aid. Whenever steps are taken to reduce this expenditure, for example in simplifying procedure, or in transferring work to a lower court, one observes the legal profession negotiating a higher hourly rate,[3] or increasing the number of applications made in respect of

---

[1] This argument has also been advanced in relation to criminal trials, most powerfully in a seminal article by Nils Christie (1977).

[2] A recent illustration of this is the practice direction which instructs judges and registrars to consider referring contested cases to local conciliation sevices where these exist (*Family Law*, vol. 16, 286). This is likely to place a further barrier in the way of divorcing couples' access to judicial determination.

[3] In the 32nd Legal Aid Annual Reports (1981–2), the Lord Chancellor's Legal Aid Advisory Committee applaud the recent 'rationalisation' which facilitated the transfer of proceedings from High Court to County Court, thereby increasing the County Court jurisdiction (para.73). But the Committee's comments on the consequences of this change (para.74) have a decidedly plaintive air: 'One feature of the change in the County Court jurisdiction we find disturbing, however. We understand that the change was secured only at the price of an uprating of the County Court scales of costs aimed at ensuring that there was no substantial alteration thereby in the remuneration of the profession or in the cost to paying parties, including the Legal Aid Fund. While the County Court scales may have been too low, that is a wholly separate issue from that of the reform of the jurisdiction. We would be concerned if it was in any way generally accepted that no procedural or jurisdictional reform should be allowed to affect the average cost of cases, since it is only thus that there can be any prospect of a more economical use of legal aid resources.'

other matters,[4] or simply managing, within each case, to locate more chargeable work.[5] Short of some natural catastrophe which decimates the number of fee-earning matrimonial lawyers, the demands on the Legal Aid Fund will continue to rise. Mediation cannot change this.

The current preoccupation with 'savings' reflects a climate of retrenchment. This effectively rules out any radical reappraisal of the present legal framework; one simply looks for a marginal reduction in the cost of existing commitments. In fact, the introduction of cost arguments at an early stage of any debate concerning new services (as, for example, in relation to the proposed 'Family Court') generally indicates that these are being used as a cover for less rational objections, or to protect vested interests (Murch 1980, 239). The report of the Inter-departmental Committee on Conciliation provides perhaps the clearest illustration of this approach, the savings test being used as a fig-leaf to cover up a reluctance to address more fundamental issues. What has to be remembered is that there is no question of the state making money out of divorce, any more than it can make money out of the health service, or education. It can only *spend* money. Any new service has to be judged on its merits, rather than in terms of its impact on current expenditure.

One might also ask what this tendency to employ conciliation in the service of courts is doing to the image and the practice of non-coercive, independent mediation schemes. Most writing on the subject has focused on the consensual elements, almost ignoring the role of coercion and power (a point made by Merry 1982). But as mediation comes to be accepted as the 'proper' way of resolving divorce disputes—and as some elements of the idea become enshrined in legal process—it is likely that mediators will become increasingly impatient with recalcitrant or 'unreasonable' parties. Those who persist in

---

[4] Following the withdrawal of Legal Aid from undefended decree proceedings in April 1977, the number of Matrimonial Legal Aid certificates declined considerably, from 119,030 in 1976/7 to 55,775 in 1977/8. (This was because Legal Aid was limited to cases involving dispute.) For some unexplained reason, there then followed a dramatic increase in the number of divorce 'disputes'. This was of the order of 100 per cent over 3 years, the number of certificates issued rising to 100,690 in 1980/1, a period in which the divorce rate remained constant. (Source: 32nd Legal Aid Annual Reports, 1981–2, The Law Society's Report, Appendix 2A(i).)

[5] In the 32nd Legal Aid Annual Report (1981–2), the Lord Chancellor's Legal Aid Advisory Committee note (para.14) that whilst 20 per cent fewer matrimonial Legal Aid bills were paid in 1981/2 than in 1977/8, 'there was nevertheless little difference in (deflated) total costs between these two years, the reduced volume of bills being almost wholly balanced by their higher (deflated) average unit cost.'

seeking a court adjudication will suffer the stigma of having rejected or failed at negotiation. The following account (by an Australian barrister) gives a fascinating insight into the unexpected ways in which mediation may be employed—for example, as a form of punishment:

I sometimes suspect that some judges direct parties to attend these confidential conciliation conferences in custody and access matters in much the same way as a school teacher may keep difficult children back after school as a punishment. Sometimes the judges ordering these conferences seem to be saying: 'If you two people are both so silly and difficult as to want to fight about this question I am going to indicate my disapproval by condemning you both to spend a couple of hours talking to each other and a court counsellor about the problem.' I suspect that some aspects of access disputes are occasionally settled because the parties wish to avoid being 'kept in after school'. (Broun 1983)

It might be thought that the recent enthusiasm for 'conciliation' is in tune with the case made by Brigette and Peter Berger for a 'restoration of the private' (1983, 206 ff.). To some extent that is so, but conciliation is such an amorphous concept that it can easily be hijacked by existing professional groups. It may, in certain contexts, be transformed into a highly coercive activity, although, fortunately, this potential is not always realized. But there are signs within the present conciliation movement of a wish to give people what is good for them, without first checking that this is what they want (as noted by Nader 1984). This was confirmed by our own research: some of the parents interviewed in the course of the 'Conciliation in Divorce' project simply wanted to get out of their marriage and were annoyed at all the hoops, including certain forms of conciliation, which they had to jump through in order to achieve this.

Looking ahead, to California, one finds that there has recently been enacted a 'mandatory mediation law' which is intended 'to overcome the substantial attrition rate that most voluntary programs experience' (Pearson and Thoennnes 1984a, 514). One might well ask: how can such a distortion arise? Part of the problem lies in the financial and adminstrative pressures to which I have already referred. But one must, in addition, consider the values and aspirations of the new mediators. The conciliation movement has brought together two groups, lawyers and social workers (or 'counsellors'), who are not noted for a particularly favourable view of one another's activities. Nevertheless, this boundary-crossing helps to explain the success of the idea. It has enabled these two groups to employ the same language to describe what are in fact very different approaches and modes of thought.

The apparent bridging of this professional divide enables mediation to be construed as an attempt to marry the lawyer's awareness of issues of justice and accountability with the social worker's sensitivity to the emotional impact of divorce. The risk, of course, is that what will actually be on offer is the somewhat less attractive blend of the court's preoccupation with settlement-seeking, cost-savings and administrative efficiency, and the social work profession's therapeutic aspirations and supposed child welfare expertise.

It is typical of professional groups that they do not take a new idea at face value; they retain the language, but change the practice in order that it may fit in with what they do already. The social workers/ counsellors, in particular, will claim that mediation falls squarely within the area of their own specialist knowledge and expertise. Unfortunately, their training and professional orientation have led them to develop frameworks of explanation which are commonly not shared with (and would not be understood by) their clientele. Divorce court welfare officers are fascinated by the idea of conciliation, but apply this term to an activity which has as its main focus the protection of children. Such confusion has enabled one prominent critic, referring to proposals for a new 'Family Court', to observe that '(the) rhetoric is about family autonomy; the reality is of a more pervasive control than existed one hundred years ago' (Freeman 1984).

But viewed from a rather different perspective, the new mediators could offer a challenge to the aggrandizing attitude of the various professional groups involved in divorce. In law (as in medicine) one may observe some resistance to the exclusively professional definition of problems and control of services. There is a growing recognition that the treatments which are offered may create more problems than they solve. Accordingly, we see growing up alongside these professions, various fringe groups which, whilst they struggle for acceptance and recognition, seek to avoid some of the defects of more established systems. Typically, these services will draw rather more on the resources of the patient/client and less on the expertise of the 'treater'. The technology may be less impressive, but it is also less daunting.

To some extent, the question of whether established law (or established medicine) can do very much in the individual case is a matter of good or bad fortune. If, today, you contract tuberculosis, you should survive. But if you suffer from arthritis or multiple sclerosis or certain forms of cancer, there is no cure available. The same may be said of the law. It provides a remedy for certain kinds of injustice, but, in family law especially, it is often powerless to improve people's lot. If a couple are splitting up and have only one home and not much money, then at least one of them will no longer have a place of their own. Likewise, there is no remedy for the pain of having only occasional contact with one's children.

But it is only half of the picture to look at what law or medicine can provide. It is also important to consider what the client/patient can do to help himself. The problem with some diseases, such as alcoholism, is not so much that they are physically damaging (unless remedial action is taken in time) but that the patient lacks the resources to participate effectively in his own recovery. Similarly, some people's response to the ending of their marriage is so self-mutilating that no amount of law will ever provide a cure. Indeed, they use the law as a kind of pumice stone, endlessly rubbing away at their own wounds, never allowing them to heal.

This is not to deny that there may be a great relief when under stress in having all the pressures lifted—say, by a competent legal adviser. Professional control may, at times, be exactly what is required. But the desire to be taken over, if satisfied completely, is likely to prove self-defeating. This is well understood by some members of the legal and social work professions. They have given their support to these extra-legal services, not because they want to take them over, but because they recognize the limitations of their traditional role.

This point was well made by one consultant psychiatrist in a letter to a national newspaper.[6] He developed the idea of 'the wounded healer', arguing that if the professional person could recognize his own vulnerability, that he is in fact 'part client or patient and not the exemplary citizen who is 100 per cent healthy and competent', this would be an important step in making him better at this work. Referring to the four professional groups of doctors, nurses, social workers, and clergy, he wrote as follows:

Each group has specific frustrations and escape routes. Doctors are faced with massive suffering which they cannot hope to remove and which they are

---

[6] Dr Glin Bennet, Consultant Psychiatrist based at the University of Bristol, in a letter to the Guardian published 3 August 1983. Dr Bennet has since written a book (1987) in which he explores this theme.

inadequately trained to respond to effectively, but they can retreat into high-technology medicine where an illusion of certainty prevails. Nurses in hospital are restive in their conservative profession, but have opportunities to escape into community work. Social workers are already in the community, but they are landed with statutory duties and all kinds of other obligations which they cannot possibly fulfil, so they can only escape upwards into the bureaucracy. The clergy are only too aware of the social problems around them and when they have doubts about their spiritual role there is always the temptation to do something which is 'socially relevant'.

Viewed most positively, one may regard professional people's willingness to encourage and participate in extra-legal and medical services as an implicit acknowledgement, first, of the limited scope of much of their expertise; and secondly, of their own vulnerability given that they cannot possibly provide all the help which their clients or patients are seeking. Meanwhile, there will always be a tendency to employ these new approaches, not as a means of acknowledging the limitations of professional expertise, but in order to extend the boundaries of professional dominance and control.

References

ABEL R. L. (1979). 'The Rise of Professionalism' (Article reviewing M. S. Larson, *The Rise of Professionalism: A Sociological Analysis*) *British Journal of Law and Society*, 6/1.

—— (1982*a*). 'Intoduction', in R. L. Abel (ed.), *The Politics of Informal Justice*, vol.1, Academic Press, New York.

—— (1982*b*). 'The Contradictions of Informal Justice', in R. L. Abel (ed.), *The Politics of Informal Justice*, vol.1, Academic Press, New York.

AMREN, B. and MACLEOD, F. (1979). *The British Columbia Unified Family Court Pilot Project 1974 to 1977: A Description and Evaluation*, Information Services, Ministry of Attorney-General of BC.

AUERBACH, J. S. (1983). *Justice without Law?*, Oxford University Press.

BENNET, G. (1987). *The Wound and the Doctor*, Secker and Warburg, London.

BERGER, B. and BERGER P. L. (1983). *The War over the Family*, Hutchinson, London.

BERNARD, J. (1982). *The Future of Marriage*, 2nd edn., Yale University Press.

BOTTOMLEY, A. (1984). 'Resolving Family Disputes: A Critical View', in M. D. A. Freeman (ed.), *State, Law and the Family*, Tavistock, London.

BROUN, M. (1983). 'Conciliation: The Australian Experience', *Family Law Bar Association Conference*, Cumberland Lodge, London.

CHANG J. W. (1984). 'Nonadversarial Representation: Rule 2.2 and Divorce Mediation', in *A Study of Barriers to the Use of Alternative Methods of Dispute Resolution*, Vermont Law School, South Royalton.

CHRISTIE, N. (1977). 'Conflicts as Property', *British Journal of Criminology*, 17/1.

CLULOW, C. and VINCENT, C. (1987). *In the Child's Best Interests?* Tavistock, London.

COMAROFF, J. L. and ROBERTS, S. (1977). 'The Invocation of Norms in Dispute Settlement: The Tswana Case', in I. Hamnett (ed.), *Social Anthropology and Law*, Academic Press, New York.

CRETNEY S. M. (1984). *Principles of Family Law*, 4th edn., Sweet and Maxwell, London.

DAVIS, G. (1983). 'Conciliation and the Professions', *Family Law*, 13/1.

—— (1988). 'The Halls of Justice and Justice in the Halls', in R. Dingwall and J. Eekelaar (eds.), *Divorce Mediation and the Legal Process*, Oxford University Press.

—— and BADER, K. (1985). 'In-Court Mediation: The Consumer View', *Family Law*, 15/3.

212 *References*

—— and MURCH M. (1988). *Grounds for Divorce*, Oxford University Press.

—— and ROBERTS M. (1988). *Access to Agreement*, Open University Press, Milton Keynes.

—— MACLEOD A., and MURCH, M. (1982*a*). 'Divorce and the Resolution of Conflict', *Law Society's Gazette*, 79/2.

—— —— —— (1982*b*). 'Special Procedure and the Solicitor's Role', *Family Law*, 12/2.

—— —— —— (1983). 'Undefended Divorce: Should S. 41 of the Matrimonial Causes Act 1973 be repealed?, *Modern Law Review*, 46/2.

DINGWALL, R. (1986). 'Some Observations on Divorce Mediation in Britain and the United States', *Mediation Quarterly*, 11.

—— and EEKELAAR, J. (1984). 'Rethinking child protection', in M. D. A. Freeman (ed.), *State, Law and the Family*, Tavistock, London.

DOUGLAS, A. (1962). *Industrial Peacemaking*, Columbia University Press, New York.

ECKHOFF, T. (1969). 'The Mediator and the Judge', in V. Aubert (ed.), *Sociology of Law*, Penguin, Harmondsworth.

EEKELAAR, J. (1982) 'Children in Divorce: Some Further Data', *Oxford Journal of Legal Studies*, 2.

—— (1984). *Family Law and Social Policy*, 2nd edn., Weidenfeld and Nicholson, London.

—— CLIVE, E., CLARKE, K., and RAIKES, S. (1977). *Custody after Divorce*, Centre for Socio-Legal Studies, Oxford University, SSRC publication.

EPSTEIN, A. L. (1971). 'Dispute Settlement Among the Tolai', *Oceania*, 51.

FREEMAN M. D. A. (1976). 'Divorce Without Legal Aid', *Family Law*, 6/8.

—— (1983). *The Rights and Wrongs of Children*, Frances Pinter, London.

—— (1984). 'Questioning the Delegalization Movement in Family Law', in J. M. Eekelaar and S. N. Katz (eds.), *The Resolution of Family Conflict*, Butterworths, Toronto.

GALANTER, M. (1985). 'Judicial Mediation in the United States', *Journal of Law and Society*, 12/1.

GILLIGAN, C. (1982). *In a Different Voice*, Harvard University Press.

GLENDON, M. A. (1981), *The New Family and the New Property*, Butterworths, Toronto.

GOLDSTEIN, J., FREUD, A., and SOLNIT, A. J. (1973). *Beyond the Best Interests of the Child*, Free Press, New York.

GUISE, J. (1983). 'Conciliation: Current Practice and Future Implications for the Probation Service', *Probation Journal*, 30/2.

GULLIVER, P. H. (1979). *Disputes and Negotiations*, Academic Press, New York.

HAYNES, J. M. (1983). 'The Process of Negotiations', *Mediation Quarterly*, 1.

HOGGETT, B. (1986). 'Family Courts or Family Law Reform?', *Legal Studies*, 6/1.

HOWARD, J. and SHEPHERD, G. (1982). 'Conciliation—New Beginnings?', *Probation Journal*, 30/3.

—— (1987). *Conciliation, Children and Divorce*, Batsford, London.
INGHAM, M. (1981), *Now We Are Thirty*, Eyre Methuen, London.
ISONO, S. (1975). *Some Theoretical Problems in Handling Family Disputes in the Japanese Family Court*, paper delivered at a *Symposium on the Sociology of Law*, organized by the International Sociological Association, September 1975.
JOHNSTONE, T. (1972). *Professions and Power*, Macmillan, London.
JORDAN, W. (1981). *Freedom and the Welfare State*, Routledge and Kegan Paul, London.
KAWASHIMA T. (1969). 'Dispute Resolution in Japan', in V. Aubert (ed.), *Sociology of Law*, Penguin, Harmondsworth.
KING, M. (1984). 'Child Protection and the Search for Justice for Parents and Families in England and France', in M. D. A. Freeman (ed.), *State, Law and the Family*, Tavistock, London.
—— (1987). 'Playing the Symbols—Custody and the Law Commission', *Family Law*, 17/6.
LEETE, R. and ANTHONY, S. (1979). 'Divorce and Remarriage: a Record Linkage Study', in *Population Trends No. 16*, HMSO, London.
LEVY, R. J. (1984). 'Response to the Pearson/Thoeness Study', *Family Law Quarterly*, 17/4.
LINCOLN, Mr Justice A. (1981). 'Policy in Respect of Financial Relief', *Family Law Bar Association Conference*, Cumberland Lodge, London.
MCGREGOR, O. R. (Lord McGregor of Durris) (1987). 'Family Courts?', *Civil Justice Quarterly*, 6/1.
MEGARRY, R. E. (1962). *Lawyer and Litigant in England*, Stevens, London.
MERRY, S. E. (1982). 'The Social Organisation of Mediation in Non-Industrial Societies: Implications for Informal Community Justice in America', in R. L. Abel (ed.), *The Politics of Informal Justice*, vol. 2, Academic Press, New York.
—— and SILBEY, S. (1984) 'What Do Plaintiffs Want?: Re-examining the Concept of Dispute', *Justice System Journal*, 9/2.
—— —— (1986). 'Mediator Settlement Strategies', *Law and Policy*, 8/1.
MNOOKIN, R. H. and KORNHAUSER, L. (1979). 'Bargaining in the Shadow of the Law: the Case of Divorce', *Yale Law Journal*, 88.
MURCH, M. (1980). *Justice and Welfare in Divorce*, Sweet and Maxwell, London.
NADER, L. (1984). 'Dispute Resolution—Law as Marginal or Central', in *A Study of Barriers to the Use of Alternative Methods of Dispute Resolution*, Vermont Law School, South Royalton.
NEWSON, E. (1978). 'Unreasonable Care: The Establishment of Selfhood', in G. Vesey (ed.), *Human Values*, Royal Institute of Philosophy Lectures, 1976–7, Harvester, Sussex.
ORMROD, Sir R. (1973). 'The Role of the Courts in Relation to Children', *The Sixth Hilda Lewis Memorial Lecture*, delivered to the Annual General Meeting of The Medical Group.

214   *References*

PARKINSON, L. (1983). 'Conciliation: A New Approach to Family Conflict Resolution', *British Journal of Social Work*, 13.
—— (1986). *Conciliation in Separation and Divorce*, Croom Helm, London.
—— and PARKER, D. (1987). 'Conciliation and the Old Chestnuts of Confidentiality and Privilege', *Family Law*, 17/6.
PARMITER, G. M. (1981). 'Bristol In-Court Conciliation Procedure', *Law Society's Gazette*, 78/8.
PEARSON, J. and THOENNES, N. (1984a). 'Custody Mediation in Denver: Short and Longer Term Effects', *Family Law Quarterly*, 17/4.
—— —— (1984b), 'A Preliminary Portrait of Client Reactions to Three Court Mediation Programs', *Mediation Quarterly*, 3.
PLATT, A. M. (1969). *The Child Savers*, University of Chicago Press.
PRUITT, D. G. and JOHNSON D. F. (1970). 'Mediation as an Aid to Face-Saving in Negotiation', *Journal of Personality and Social Psychology*, 14.
PUGSLEY, J. and WILKINSON, M. (1984). 'The Court Welfare Officer's Role: Taking it Seriously?', *Probation Journal*, 31/1
—— COLE, J., STEIN, G., and TROWSDALE, E. (1986). 'Conciliation and Report Writing', *Family Law*,16/6.
REES, R. and WALLACE, A. (1982). *Verdicts on Social Work*, Edward Arnold, London.
ROBERTS, S. (1979). *Order and Dispute*, Penguin, Harmondsworth.
—— (1983). 'Mediation in Family Disputes', *Modern Law Review*, 46/5.
RUBIN, J. Z. and BROWN, B. R. (1975). *The Social Psychology of Bargaining and Negotiation*, Academic Press, New York.
SAINT, J. P. (1982). 'The Matrimonial Lawyer—A New Breed', *The Law Society's Gazette*, 79/42.
SCHATTSCHNEIDER, E. E. (1964). *The Semi-Sovereign People*, Holt, Rinehart and Winston, New York.
SCHELLING, T. (1960). *The Strategy of Conflict*, Harvard University Press.
SCOTT, R. A. (1970). 'Construction of Conceptions of Stigma by Professional Experts', in J. D. Douglas (ed.), *Deviance and Respectability*, Basic Books, New York.
SHAW, I. (1976). 'Consumer Opinion and Social Policy', *Journal of Social Policy*, 5/1.
SHEPHERD, G., HOWARD, J., and TONKINSON, J. (1984). 'Conciliation: Taking it Seriously?', *Probation Journal*, 31/1.
SILBEY, S. (1981). 'Making Sense of the Lower Courts', *The Justice System Journal*, 6/1.
SIMON, W. (1978). 'The Ideology of Advocacy', *Wisconsin Law Review*, 29.
SMART, C. (1984). *The Ties That Bind*, Routledge and Kegan Paul, London.
SUTTON, A. (1981). 'Science in Court', in M. King (ed.), *Childhood, Welfare and Justice*, Batsford, London.
WALLERSTEIN, J. S. and KELLY, J. B. (1980), *Surviving the Breakup*, Grant McIntyre, London.

WILKINSON, M. (1981). *Children and Divorce*, Basil Blackwell, Oxford.
WISHIK, H. (1984). 'Family Disputes: Problems Arising from the Regulation of the Legal Practice', in *A Study of Barriers to the Use of Alternative Methods of Dispute Resolution*, Vermont Law School, South Royalton.

Index